Yoga inVision 8

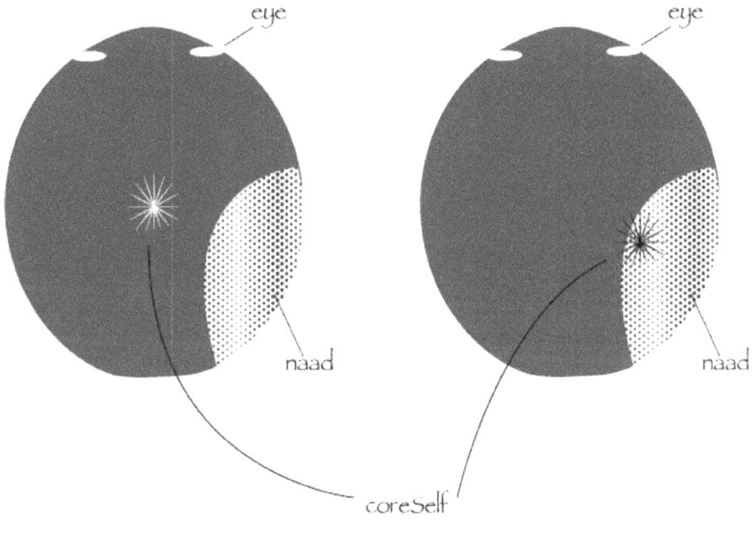

Michael Beloved

Shiva Art: Sir Paul Castagna
Illustrations: Author
Correspondence:
Michael Beloved
19311 SW 30th Street
Miramar FL 33029
USA
Email: axisnexus@gmail.com
michaelbelovedbooks@gmail.com

Paperback ISBN: 9781942887225
eBook ISBN: 9781942887232
LCCN: 2019913610

Table of Contents

INTRODUCTION 5
Part 1 6
Part 2 32
Part 3 64
Part 4 94
Part 5 123
Part 6 151
Part 7 183
Part 8 216
Index 253
About the Author 264
Publications 265
- English Series 265
- Meditation Series 267
- Explained Series 269
- Commentaries 270
- Specialty 273
- inVision Series 275

Online Resources 278

INTRODUCTION

This is the eight of the Yoga inVision series. It relates experiences and practices done in January through August, 2011. These give beginners ideas of the physical, psychological and spiritual experiences one may have when doing asana postures, pranayama breath-infusion and *pratyahar* sensual energy withdrawal. Beyond that is higher yoga, which Patañjali named the *samyama* procedures. He defined *samyama* as a combination of *dharana* deliberate focus, *dhyana* spontaneous focus and *samadhi* continuous spontaneous focus. During practice, these progress one into the other. If one is expert at *pratyahar* sensual energy withdrawal, one may graduate to *dharana* which is deliberate focus of the attention to a higher concentration force or person. As soon as one masters *dharana* one may slip into *dhyana* which is an effortless focus on a higher concentration force or person. Once you practice *dhyana*, *samadhi* happens as the continuous effortless focus on a higher concentration force or person.

Many persons on a spiritual path feel that they can construct a process as they advance. This idea denotes failure. After all, if the supernatural and spiritual environment, is not already there, no one can create it now. It is either there or it is not. For instance, if one intends to moves to a different country, then of course one will fail if the country intended does not exist. It has to be there prior. Similarly, what you aim for as spiritual life, must be there already, or one will find that the aspiration is incorrect. This is why I speak of a concentration force or person. I could have said concentration person or divine person, or God. I did not because I do not know how anyone's spiritual path will develop.

One may leave an island in the safest boat and still the vessel may sink. One should keep one's mind open and be willing to work with fate. In spiritual development, there is providence too. What one desires to have one may not achieve. What one wishes to see may never appear.

These Yoga inVision journals show how sporadic my course of yoga was. This is after years of practice. It gives some idea of what to expect. Once you get through the lower yoga practice, you will see advancement in a more stable way but it may be incremental, accruing little by little, with bright flashes here and there.

Part 1

Infusing the intellect (February 2011)

Rishi Singh Gherwal gave a procedure for achieving the second sutra of Patanjali regarding the suspension of the vrittis which is the curtailment of the natural operations of the intellect. Even though unseen, the intellect is a psychic orb. Even though students may not perceive the intellect visually they should be confident that it exists. To do this procedure one must accept that thoughts occurs in a specific location in the mind. This is about mental space location. One should trust my information that the intellect is a subtle object. The observing iSelf is also a psychic object in the mind. Once the intellect's location is known one can do this procedure.

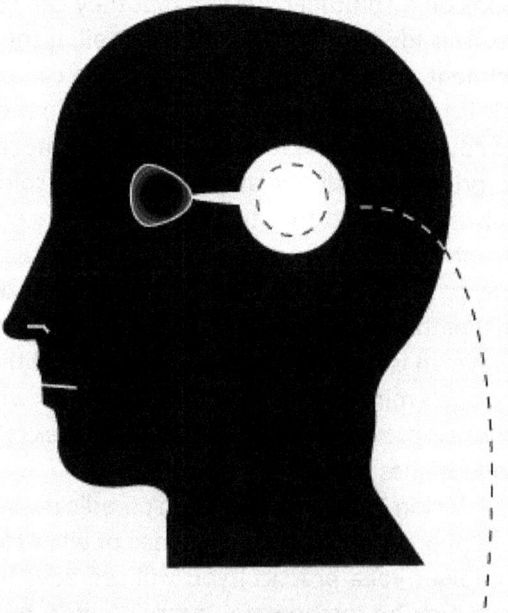

core-self
surrounded by focused sense of identity
which touches intellect orb

Sit to do rapid breathing. Use either posture as shown in the illustrations which follow, or use another sitting posture.

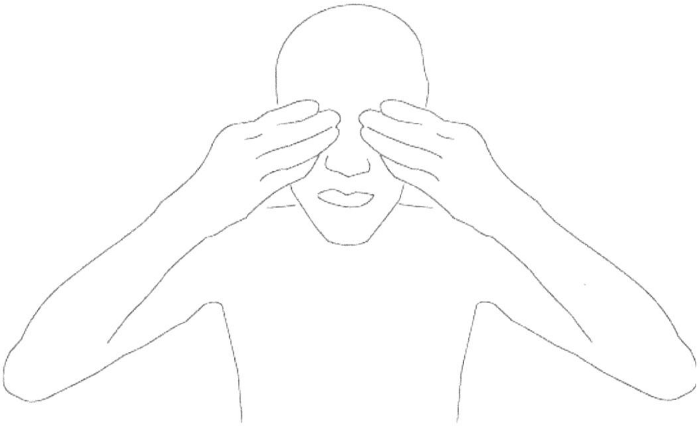

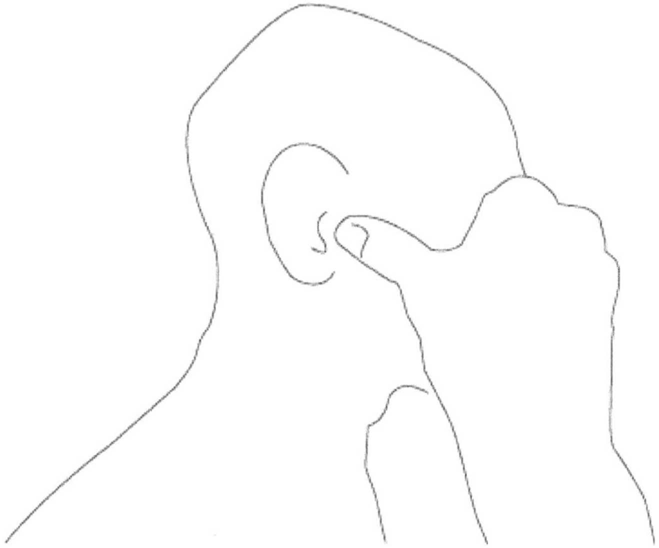

This should be done after infusing the spinal column with breath energy. Place the four fingers over the face as shown. Use the thumb to compress the ear canal. Press down firmly on the eyes. Once you are in that posture, make sure that the thumb compresses the ear canal. Begin rapid breathing but make sure that you find the location where thoughts are usually displayed mentally. Focus there. Direct the infused breath there. Do this for some time. Then meditate.

If this is done correctly one will find that the mind ceased the thought process or that its impulses slowed considerably and with much less compulsion or demand for one to view ideas. Thoughts which usually flow rapidity with a compelling energy for viewing, now move in slow motion with a weak compelling force which one can dismiss easily. Keep the attention on the location of the intellect even though it is not perceived visually. Be confident that though invisible, the intellect is located where the ideas would arise in the mind. Insist that no thoughts be generated. There should be no focus on the breath. No mantra is used during this meditation. To infuse the intellect breath is used for rapid breathing in the first part of this practice Then there is no more focus on breath.

For me, during the infusement process, there were no thoughts or images. After a few minutes of forceful breathing, I saw a large glow of light forming in the space ahead. When I looked at it directly, it moved and disappeared. This glow sometimes appears to increase in brightness (almost yellowish in color). When one is fascinated with the brightness and peers deeper it moves. When one tracks, it disappears.

February 2011

Initially one can expect that there will be mental chatter during breath infusion exercises. There may be hesitation from not knowing which sequence of postures to use. However, once a sequence is established, one will find that mental chatter decreases. If one is not consistent with a daily schedule, this problem will remain. Mental chatter is nature's harassment. It is not just humans who are plagued with that. Other species even the most primitive have that problem. All species think even though all species do not have the equipment to vocalize thoughts. By nature's grace mental chatter is permanent. It will leave only by long endeavor in the practice of thought suppression. Patanjali declared both correct deduction and erroneous notions as stumbling blocks in meditation. The more one meditates the more one understands how plagued one is by involuntary thinking and ideation.

The more one practises, the more one may observe how one is controlled by thoughts. Any beginner who gets the idea that overnight he or she will conquer the thought harassment system will be disappointed. That may happen after consistent and sincere practice for many years. As soon as one is inattentive, nature will resume the harassment.

Some who know that I have little or no interest in social affairs, do not hesitate to enlist me in social services. In fact, some make demands with force. That is the way it is for every yogi. Even though during the infusement when one is occupied ingesting the breath energy, one may not notice thoughts, there will come a time if one persists where one will infuse the system and also notice thoughts. Not noticing thoughts does not mean there are no ideas. The stage of no thoughts is rare, just as when people say that they do not dream, the fact is that they have no memory of dreams. When one does breath infusement, the attention is occupied doing that. Even though thoughts arise one may not detect them.

The thinking process is in part involuntary where one may become aware of thinking which transpires even before one could observe it happening. When one reaches the stage where one becomes aware of thoughts during the breath infusement session, one should send some infusement energy into the location in the subtle head where the thoughts occur.

Navel Area Design

If one changes the design of the navel area, so that the energy ingested does not coalesce there, and instead goes to muladhara base chakra without having interest in the sex-reproduction apparatus, then the spiritual struggle is over. Review these drawings.

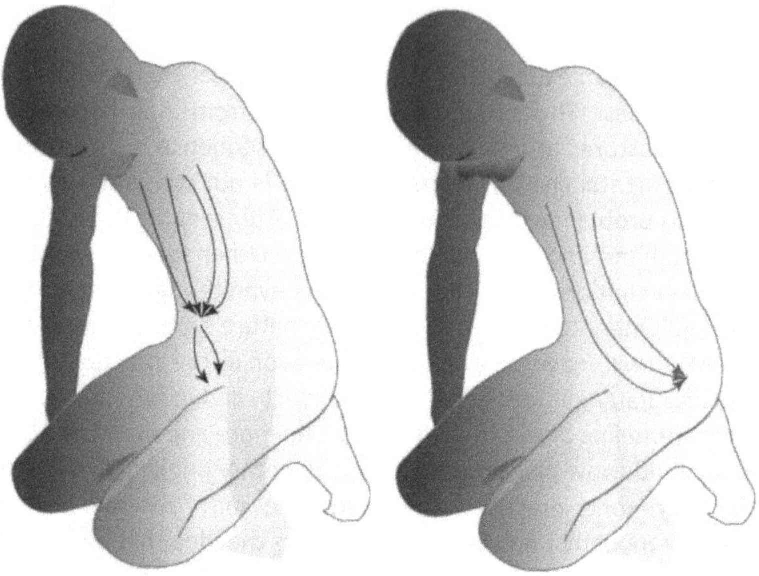

Dreams (May 2011)

Regarding dreams, I think that lucid dreams are those in which the astral body is not displaced from the physical one. Astral projection is when the subtle body is displaced. But one may have an astral projection and then immediately after find oneself in a lucid dream. The reverse may also occur. In lucid dreaming the individual becomes aware of either the astral form or the astral and physical systems simultaneously.

This is in contrast to normal consciousness where the person is not aware of the astral body and feels that everything about himself or herself is physical. In a situation where you find yourself located as the physical body but you find that you are not acutely aware of that form and instead is distinctly aware of the subtle body which is interspaced in the physical that is one of the two types of lucid dream experience. The other type is when you find yourself located in the physical body but you are distinctly and unambiguously aware of the subtle and physical ones. You feel that the subtle one is a separate energy form which interspaced in the physical system.

Another way to look at this is the situation of a live wire. In the live wire there is an invisible but real current flowing. Yet there is no visible change of appearance in the wire. When the current is switched off, the live wire appears to be the same, even though it is quite different since no current is transmitted. A lucid dream experience may be compared to the live wire situation, where there is an invisible body of energy inside the physical system. One becomes aware of that invisible force while it is still interspaced in the body.

Let us take this a step further. Suppose somehow the electricity in the live wire, were to jump out of the wire and flash in the air like a static charge or lightning in a cloud. That would be similar to astral projection, because the charge left the wire and was experienced outside of it

Psychic Perception Encouraged

Here are verses from *Uddhava Gita.*

श्री-भगवान् उवाच
सिद्धयो ऽष्टादश प्रोक्ता
धारणा योग-पार-गैः ।
तासाम् अष्टौ मत्-प्रधाना
दशैव गुण-हेतवः ॥१०.३॥
śrī-bhagavān uvāca
siddhayo 'ṣṭādaśa proktā
dhāraṇā yoga-pāra-gaiḥ
tāsām aṣṭau mat-pradhānā
daśaiva guṇa-hetavaḥ (10.3)

śrī-bhagavān – the blessed lord; uvāca — said; siddhayo = siddhayaḥ — mystic skills; 'ṣṭādaśa = aṣṭādaśa — eight and ten, eighteen; proktā — state; dhāraṇā — the linking of the attention to various concentration forces; yoga — yoga; pāra-gaiḥ — one whose interest has progressed the farthest; tāsām — of them; aṣṭau — eight; mat-pradhānā = mat-pradhānāḥ — prominent in me; daśaiva = daśa — ten + eva — indeed; guṇa – influences of material nature; hetavaḥ — causes.

Those who progressed the farthest in yoga, state that there are eighteen mystic skills, and eighteen types linkage of the attention to eighteen types of concentration forces. Eight of these are prominent in Me, the remaining ten are caused by a particular influence of material nature. (Uddhava Gita Explained 10.3)

अणिमा महिमा मूर्तेर्
लघिमा प्राप्तिर् इन्द्रियैः ।
प्राकाम्यं श्रुत-दृष्टेषु
शक्ति-प्रेरणम् ईशिता ॥१०.४॥
aṇimā mahimā mūrter
laghimā prāptir indriyaiḥ
prākāmyaṁ śruta-dṛṣṭeṣu
śakti-preraṇam īśitā (10.4)

animā — becoming atomic; mahimā — becoming cosmic; mūrter = mūrteḥ — pertaining to form of the yogi; laghimā — technique of weightlessness; prāptir = prāptiḥ — acquiring or experiencing; indriyaiḥ — through sense organs;

prākāmyam — enjoying almost anything desired; śruta-dṛṣṭeṣu = śruta — of what is heard of only + dṛṣṭeṣu — what can be seen normally; śakti-preraṇam — the ability to manipulate mundane potency; īśitā — power of ruling others.

Becoming atomic, becoming cosmic, pertains to a form of the yogi, as well as being weightless, acquiring or experiencing through the sense organs of others, enjoying what was heard of and what was seen normally, manipulating mundane potency, ruling over others, (Uddhava Gita Explained 10.4)

This is from *Yoga Sutras* of Patanjali.

कायाकाशयोः सम्बन्धसंयमाल्लघुतूलसमापत्तेश्चाकाशगमनम् ॥४३॥
kāya ākāśayoḥ saṁbandha saṁyamāt
laghutūlasamāpatteḥ ca ākāśagamanam

kāya – body; ākāśayoḥ – of the sky, atmosphere; saṁbandha – relation; saṁyamāt – from the complete restraint of the mento-emotional energy; laghu – light; tūla – cotton fluff; samāpatteḥ – of meeting, of linking; ca – and; ākāśa – atmosphere; gamanam – going through, passing through.

By the complete restraint of the mento-emotional energy, while linking the mind to the relationship between the body and the sky and linking the attention to being as light as cotton fluff, a yogi acquires the ability to pass through the atmosphere. (Yoga Sutras 3.43)

Sometimes the entire astral body shrinks to an atomic size. Sometimes the astral body remains its usual size which is about the size of a human form. It may have atomic vision. Usually, these experiences happen at random. They occur suddenly without personal control. What Krishna and Patanjali described has to do with the deliberate assumption of those mystic powers. Way back in 1973, I was once using the astral body. Suddenly a probe like proboscis emerged from the third eye. Through it I saw on the microscopic level. While that probe was in effect, I could not see anything on the normal size. I could only see through the probe and could only see as if a microscope was strapped to my third eye.

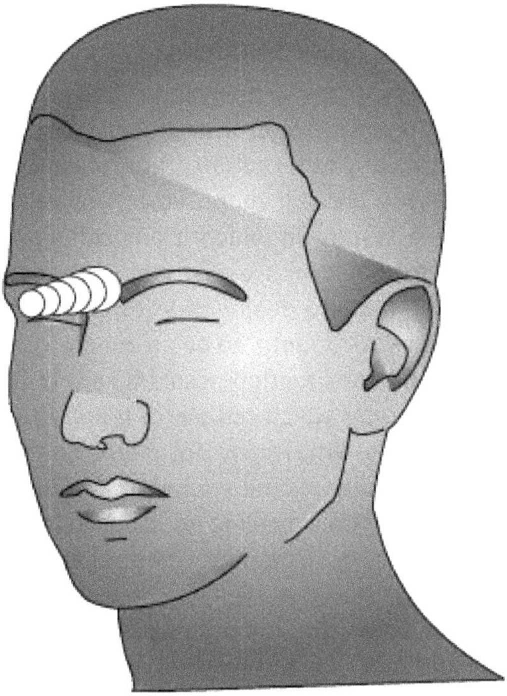

The astral body has many unusual abilities. One should have confidence in that with the understanding that in certain dimensions, the perception varies and that causes various types of mystic skills.

Time Warp

What we experience as a lifetime on earth, may be experienced as a moment or two in the astral world in some of its accelerated dimensions. Sometimes it happens, that just before passing from the body, a person has a flash in the mind and sees his or her entire life in a second, just as if the whole thing happened for a moment only, even though it was experienced as seventy or eighty years in the physical world.

Neutralizing Penetrating Thoughts

Nothing is ever done in total privacy. There can always be someone in this or in another dimension who looks in on what someone does in private. As soon as someone thinks, an energy from the thought vibration is expressed. It can be read accurately or interpreted inaccurately by the mind of another person. On the high end of meditation practice, one reaches a stage where one causes the outer membrane of the mind chamber to be a neutralization zone, such that any thought or image energy which is from certain levels of energy, is immediately neutralized. This is better than having to deal with lower energies and having to react to them every time they come into the mind.

To be realistic, imagine that you are responsible for protecting a country which has a powerful enemy. You get instructions from the leading council that you should not attack any other country, nor retaliate to any attack from any other country but you are still supposed to neutralize all attacks. You would have to create a system in which if any other country launches a missile, you would destroy that missile or disable it before it impacted your country. You would also have to deal with internal threats from agents of countries which consider your country to be an enemy.

In yoga practice a similar situation occurs where one must protect the psyche from external energies which can pierce it and alter its behavior, but you must watch for energies which may not pierce but which would affect just the outer layer of the mind. Some energies have a charge within them, which causes them to burst into a piercing explosion when they make contact with the mind's outer layer. One must neutralize these psychological projectiles.

Meditation begins when the mind stops access to and formation of thoughts. Patanjali did not list observation of breath and thoughts as meditation. It is better to regards thoughts observation, breath observation, thought control and breath control as preparation for meditation.

Astral Travel

The astral body has access to many places where the physical body cannot access. This helps tremendously in yoga because a yogi can fulfill many desires using the astral form alone, such that he does not have to endeavor for those things with the physical form. An example from my life, is that I do not go to India to see gurus there. Yet, I go there astrally and take valid instructions through the astral body. That made it easy for me to advance without having to acquire funds for travelling physically to India.

It is a huge convenience if a person can become aware of the activities of the subtle body, since then there would be satisfaction from fulfillment of many desires. One would not have to hanker for those aspects physically nor feel that one lacks that. Too much reliance on the physical body causes general frustration. It causes a person to have unreasonable demands which providence ignores. In the astral existence language is irrelevant, because the astral body comprehends an original idea before it is converted into language. Thus, it does not matter what language the other person uses, one understands what is indicated. Some distortions may occur if the astral body has cultural prejudices which it developed while using the physical form. We carry psychic containers of cultural prejudices from many previous lives. Each is in a separate memory compartment. If one is accessed during an astral experience, it may cause prejudices to surface. That will tarnish or embellish the astral experience.

One can eavesdrop on a friend or enemy. One can eavesdrop on someone whom one is neutral towards. Which is which? Is the reaction to each the same? Astral travel is wonderful because it can free a person from the ignorance of what that person is and can be without a material body. Astral travel allows one to realize many hidden areas of existence.

During 1973-1974, I consciously astral travelled daily without fail. The third eye opened regularly. I left the earth and went into outer space but it was not easy to do so, because the astral body went into the sky to about 300 to 1000 feet. Then it would rise no further. At about 40 feet it travelled at a rapid speed if I wanted it to. Sometimes I would be in a parallel world. Everyone there except myself would walk on the ground while I flew about.

Some person noticed my flying ability and yelled to others to show what I did. People became angry and try to cause me to fall to the earth. Some would run, jump and try to pull me down. Some try to do so with willpower. After a time, I made my astral body unseen. I would be in the sky but someone in that parallel dimension could not see that I was present. On one occasion when I tried to go up beyond 1000 feet, I found that I could do it.

Then, something happened that altered the buoyancy of the astral form. I went up and up and up. I found myself looking into a spaceship window viewing an astronaut. From that I knew for sure, that the scientists did in fact put these vehicles into orbit around the earth. The astronaut could not see me because I was in a dimension which his eyes had no access to. All the same even though I could see him and the spacecraft, I could not do anything to affect that. My astral body had visual access only.

Naad Advanced Meditation (May 2011)

Those who practice kriya yoga meditation or the Patanjali system of meditation, should use naad sound as their mantra and main centering device. This sound is automatically there and does not require any endeavor for its usage. Rishi Singh Gherwal asked me to make sure that this instruction is recorded. He said that there are many mantras from India which are divulged in a misleading way. Yogis, he said, should not waste their valuable time using the majority of these mantras, except for perhaps a few like *Om namo Shivaya, Om mani padme hum, hansa, Om* (by itself), *Om namo bhagavate vasudevaya, gayatri* mantra, and tantric guru imparted mantras like *Om Hrim*. He said that ultimately no mantra should be used and only naad sound should be the shelter for the yogi. Rishi is of the view that if one studies

Patanjali Yoga Sutras and also understands and agrees with Krishna's Universal Form, every problem will be solved.

To understand the Universal Form, one has to study the Bhagavad Gita with great care and respect. He emphasized the following:

> *"Since the material world is pivoted away from the spiritual level of existence, one cannot expect to transcend the material world by focusing on it. Naad is important because it comes from the spiritual domain. It is not created by the human vocal organs or human low-level mind. If one fails to take help from the Supreme Being, one will never be liberated because it just happens to be the case that without getting the assistance of the Supreme Being one does not have the strength to shift from the mundane energy. It is a practical matter, where one does what is necessary to complete an objective. Help must be taken from Krishna, regardless of if one likes Krishna or not. This is because a limited spirit does not have the power to lift itself away from these physical and subtle energies which surround it on all sides."*

In reciting a mantra verbally or within the mind mentally, one should give attention to the recitation. The most powerful mantra for this purpose is the age-old standard mantra, *Om*. There are many other mantras but ultimately for meditation, *Om* is the ultimate sound. When *Om* is reduced, naad is heard as the final irreducible resonance.

The problem with chanting is that it requires attentive energy to generate the sound. When using naad the yogi does not generate the sound. It is produced causelessly by the clash between the material existence and the spiritual one. Beyond Om there is the naad sound which is the final mantra. It is free. It does not require endeavor for producing it mentally or aurally. It is there for the taking once you can make contact with it.

I feel duty bound to make this statement since I will not be physically present for very long. The body I use is sixty-eight years of age. Naad is a vital hint. The only person who said that outright during the 1960's and early 1970's was Sri Siri Kirpal Singh Sahib. He was a Sikh by religion but in terms of yoga, he was in a lineage of yogis who used naad and stressed its importance. Kirpal addressed naad as the sound current. As a river is called a current of water, the naad is called a current of sound. It was mentioned by Patanjali and also by Krishna to Uddhava even though it is not mentioned in the *Bhagavad Gita*. Details of its value and usage are given in the *Hatha Yoga Pradipika*.

Krishna's instructions to Uddhava in the *Srimad Bhagavatam* or *Uddhava Gita* are higher instructions for isolated yogis. In this body I personally researched and practice this and tested other processes. Most mantras except for *Om* are trivial. This does not mean that they should not be used. If you are attracted to a mantra, use it. Find its worth. The quicker you practice what you are attracted to and what you believe in, the better off you are, because you can free yourself from mere belief and actually know the worth of the process. You are then freed from prejudices and can test something else.

Ultimately most mantras are props. In the end however to be successful one has to move into naad focus. From there one can get the mind where Patanjali requires it to be. At first one should remain in the coreSelf's default position and listen to naad. When that becomes a habit, one should move the coreSelf from its default position. Move it into the naad which is usually on the back right or left side near an ear. Location of naad may be different for each yogi. Usually naad is a shrill frequency sound which is like the sound of crickets in the dead of night. It resonates continuously even when one is unaware of it. Once you get used to it and can find it easily when meditating, and once the coreSelf gets used to it and accepts it and prefers to focus into it rather than focus on images and thoughts, one should try to move the coreSelf into naad zone.

In the beginning there will be resistance. The core will refuse to move, but one should keep trying to relocate. Eventually the resistance will slacken. One will move the core into naad sound, in the left or right back part of the head. Keep doing this for some time, until the core voluntarily complies and stays there on its own in meditation.

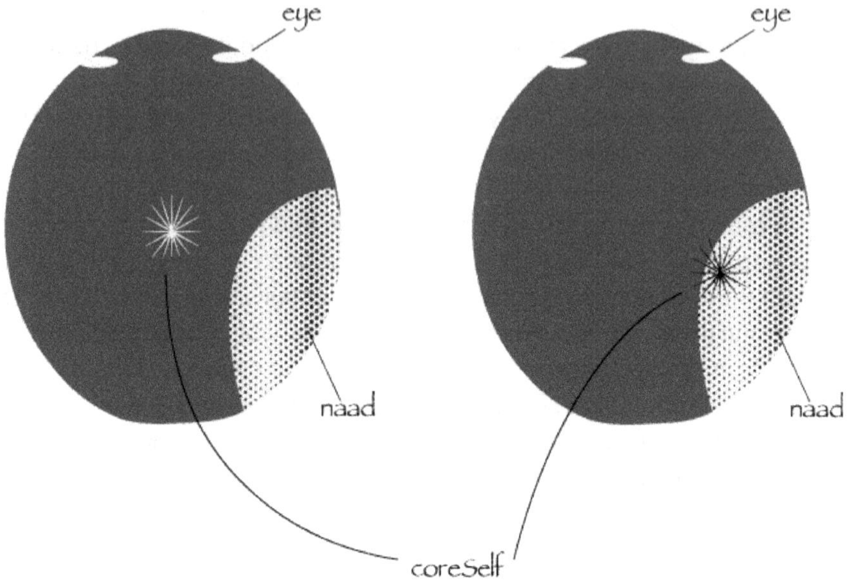

Once you attain that the next stage is to let the core remain in its default position but also note that while it is there it does not adhere to that place as before. It will stay there but with the freedom to move, so that if you relocate there is no flyback, where it wants to return to the default position. At that stage the core should remain in the default position and listen to naad. You may find that naad comes to the coreSelf. Before when the coreSelf was in its default position, the core focused on naad from a distance, but now naad sound comes to the coreSelf of its own accord.

This is the stage where one will meditate like this for some time, until this becomes a settled normal meditation without effort. In this state the mind should not produce images or thoughts. The breath should not be observed. The only thing being observed at this stage is the naad sound. Once settled into this practice, one should focus forward into the intellect organ or into the brow chakra. This may take years to master but one should practice to attain it.

Astral Desire (May 2011)

The astral body has desires and tendencies which have nothing to do with one's conscious desire or willpower. There is this idea that the astral is under our control but that is not the truth. Take the physical body for instance, is that under control? Can anyone stop its deterioration and death?

If the body is seventeen years of age, it is youthful. The faculties are sharp. Now sit on a bench. Using two hands alone, count the hairs on your head. Even though you have the advantage of two hands, you cannot do it. A simple task like that cannot be done by anyone. These bodies, the physical and astral ones are to a greater extend beyond control.

Recently, I had a superficial surgery in South Korea. It concerned a recurring cyst and a tube which vented it through pores, a fistula. It is not something I designed and wanted. It developed involuntarily according to the biological functions of the body. It never had my permission to be there. It never cared of my rejection of it. It only had this sense of doing what it had the authority to do. There are many things in both the physical and astral bodies of which we have no control now and will have no control over in the future. Part of the operation of the body we do control but it is not enough to say that we have absolute privilege.

Suppose I lose my body tomorrow, then if I take an infant form somewhere, how will I control it? I will be totally helpless when that new body is born, being dependent on medical professionals and relatives and also on the political and social circumstances in the area where the body lives. The astral body is an impulsive form, even more so than the physical one. In the physical body for instance after it develops sexual maturity, it pursues sexual indulgence no matter what. It does not care about the responsibilities implied. When it is an infant it goes crazy over what it wants. It harasses the mother, father or guardian for many things. It behaves badly to intimidate the parent when it cannot get what it desires. But that is nothing compared to the craziness of the astral form.

In yoga, we are not afraid of the impulsiveness of the physical body. The formidable fear comes from the impulsiveness of the astral body because by that a yogi can, in a jiffy, lose the spiritual advancement. The astral form craves the fulfilment of desires. It is crazy and has no inhibitions. If you have some basic morality, even if you are an aborigine, you may be disincllined to have sex with your mother or sister, but the astral form may care less about physical morality.

There is a story in the Mahabharata. An angelic woman who was Arjuna's aunt petitioned him for sexual service. When Arjuna brought it to her attention that she was like a mother to him, the lady cursed him to lose the sex drive when he would return to the earth. That is how impulsive the subtle body is. inSelf Yoga™ has as one of its objectives, the curbing of the subtle body. Unless it is curbed, there is no chance for going to a higher existence permanently. One is doomed to haphazard births and deaths, taking one embryo after another to fulfill the desires of the subtle body for physical participation. In fact, when we say that a person reincarnates what we really mean is that the astral of that person develops one physical form after another, in the hope of making its impact in the physical world because the self cannot act in the physical history except through a physical body.

The subtle body has desires of its own. It does not need nor require the coreSelf's approval for the fulfillment of desires. It is in the habit of confiscating the self's authority. What one has as desires in one's conscious purview is only a fraction of the desires in the psyche. From time to time one may be compelled to fulfill odd desires which are not in one's interest. The realization is that unless a person can eliminate the unwanted desire-energies from the subtle body, he or she is doomed to fail in the spiritual quest.

I refer to desires and desire energies which are the subconscious basis of full-blown conscious desires. The subtle body is an escapist form. If the government arrests someone and puts that individual in solitary confinement, his subtle body will escape anytime the physical form sleeps. In the astral environment it will travel and do what it desires, free of the confinement. For that matter the more restriction one places on the physical body the more freedom the subtle body takes. Yogis put this trait of the subtle body to use, by remaining isolated, since then the subtle body increases its travels. In the astral world the yogi can fulfill many desires. He can do many things which otherwise could not be done. When I am in South America, some people in the USA think that I should travel abroad. When I am in the USA, people in South America think that I should travel to those places. Little do they know that I travel astrally and relate in dreams.

Compelling Astra Travel

These are pressures may cause the astral body to travel to another country:

- desire for meaningful or casual relationships with persons in that other location.
- desires of relatives and friends for one's association
- desire to participate in the history of the other country

Freaky Astral Realms

There are freaky places where some particular tendencies and characteristics of a person show in weird forms which either project out of the astral body or show in the astral form in various ways. Usually one does not go to these places but if one takes narcotics especially opium, heroin and morphine, even LSD, one may be transferred to these places and witness one's form and the form of others in lower astral realms in frightening configurations. You may discover yourself there even if you do no opiates and sedatives but it will happen infrequently. It may happen to someone who used the narcotics previously but has relapses from time to time. The astral body is pulled into those places by the dimensional traces which were established previously under the influence of the drugs.

For some reason I transitted to similar places in the astral world. My subtle body strayed there. I have a mission to review those places so that I can describe the situations in books. Even though I am advanced in meditation and astral travel, I dread going to such places. There is always the danger that one may enter such a place and not have the power to exit. The smoking of ganja, hashish and other mind-altering herbs may cause a person's subtle body to journey to such places.

Subconscious Mind/Causal Body Penetration (May 2011)

There is a yoga practice which can be used to enter into the subconscious mind which hold memories which are off limit to the conscious self. One can use this process to enter the causal body, which is not a body but which is part of a space in the cosmic causal energy which one is assigned to. Just as on this planet there is land, and a piece of that land may be called a continent, a piece of which may be called a country, a piece of which may be called a county, a piece of which may be called a property, so there is a causal energy which is inhabited by trillions of living entities, individual selves. To enter the subconscious mind or the causal body, one should reach a plane where thoughts and images cease occurring in the mind. If one has to observe or resist thoughts, one will be unable to do this. As soon as one finds that one is in a mental place or space, where there are no thoughts in the frontal part of the subtle head, one should go down through the neck as if one descended a funnel.

Usually one will find that one cannot do this, as if there is a resistance that prevents one. One should persist in the effort and meditate, practicing this for some time, until the resistance to the downward movement is no longer there. This should be an actual psychic movement not an imagined movement or a visualization of a movement. One should feel that the iSelf moved downwards. It is important to lose the vague idea of the coreSelf and to know what it is and where it is located in the subtle head. When one enters the neck, one is in the subconscious region and when one goes lower and enters the chest region, one is in the causal body. Since there is no sensual facility there like eyes, ears and nostrils, being there may seem like no achievement. The only thing one finds is concentrated energy. However, that energy is compressed subtle information. In the subconscious there are compressed memories from many past lives. In the causal body, the transcendental impetus that drives the numerous lives and numerous bodies we take, is there as well.

These energies however can be translated into the conscious mind so that a person can see, what they would burst out as, in real time in a life experience. If one practices this meditation regularly, there will come a time, when one will find that after moving from the neck or chest, one begins to see images and scenes, even live scenes of the things which happened as well as incidences that will occur in the future. In other words, the informational energy which one carries back into the conscious mind, will burst out into real circumstances. Then one can see past lives and also future time. This is sometimes called reading the akashic records.

Kundalini Sex Urge (May 2011)

When one meditates more and becomes more sensitive to the psychic side of life, that allows one to observed psychic actions which were unconscious or misinterpreted. The differentiation between the actions of kundalini and that of the analyzing faculty in the head is important. Because they consider the psyche to be themselves most people do not know the distinction. They have no idea of distinct psychic components, like kundalini which is based in the lower spine and the analytical faculty which is based in the head.

As one meditates more and more one can sort the components in the psyche. One can observe how they interact. One will know how resistant they are to one's willpower. Regardless of whether one's intuition is correct or not, it is a fact that one partner may sleep near to another in the same bed, and that partner may be engaged in sexual intercourse with someone else who is not present in the bed physically but who may be there on the subtle side or existence. In the yoga practice, there are prohibited activities and approved behaviors. One of these is celibacy. Patanjali gave this alert.

जातिदेशकालसमयानवच्छिन्नाः सार्वभौमा महाव्रतम् ॥३१॥
jāti deśa kāla samaya anavacchinnāḥ
sārvabhaumāḥ mahāvratam

jāti – status; deśa – location; kāla – time; samaya – condition; anavacchinnāḥ – not restricted by, not adjusted by; sārvabhaumāḥ – relating to all standard stages, being standard; mahāvratam – great commitment.

Those moral restraints are not to be adjusted by the status, location, time or condition. They, being the great commitment, are related to all stages of yoga. (Yoga Sutras 2.31)

The yama and niyama processes involve a great commitment *(mahavrata)* to complete the approved behaviors and to squash the prohibited activities for the purpose of advancing spiritually. When a yogi becomes sensitive on the subtle side of existence, he/she can gage as to whether the subtle body complies with Patanjali. The yogi usually finds that the subtle body is crazed for enjoyments and does not give a hoot about moral commitments.

It is then that a yogi understands his miserable plight. He takes seriously to yoga disciplines, to bring the subtle body under control and to make it comply with the request of the yoga teacher.

One should observe the sexual developments in the psyche so that one can plan how to monitor the overwhelming influence of kundalini. To increase its power kundalini takes help from the coreSelf, but when it reaches a certain content of energy, it pushes the coreSelf aside and takes control of the psyche. It fulfills its desire even if the core becomes tagged with the liabilities for sexual involvement. Those liabilities are:

- a fetus
- emotional trauma
- involvement of relatives
- development of a livelihood if there is a fetus
- years of commitment to the infant who takes birth
- absorption of hostilities from relatives and friends who oppose the involvement

Kundalini does not care if any of these are obstructive. Its only interest is to increase its power, cast the coreSelf aside and fulfill itself with an explosion of the sexual force. In addition to kundalini but unseen to physical perception are ancestors who inhabit the sexual energy and take advantage of sexual intercourse to derive embryos.

Subtle Sex (May 2011)

Having or not having physical sexual contact with someone may or may not be related to having subtle sexual relationship with that someone. The two experiences are worlds apart but as the subtle body is usually interspaced into the physical one, it is hard to distinguish subtle activity from physical actions, except in dreams when the astral form is disengaged from the physical system and may or may not have transmission influence. Sex between subtle bodies does not produce children. Sex between physical forms may cause progeny. One may have sexual relationship with someone whom one did not have physical contact with. For that matter one can have sex with someone in the astral world, whom one did not meet physically in the current life.

The subtle body specializes in breaking through moral and social restrictions. If there is an attraction to someone but the moral or social environment prevents sexual linkage, the subtle body may supersede that and find a way to express the sex in the subtle world, on the astral level in dreams. In the astral world, one can be next to someone and not perceive that person. This happens because the astral body may have a slightly different frequency in reference to the other person. That other person cannot perceive one unless his/her astral form also switched to that other frequency. The astral world is a *hide and seek* environment. That is evidenced by the fact that most species which developed on this planet developed color markings which caused the body colors to blend with the environments. Examples are white polar bears on white ice, and straw-colored tigers in the African savannahs. This means that the subtle body expresses camouflage.

When one has a sexual dream, or astral projection and then finds that the physical body secreted sexual fluids, this is a physically registered sexual dream. That is a situation where there is sex using the subtle body, but the information from the subtle body is transferred into the physical system which mimics the subtle act.

Questions of Self

Meditation is for researching, controlling and making psychic use of the mind. In meditation one should discover the psychic components of consciousness and transcend what is physical about the self. Some important questions which meditation should clarify are:

- What is the mind?
- What is the self?
- How are thoughts and images produced in the mind?
- Can the self exist apart from the physical body?
- How is emotion generated in the psyche?
- Are there psychic organs in the mind, just as there are physical organs in the head?
- Are thoughts and images produce by a psychic organ?
- Does another psychic organ produce emotions and feelings?
- Can the self live outside of the mental space which it currently inhabits?
- Can the mind exist outside the brain?

Astral Projection or Dream? (May 2011)

Since a person cannot prove astral travel with scientific precision, we must approach verification in a different way. There is real astral travel. There is real imagination during dreaming. Both are psychic actions. If someone sits on a bench and imagines that he is with a friend that is imagination. The person imagined is not there in fact. Friendly feelings are experienced in the friend's absence. The emotions created suit what is imagined. The person knows that it is imagination and is unrealistic. On the following day he sat on the same bench. This time, the friend was present. Similar emotions arose. He had a similar experience but it was more intensified. It was reinforced by objective reality. In the same way a person who is honest and who endeavored in meditation for some time, should differentiate between an imagination, a lucid dream or an astral projection experience. The more astral projection one does, the more the imagination dreams cease. One who does not astral project consciously will have mostly imagination dreams.

How do we know that someone can distinguish between an astral projection, a lucid dream or the creation of imaginative events in the mind? We do not know except for our reference to incidences like the bench experience. We must rely on that and not think that we should have proof like in scientific experiences which are verified physically.

During imagination dreaming, everything takes place in the imagination faculty in the mind. That is the faculty in which we daydream, in which we experience ideas. A person can have an experience in the imagination chamber in the mind. That experience may be a creation of the mind only. A lucid dream is different in that in such a dream, the person is not in the imagination chamber of the mind but is in a subtle world, in another dimension. He experiences the reality of that place. The same mind is used to have that experience. What is the difference? How do we know that it is not an imaginative sequence created by the mind?

Just as there are physical objects outside the physical body there are astral objects which are present outside the astral body. In lucid dreaming the occurrences happen outside of the imagination faculty. In an imagination dream, they occur within that faculty. In an astral projection the same thing occurs except that the astral body is displaced from the physical one. It is not interspaced into it as it is in a lucid dream.

Let me review this.

- imagination dreaming occurs in the imagination chamber in the mind
- lucid dreaming occurs outside of the imagination chamber of the mind while the astral body remains interspaced in the physical body
- astral projection occurs outside of the imagination chamber of the mind while the astral body is displaced from the physical one, separated from it

Speed of the Astral Body (May 2011)

The astral body can travel according to the energy level it is synchronized into. If it is synchronized at a light frequency, like sunlight for instance, it can travel at the speed of that energy. Because we use physical bodies, it is hard to accept that this may be possible but actually if one thinks a little deeper one can see that even though we are stationary and bound by gravity, the mass of the earth rotates at a rapid speed. The earth itself rotates and it orbits the sun at a rapid speed. It is not stationary. The galaxy we are in moves at a tremendous speed and still we are not aware of it.

The astral body is sometimes moving slowly and sometimes rapidly depending on the level of energy within it. The procedure of breath infusion is a method for rapidly changing the frequency of the astral body so that it can reach tremendous speed and go to much higher levels of existence. But even normally, the astral body is sometimes experienced to travel rapidly. For instance, a person who lives let us say in the USA and who takes a job in Burma, may find that there are dreams of going to the USA to meet friends and family. In these dreams that person feels the need to return to work in Burma. In the dream the person, may not realize that it was an astral projection. He may think that it is physical. He may attempt to board a plane to return to Burma and may even be worried in the dream about arriving late. But suddenly that person will find himself awake as the physical body in Burma. Most of these experiences happen astrally, where like a cell phone signal, the subtle body travels in a few moments across the Pacific, from the USA to Burma, but the dreamer may rationalize that it was just a dream. He cannot distinguish between subtle experience and imagination dream experience.

Mukti Baba (May 2011)

Kundalini rose this morning in a balanced way through the trunk of the body and into the neck. It felt like tiny pearl drops of electric bliss force compacted together tightly. I infused the space around the intellect. When this is done the orb spins rapidly. Thoughts which were manifesting disappeared. After the exercises when I sat to meditate, I heard naad sound. About three seconds after I became aware of an astral level where there were thousands of Indian (India) people. One person walked by them. They shouted, *"Mukti Baba! Mukti Baba!"*

That is Hindi for *free us father, liberate us father*. In that dimension, the astral body does not use language. It processes the precursor of language which is the actual communication without distortion. Even though I never heard what those persons said in Hindi, as soon as their voices rang out, my mind translated their expression-energy into the language which I would have heard if I heard that in physical surroundings. Soon after a man with an afro came to me. He expressed this, "I am unable to get free of this."

It was Sai Baba who recently was pried loose by fate from his physical body. In reply, I said to him, "That is what happens when you mislead people." He did not reply. He kept gliding down the astral roadway. The people kept coming. They chanted, *"Mukti Baba!"* with a look of great anxiety on their faces.

This all happened as my body sat in a cross-legged posture, with the legs crossed under the body since due to a superficial surgery, I was unable to do lotus posture. Usually one cannot astral project from a sitting position. Usually one has to recline the physical body. However, if one practices sitting for a long time, eventually the kundalini relaxes sufficiently for the astral body to separate from the physical one in a sitting pose.

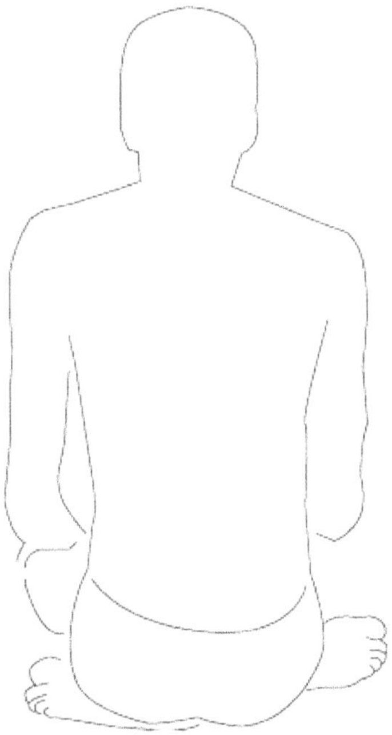

Kundalini: Lack of Sensitivity (May 2011)

Sometimes during kundalini yoga practice, one fails to note the various paths the energy takes. For one thing, unless one developed a high degree of psychic sensitivity, one will miss most of the small charges and movements of kundalini. Even in routine actions of the physical body, there is involvement of kundalini that goes unnoticed. Take for instance if one needs to urinate and fails to do so, the bladder becomes inflated with liquid, until one must urinate. One is compelled to do so, regardless of if one is at the proper location or not. Then there may be a burning sensation or an electrical sensation in the bladder. That is a feeling of kundalini. During sexual arousal there is kundalini energy surging, accumulating and discharging like the arc of a spark plug.

Unless it discharges and acts sensationally as in sexual climax and in its rush into the head of the body during kundalini yoga exercises, a lack of psychic sensitivity makes it impossible to realize kundalini.

Laser Kundalini (May 2011)

During exercises this morning, kundalini rose in an unusual way which was up and then down. First, I raised kundalini through the trunk of the body evenly. This happened because under Rishi Singh's direction, I did this for the past six months. His instruction was to work with kundalini in the trunk of the body and defocus from getting kundalini into the head. This instruction was to force kundalini to find the nadis in the trunk and to cause it to flush through those channels, instead of avoiding them. The entire psyche must experience a transformation from lower to higher energy.

If just the head of the subtle body is energized, the rest of the system will affect the head negatively. The system must be energized for success to relocate to higher planes. A person can wait to see what will happen at the time of death or he/she can endeavor industriously to move the psyche to a higher plane before the physical body dies in order to be sure that the transition occurs. People with strong faith rely on a deity. Some rely on willpower and visualization to take them to a higher plane. Others hope for a dissolution of ego consciousness and an assumption of universal identity. To follow the Bhagavad Gita and even the Yoga Sutras, one must shift the self from the mundane universe.

Krishna said this:

उद्धरेदात्मनात्मानं
नात्मानमवसादयेत् ।
आत्मैव ह्यात्मनो बन्धुर्
आत्मैव रिपुरात्मनः ॥६.५॥
uddharedātmanātmānaṁ
nātmānamavasādayet
ātmaiva hyātmano bandhur
ātmaiva ripurātmanaḥ (6.5)

uddhared = uddharet — should elevate; ātmanā — by the self; 'tmānaṁ = ātmānam — the self; nātmānam = na — not + ātmānam — the self; avasādayet — should degrade; ātmaiva = ātmā — self + eva — only; hyātmano = hyātmanaḥ = hy (hi) — indeed + ātmanaḥ — of the self; bandhur = bandhuh — friend; ātmaiva = ātmā — self + eva — as well; ripur = ripuḥ — enemy; ātmanaḥ — of the self

One should elevate his being by himself. One should not degrade the self. Indeed, the person should be the friend of himself. Or he could be the enemy as well. (Bhagavad Gita 6.5)

बन्धुरात्मात्मनस्तस्य
येनात्मैवात्मना जितः ।
अनात्मनस्तु शत्रुत्वे
वर्तेतात्मैव शत्रुवत् ॥६.६॥
bandhurātmātmanastasya
yenātmaivātmanā jitaḥ
anātmanastu śatrutve
vartetātmaiva śatruvat (6.6)

bandhur = bandhuḥ — friend; ātmā — personal energies; 'tmanas = ātmanas — of the self; tasya — of him; yenātmaivātmanā = yena — by whom + ātmā — self + eva — indeed + ātmanā — by the self; jitaḥ — subdued; anātmanas — of one who is not self-possessed; tu — but; śatrutve — in hostility; vartetātmaiva = varteta — it operates + ātmā - self + eva — indeed; śatruvat — like an enemy

The personal energies are the friend of the person by whom those energies are subdued. But for one whose personality is not self-possessed, the personal energies operate in hostility like an enemy. (Bhagavad Gita 6.6)

Sitting around waiting on faith and hopes is not recommended. When kundalini arose in a strange way which was a little up and then down, I could not trace its every move. This carelessness occurs when one is distracted. There are basically two types of distraction during kundalini yoga practice. One is external stimuli. The other is internal stimuli. In this case it was an internal thought which came into the psyche from an external source. Sometimes there is an internal thought which is created inside the psyche. In this case this was a thought from someone outside the psyche which penetrated the psyche. When it did so, it caused other thoughts to be activated from memory. These psychic movements cause one to advance slowly. Over time, one can get this under control. I tracked the downward movement of kundalini which was a movement downward from about four inches in the center of lower trunk downward though the reproduction chakra of the body. This happened in the subtle body.

As kundalini moved downward it took the form of a white laser beam which splintered and sparkled. It produced blue-white microscopic sparklets. After this kundalini rose into the trunk evenly but it was like shattered windshield glass moving upwards with bliss energy. These actions of kundalini are vital for the removal of old subtle energies which keep the psyche in a dull state of subtle mass ignorance.

Disembodied Souls Enter Parent

There are several passages used by disembodied souls who enter a potential parent body. I gave clarification about this in the *sex you!* book. Here is another detail about a specific passage used in my body recently. A relative of mine who is now deceased for several years, came to me astrally and asked about getting as a body through me. I explain that at sixty years of age, that was not likely. I said that it is known that males of sixty years may sometimes beget children but apart from that I was not in a socially suitable situation. Even though I explained, the person looked in my subtle body through a passage which went from the intestines through the center of the lower trunk and through the reproductive organs.

This is a passage I had not seen in recent meditations. The only reason why I saw it was due to my looking through the subtle perception of that deceased relative. In the astral body, one can sometimes see through the other person vision like looking through a pair of binoculars. There was one tube on the left of the central one and one on the right. The disembodied person took the central one. Before going through that passage, the person fused into my hormonal energy. That was interesting because when the person first appeared the subtle body of that person was like a full-size human form. However, during the procedure when the person tried to enter that subtle body converted into a curved form like a curve fetus. Gradually over a period about fifteen minutes, it merged into my hormonal energy. Then the combination energy went downward to the reproductive location. I did nothing to stop the process because this relative had rights to take birth in the family in which I am a part. I mentally told this person, that I would do my best to facitate a transfer to a younger relative in the family.

Time Limit

A yogi must know that providence places a time limit on everything. No one has an unlimited span of time to achieve. Even the resources in the universe are limited even though it is not possible for any limited being to exhaust these. We find that providence puts us in slots where we cannot realize the extent of certain things. For instance, in the case of electric energy which now powers practically every home in the world, there is a limit to how much we can produce. There is an unlimited amount of electricity in the cosmos, but we are not in a position to exploit it. We have a sun which, relatively speaking, has an unlimited supply of energy for earthly needs. It emits an unlimited supply moment after moment and still we cannot use it except for the distribution of daylight to our planet.

One tiny nuclear explosion in the sun can supply a city like New York with electric power for years, but still we cannot exploit it. Knowing of this unlimited supply in no way give us the power to utilize it. Time is infinite but still the body we use currently will deteriorate in one hundred years. A bug may have two weeks or months to live. Then its body dies. Using its subtle form, it must transmigrate. Time does not allow it perpetual access. When one is transferred to another zone at death, one may have no authority in that place. One's easy life here and the philosophical basis here which was connected to the sense of security one has in the social world here, is finished more or less when time shifts one into another domain.

For that matter one does not know what level of consciousness one will be on, or if one would be objectively aware with insight or memory of the previous life. A yogi should utilize as much time as he/she can for meditation practice, so that he/she may gain insight about the hereafter.

Part 2

Purpose in Life (May 2011)

When one assumes a body and emerges as an infant, one is lost and does not know what one is about. This is due to having lost the point of reference from the previous life. We can understand this by observing what happens to those who are use elderly bodies. They become afflicted with Alzheimer or dementia. They do not know who they are. They do not recognize even the next of kin. As an infant one is without reference. One feels that it is the first time existing. Later as the body matures, one becomes dissatisfied with the conditions and figures what this is about.

Many persons go through the process of waking up to the fact that there must be a deeper meaning to life. Nature has everything under its wings. One should respect that and simultaneously get to a deeper level through reflection and meditation. Read books about spiritual life. Gradually over time one may regain the faculties from past lives.

Regarding negativity. That comes about if one does not have a purpose in life or if one is in an environment which seems to be disharmonious with one's nature. The remedy is to gain a purpose for living. Negativity also comes about because of an innate drive to get satisfaction from the circumstances of life. If life refuses to accommodate what a person desires, that someone feels dissatisfied. The fact is that life is a bigger factor than the self. Life does not have to kowtow to the needs of a limited self. Thus, the self needs to find something in life that it can do in harmony with the flow of time and life. We recently arrived in a universe which astronomers estimate to be some 13 billion years in the making. It is insanity if we think that this should be centered on us or that it should please us.

Most people are materialistic and have no interest in researching the basis of consciousness. We should accept that and be cordial to these people despite the fact that their main business is the physical world and the maintenance of it. Even though they have little interest in spiritual life and they become hung up either in science without spiritual evaluation or in religious beliefs without scientific application, still they should be respected. They work to build roads and buildings, to provide electricity and many things which are useful. The trick is to appreciate them and simultaneously not allow them to keep us bogged down in the materialistic way. Since we use their utilities it is only fair that we appreciate them. A person may be a total egghead from the spiritual perspective and be valuable from the materialistic viewpoint.

Default Condition of the Mind (June 2011)

Sometimes on occasion one finds that meditation is clear, just as on occasion but more often than not, one finds that meditation is a sham, a failed effort. This means that nature's influence is irregular. By our actions, associations and carelessness we inadvertently position ourselves for success or failure.

Consider this. Last night suddenly around 2 am, I got an inspiration to meditate. It was sudden and abrupt. I had not done yoga postures. What I did was to retire early. Somehow by the grace of providence I had no bothersome astral visitors during the night. When I first put the body down to rest there was one astral visitor who wanted to meditate and listen to naad. That was unusually since most visitors have no interest in that.

That person was an encouraging astral association in terms of spiritual progress. When at 2 am I got the inspiration to meditate. I immediately checked the condition of the mind, the way a businessman would check his office after entering his business early in the morning. He checks to see if anything is amiss. Was there a burglar during the night? Did a rodent chew paper? Were there phone messages by eager customers? Did a competitor break into the safe and steal the trade secrets?

Checking the condition of the mind, I was surprised to see that everything was in order. There were no thoughts. Naad sound was loud and clear. Instead of speckled darkness there was clarity and even a diffused light in the mind. I created a thought which ran like this.

This feature of mind should be the default condition.

Unfortunately, it is not so. Anyway, I listened to naad and considered how I could advise students to have this mental state as the normal condition.

Naad Absorption

Read about naad sound. It is called *pranava* Om sound in the yogic books. It is different to tinnitus which is an unwanted medical condition. Naad sound is not a mental nuisance. It is the ultimate unpronounced mantra.

Even though it is described as coming from the right side by the right ear, it may be heard from the left side. Sometimes it comes from all sides. Sometimes it comes from the sushumna nadi and spread into the head as if it is broadcasted from the neck or from inside the back part of the head.

When one reads about this in the Upanishad or in other literature from India, it will be called naad or *pranava* or *sushumna shabda*, the unstruck or unuttered Om, non-resonant Om, *anahat* naad. This is a real Om sound which is never uttered by a human being. It is the ultimate mantra. It is free. Here is a basic procedure for using naad sound.

- Sit to meditate
- Close eyes and focus on naad sound.
- If you cannot find it or cannot hear it, go to the back of the head. (This means to actually move the coreSelf to the back of the head. It does not mean to visualize that you are there or to imagine that you are there.)
- If you can only visualize or imagine it means that you should practice how to relocate the coreSelf in the head. It has a default position according to the dictates of Nature, but by mental practice you can nudge it.
- How long will you have to practice? For as long as is necessary.
- Once you get to the back of the head, once you moved the coreSelf from its default position, what should you do?
- The first action is to realize if you are turned about in the back or if you are face forward from the back. If you face forward remain in that position in the back. Listen to naad there. Determine its origin point.
- If you face backward, turn about while staying at the back. If you find that when you try to turn the coreSelf resumes its default position, keep trying until you can achieve the turn and remain in the back looking forward. It may take some days, weeks or months of practice to master that. Do not be discouraged.
- Once you locate naad's original point, apply attention to that place. If naad is all-pervasive which means that it appears to have no origin point, focus the coreSelf in naad sound while remaining at the back of the head.
- If you find an origin point or if the origin point seems to be in another dimension, go to that location and remain as the coreSelf there. Stay there as long as you can. If you find that you are projected from the naad influence, check to see what happened in the frontal part of the head. If it is involved in the usual images, thoughts and ideas, retreat to naad again. If, however the front area is silenced and if it has a glow of light, or a moving form of light or transparent images, look forward with a slight focus while remaining in naad.
- Eventually, the intellect will open as a vision instrument or the third eye brow chakra will open as a window to another dimension. In some experiences, a bliss energy will surround the

coreSelf while it listens to naad. Be vigilant so that the intellect in the frontal part of the head does not pull the core out of naad.

With naad each yogi has a particular way in which he or she hears it as well as a particular zone for it which is the most frequent location, except when one enters into deep meditation and strange things happen. Honestly, I rarely hear naad from the lower part of the mind (brain). It rarely approached me in a dual fashion but such experiences are all the wonder of it.

When being absorbed in naad it is best not to apply strong focus into the front, into the third eye, or the space between the coreSelf and the third eye. Always apply a mild focus and only when that area is in quiescence without the idea-image-thought panorama. If when you apply that slight focus there is the image-idea-thought stuff going withdraw the focus. Return to full naad focus. If you find that the idea-image-thought ceased, keep the slight focus forward while listening to naad. Patiently wait for other developments.

Meditation Focus (July 2011)

Apart from naad sound there is the focus on diffused, streaming or shining light. The most common light focus is the one of diffused light but the others like a streaming force entering the psyche or going out of it, and a shining light in the psyche or outside of it, are more advanced forms of absorption meditation. The normal state of mind is that of blackness with speckled pieces of light scattered at random. When one is in that state, the best focus is the naad sound. As soon as one focuses definitely on naad sound, one loses focus on the light speckled blackness, unless one makes a deliberate attempt to keep both in focus.

From time to time when in naad, one may drift from it. This happens because the default position of the observing self is to be looking into the imagination chamber of the mind. This chamber is usually located between the self and the frontal part of the head. Even though it appears to be a chamber, it is actually a psychic organ which is the intellect.

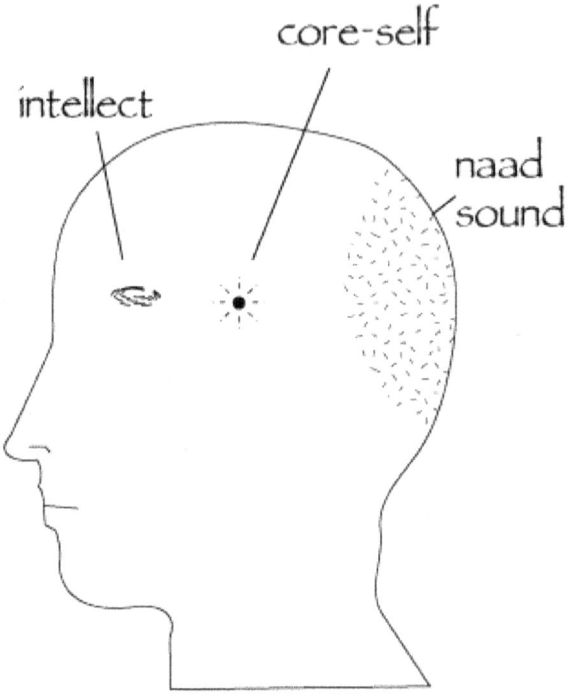

There is a course in yoga for reforming and upgrading the intellect. It is buddhiyoga which is explained by Krishna in chapter two of the Bhagavad Gita. This is so important that Krishna taught it to Arjuna just after Arjuna's depression. It was actually the third teaching told to Arjuna, the first being a reminder that since Arjuna was in a high caste, he should act honorably. The second was that despite forgetting the past life, Arjuna should know for sure that he had many lives previously.

Usually when one is in the speckled darkness, it is best to locate and adhere to naad. A question may arise as to what to do next. Should one be positioned there and adhere to the sound forever? The answer is that when one is absorbed in naad if one finds it to be unattractive and that is not deep or getting increasingly deeper, one is at the surface level of naad. One may infuse the subtle body with breath energy before doing the meditation.

Thought Cores as Closed Bubbles (July 2011)

This morning's meditation consisted of the first ten minutes of distraction with thought core bubbles which did not burst out. To understand what a thought core is, consider if you dive into a pond where they are bubbles rising from the bottom. As these bubbles rise, they move to the surface where they burst and are expressed in air. But consider that somehow as you dive you find that the bubbles remain suspended in the pond, without ever reaching the surface, without ever bursting. This is similar to the first ten minutes of meditation this morning, where there were thoughts bubbles. I was near them but they never burst.

To be more precise on what happened, let me give some locational details. I did breath infusion and because my back was pained, I did not do every required posture. I did however do a good session of breath infusion but only in a few postures. Once after an infusion, I arched to the left and kundalini rose on that side. I did more infusion and arched to the right and kundalini rose on that side.

Two women whom I knew in Trinidad during the years of 1966-1967, came there. These women are deceased. They did the exercises just as I performed. When they were in physical bodies in 1966, they were not interested. Now they are deceased, they developed interest. Their subtle bodies are not as stiff as the physical forms were. They are freed from the social disapproval which came from their neighbors years ago.

After I saw them doing the exercises, I gave instructions since female bodies operate differently to male ones. Some postures are different because of the structural difference in male and female anatomy. After instructing them for fifteen minutes, I refocused on my energy. These two persons used subtle bodies only.

After completing the exercises, I sat to meditate. During the exercises, I wrapped a dark colored cloth over my head and eyes. I do the same during meditation. This is to be sure that no physical light enters the brain and that it is not distracted by sensual stimuli from physical existence. As soon as I sat to meditate, I was distracted, so much so that it took ten minutes to realize that I was.

During that deviation I was involved in the frontal part of the head with thought bubbles which did not expand into thoughts. These were ideas which remained in a compressed form like seeds which had no opportunity to sprout.

This is weird but it has great value for those who want to understand the causal level. On the causal plane, there are many seed thoughts in a microscopic compressed form. They are not in the form of bubbles even. They are compressed concentrated energies which when released, become full blown desires in the subtle and physical worlds. One microscopic bit of energy on the causal level may have within it the total motivation for me to live one thousand physical life-times.

Due to the rising of kundalini and the infusement of breath energy into the subtle body, the intellect in the subtle head was disempowered and could not in its usual way illustrate the compressed ideas or desire energies which came from the sublimal and subconscious zones. Thus, even though the energy were there the intellect could not process it.

The coreSelf which is usually like a passive addicted observer peered to see what would be shown by the intellect but in that case, because the intellect could not decipher the expression, the coreSelf realize that it was stunned for ten minutes after which it began to hear the naad sound.

This is similar to sometimes when a person loses a body, the person may not realize that this happen for some time, for hours, days or even months, because of having the objectivity suspended due to an action on the intellect. After I found myself in naad sound, I gained possession of my objectivity and began to focus on naad on the right back side of the head near the right ear.

At that time a few yoga students from Guyana came in their astral bodies. One person was offended because he tried to get me to be his teacher and I avoided him.

Astral to Physical Shift (July 2011)

Experiences take place daily in the astral world with no or very little awareness of that on the physical side. This is because our minds are tied to the physical as the reality. The mind regards everything besides physical reality as being insubstantial. It is actually the other way around, but nature has us in a spell. We are fused to the physical and have little or no awareness of the subtle places.

One should increase psychic perception by meditation and by the effort to de-emphasize the physical. I repeatedly asked students to focus on the subtle side since at the time of death of the physical body, all that will be available is the psychic existence.

People are confident that the religion, philosophy or belief will carry them safely to the other side after death and that things there will be in their favor. When I ask students to deemphasize the physical, they usually ignore the request. Review your experience. See how difficult it is to focus on the subtle side? When this body dies, one will be transferred to that side permanently.

Consider how strange some relationships are on that side in contrast to what they are or were on this side. All funny feelings, neglects and sentiments, will transpire on the subtle side when one leaves the body. It is in your interest to review the psychic situations now and take steps if one can to be in an advantageous position hereafter.

Psychological Environment

According to the Bhagavad Gita, we currently living in a psyche, a psychological residence. Krishna used the word *ksetra* which means arable land, environment, a place to settle down. Here are verses.

अर्जुन उवाच
प्रकृतिं पुरुषं चैव
क्षेत्रं क्षेत्रज्ञमेव च ।
एतद्वेदितुमिच्छामि
ज्ञानं ज्ञेयं च केशव ॥१३.१॥
arjuna uvāca
prakṛtiṁ puruṣaṁ caiva
kṣetraṁ kṣetrajñameva ca
etadveditumicchāmi
jñānaṁ jñeyaṁ ca keśava (13.1)

arjuna — Arjuna; uvāca — said; prakṛtiṁ — material nature; puruṣaṁ — person; caiva — and indeed; kṣetraṁ — the living space; kṣetrajñam — the experiencer of the living space; eva — indeed; ca — and; etad — this; veditum — to know; icchāmi — I wish; jñānaṁ— conclusion; jñeyaṁ— what is to be experienced; ca — and; keśava — pretty-haired one

Arjuna said: What is material nature? What is the person? What is the living space? Who is the experiencer of the living space? I wish to know this. What is a conclusion? And what is experienced, O Keshava, pretty-haired One? (Bhagavad Gita 13.1)

श्रीभगवानुवाच
इदं शरीरं कौन्तेय
क्षेत्रमित्यभिधीयते ।
एतद्यो वेत्ति तं प्राहुः
क्षेत्रज्ञ इति तद्विदः.॥१३.२॥
śrībhagavānuvāca
idaṁ śarīraṁ kaunteya
kṣetramityabhidhīyate
etadyo vetti taṁ prāhuḥ
kṣetrajña iti tadvidaḥ(13.2)

śrī bhagavān — The Blessed Lord; uvāca — said; idaṁ— this; śarīraṁ— earthly body; kaunteya — O son of Kuntī ; kṣetraṁ — the living space; iti — thus; abhidhīyate — it is called; etat — this; yo = yaḥ— who; vetti — knows; taṁ— him; prāhuḥ — they declare; kṣetrajña — experiencer of the living space; iti— thus; tadvidaḥ — of those knowledgeable of that

The Blessed Lord said: This, the earthly body, O son of Kuntī, is called the living space. Those who are knowledgeable of this, declare the person who understands this to be the experiencer of the living space. (Bhagavad Gita 13.2)

क्षेत्रज्ञं चापि मां विद्धि
सर्वक्षेत्रेषु भारत ।
क्षेत्रक्षेत्रज्ञयोर्ज्ञानं
यत्तज्ज्ञानं मतं मम ॥१३.३

kṣetrajñaṁ cāpi māṁ viddhi
sarvakṣetreṣu bhārata
kṣetrakṣetrajñayorjñānaṁ
yattajjñānaṁ mataṁ mama (13.3)

kṣetrajñam — the experiencer of the living space; cāpi = ca—and + api—also; māṁ -me, viddhi—know; sarvakṣetreṣu — I all living spaces; bhārata —O man of the Bhārata family; kṣetrakṣetrajñayoḥ — of the living space and the experiencer of it; jñānaṁ — information; yat — which; tat — that; jñānaṁ —knowledge; mataṁ -considered; mama — by me

Know also, that I am the experiencer of all living spaces, O man of the Bharata family. Information of the living space and the experiencer of it, is considered by Me to be knowledge. (Bhagavad Gita 13.3)

तत्क्षेत्रं यच्च यादृक् च
यद्विकारि यतश्च यत् ।
स च यो यत्प्रभावश्च
तत्समासेन मे शृणु ॥१३.४॥

tatkṣetraṁ yacca yādṛk ca
yadvikāri yataśca yat
sa ca yo yatprabhāvaśca
tatsamāsena me śṛṇu (13.4)

tat - tad — this; kṣetraṁ — living space; yat — what; ca — and; yadṛk — what kind?; ca — and; yadvikāri = yad —what + vikāri— changes; yataśca - yataḥ— what causes?; ca — and; yat — what; sa = saḥ— he; ca — and; yo - yaḥ— who; yatprabhāvaḥ- yat (yad) — what + prabhāvaḥ— potential + ca — and; tat = tad — that; samāsena — with brevity, in brief; me — of me; śṛṇu — hear

As for this living space, as for what is, as for what kind of environment it is, as for the changes it endures, as to what causes it to change, as for he who is involved, as for his potential, hear from Me of that in brief. (Bhagavad Gita 13.4)

We need clarification. Either Krishna does not know or he does. Many modern psychologists feel that the individual social person is a singular thing but Krishna revealed it as a living space and an experiencer of the living space. Patanjali also described it into a seer and perceiving equipment, like saying we have a researcher and his binoculars. Some object. They feel that the researcher and his binoculars is one and the same. They detest partition because that causes conflict and duality. Anyway, let us begin the discussion with admitting two environments. One is the external environment which we know very well which is the environment outside the body. Then there is the internal environment inside the body which by the grace of nature we do not have to attend to, because nature maintains that. Nature maintains the physiology until there is a sickness which nature cannot suppress.

When we have trouble with the environment, we consult a physician. When it is psychological and if one is in India, one consults a guru. If one is in USA, one takes advice from a psychiatrist. When one is in a tribal situation, one may consult a shaman. If one has trouble with unwanted tenants in the mind, one may consult a priest to get an exorcism. When one is depressed one may take a physical pill which has psychological effects. One may purchase from a whiskey manufacturer or drug dealer. Apart from the external environment which has unfavorable weather, we have an internal environment which gives biological and psychological ailments. Yoga and meditation are mostly concerned with the psychological environment.

Sex Chakra

This morning during exercises, I focused on the second chakra. This is not the sex organ chakra. It is the sex chakra which is on the spine. The one on the spine is the chakra of interest because it monitors the sex organ chakra. Those who have sexual addiction should reform the sex organ chakra before doing anything with the sex chakra on the spine.

The sex chakra on the spine is involved with changing air into liquid. The base chakra is concerned with compressing moisture to create solid materials. Sometimes when one arrives at the base chakra one feels density; one feels a heaviness but one may not see anything visually. At other times at the base chakra one sees a darkness or a dark-brownness. The main thing is the feeling of being at the bottom of something, as being dense and heavy. The second chakra gives the feeling of being like a cloud or being like vapor floating over water or vapor which formed in air and converts into water. Vapor may be in the air and it may not be seen, but if it condenses further, it is seen. This is like someone in the astral world awaiting rebirth. During the interim period, people in the physical world do not see that astral person, but as soon as an embryo is formed, people realize that there will be a baby.

Some people welcome a pregnancy with smiles but in some instances, people shun it. They whisper, "Who is the father? With whom did she have a penetration? Who will raise the child?

When I worked on the second chakra, the sex chakra on the spine, it did not respond. I compressed some more breath infused energy into it. After a time, it assumed an airy feeling. There was a blank space with some light like when sunshine suddenly penetrates a dark overhanging cloud. Kundalini is a nuisance but it has to be elevated. It should not be ignored. All students who work on it day after day will get results from the efforts while using this body, and after relinquishing this body at its death.

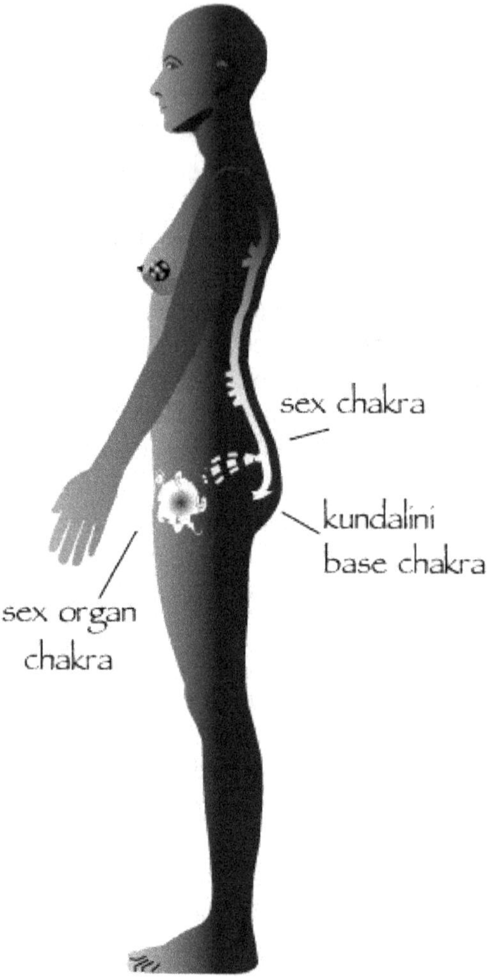

Astral Slavery

During the night I found myself in an adjacent parallel world with five people. At that place for some reason I became conscious of myself working in a precious metals mine. This is just like when one takes a body and then gradually one becomes conscious of the self as the son of a couple. Or even when one finds oneself as the son of a prostitute who does not know the specific person who was the father. At first when I found myself in that place, I was with three men. We worked for a man at precious metals mine. We used explosives to pulverize certain areas of a mountain face. The other three men were scared that somehow the explosives would detonate accidentally and damage their faces since this happened previously to other workers.

For some reason, there was a force which compelled us to keep working despite the danger. Suddenly I found myself with a man who was the overseer of the mine. His astral body was deformed so that he moved in a twisted way but he had a smile on his face which was from the fact that even though he was deformed, he was the boss. He benefited the most from the precious metal extracted. He was friendly with me and signaled that I should follow him to get registered as an employee and to get my rations and tool kit.

We moved up the side of a mountain on a slender path, below which was a sheer cliff but neither of us was afraid because the bodies we used could not fall as a physical body would. Along that path there were berry trees which grew upward from crevices in the mountain. These astral trees were the strangest vegetation because they bore more than one type of berry on one single tree. On the earth, one tree only bears one species of fruit but in that world, the trees have a power to produce other fruits. These trees had a native fruit which was found near the bottom of the tree but as one looked up higher there were other fruits which the trees bore but which were fruits which they envied in other plants and which they confiscated the psychic genetic code for producing these other fruits.

This is like when in this world, a person develops a criminal mentality and steals from another person, confiscating the property of the other. As the overseer went ahead of me on the path, I stopped for a moment to pick some fruits from the top of one tree. As I tugged to take it the fruit tree did not release the fruit even though the fruit was ripe. On this planet when a fruit is ripe it can be separated with a just a tug but as I tugged and tugged, the plant did not release the fruit. I then got a thought from the plant which read in language like this, "These are not for human consumption. These are to give me the satisfaction of bearing fruits of plants I envy."

After this happened, I realized that the overseer was far along the path. I left that place and instantly found myself at the house of the overseer. In there a lady who was his assistant spoke to me about my work kit and the required clothing. The overseer then told me that I would use explosives like the other miners. He stated that there was a quota which I had to fill every day and that I was to return to his place for sleeping at night. After this happened, my astral body suddenly changed frequency and I found myself near my physical form in this world.

Some questions may arise as to this experience.

Since one forgets one's earthly profile and cannot realize it while in such a place, how can one escape from such a place if one's astral body is stuck there for a time?

How long will the miners stay at that place?

Was the crippled overseer an astral police warden?

What force attracts the astral body to such a place?

Kriya Yoga Origins (July 2011)

I was asked for an opinion on Bikram Yoga. This yoga was founded by Bikram Choudhoury who was a disciple of Vishnu Ghosh who was a brother of Paramhansa Yogananda. Yogananda is famous from the kriya lineage which was established to spread the ideas of Sri Babaji Mahasaya, the person who inspired my book, *Kriya Yoga Bhagavad Gita*.

Choudhoury copyrighted some methods and that is crazy, because the postures and methods are natural practices. I have some particular techniques which are in my book, *Meditation Pictorial*. These are nowhere else. No other teacher gave certain methods which are in that book. No one else presented some diagrams in that book. I know this because I am with Siddhas in the astral world who marvel at some of the diagrams and wonder how I was able to put those things into print.

Still it would be a farce if I were to take those diagrams and try to monopolize then and sue people about the use of them. One does this kind of legal maneuver either to make money by monopolizing or to stop others from doing the same while they use one's process. At the time of this article I began a book called the *Anu Gita*. This is a discussion between Krishna and Arjuna, after Arjuna's brothers won the Mahabharata war. Arjuna asked Krishna to again show the Universal Form.

This is a very interesting discourse because Krishna refused to manifest the apparition again. He claimed that it was through special yoga technique that he manifested it and he could not do it again. He more or less cited that Arjuna was a terrible disappointment because Arjuna lost track of the apparition. Krishna said he was disgusted with Arjuna. Currently I translate that book. It is a small book. Why am I doing this? It is because in the astral world Rishi Singh Gherwal asked me to translate it. Then he left as if to say, that he would see me again when I got this book in print as well as another book, which is also from the Mahabharata.

The other text is one about the Yogi Markandeya, who entered one of Krishna's supernatural bodies and spend billions of years transmigrating in it as a human bacterium. Can you imagine, becoming a bacterium and then entering someone's body and moving through his tissues for years. After that intrusive journey Markandeya was evicted from Krishna's body.

That book was told to Yudhishthira in the Mahabharata. Why am I doing that book? In this life, the first time I read the Mahabharata or a part of it, was when Arthur Beverford handed me a tiny book which was Rishi Singh Gherwal's publication of that story of the microbe yogi Markandeya. That book is out of print. I cannot find a copy anywhere. I used to have a copy around 1972. Rishi Singh requested that I translate that book again. Should I claim that anyone who tries to use that book without my expressed permission should be sued?

You can see how ridiculous that would be. Anyway, the Bikram Yoga system is taken from two systems. The first is Patanjali Yoga, which list yoga as having eight parts. The second is from the Kriya Lineage from Babaji Mahasaya which came through Lahiri Mahasaya and then came to the Western countries first through Paramhamsa Yogananda. Interestingly, there is a confusion where people feel that Patanjali Yoga is something other than the kriya system. Some teachers gave that impression but it is incorrect. Here is why. The Patanjali eight coursed system is inclusive of the kriya system. The kriya system taught by Babaji is mentioned in chapter two of *Bhagavad Gita* as Buddhi Yoga. It is laid out there in plain terms.

In the Patanjali system the kriya system is laid out as *samyama* which is the three highest courses of yoga fused into one serial system, as the sixth stage progressing into the seventh which progresses into the eighth and final stage which is extra-dimensional trance absorption. No one after Patanjali can monopolized on that system.

If anyone owns it as being the person to first delineate it, that is Patanjali. He is dead and gone. My suggestion for persons who want to follow Bikram Yoga is to study *Patanjali's Yoga Sutras*. I published a translation and commentary but there are others in print.

CoreSelf Ignored by Naad (July 2011)

A Buddha deity from South Korea explained some details about uprooting kundalini energy from the base chakra. He explained that unless the yogi yanks kundalini from the base, it is doubtful that the yogi's final departure from the body will be satisfactory. For one to be a siddha, the least requirement is the handling of kundalini from the base, by uprooting it there, holding its head there and turning it upwards.

This means that a yogi must be skilled beyond raising kundalini through the spine. He should focus on shattering the magnetic force which keeps kundalini fused into its base chakra. A yogi should know that at the time of final departure from the body, if he has not already uprooted kundalini and freed it from the magnetic force of the base chakra, he will not command it and will have to wait until the energy at the base is dissipated due to frailty of the damaged or aged physical system. This will not allow satisfactory departure from the body. It will cause the yogi to be less than a siddha.

For a yogi the idea behind taking a body, is to go with the siddhas. If a yogi cannot do this, he failed in the mission in yet another life. Still there is nothing to be despondent about. The struggle to get the upper hand over the psychic instincts of the subtle body is a big challenge for any limited being. If one failed before, one can fail again. The regret ends there.

While meditating, I descended through the lower trunk to check the status of kundalini. I grabbed the kundalini at the base and pulled it up. I used the right hand, but the Buddha deity said, "Why use the right. Use the left."

After some time, I had a feeling to check on the frontal part of the brain. When I did so, the third eye was in operation. I saw a flash of clear perception into another dimension. It was too fast to identify it. After that I checked for naad sound. It streamed in from the right ear with great intensity. It seemed to ignore my presence. It did not have time to regard the coreSelf.

In my view meditation is different to astral projection. The objective is different. In advanced meditation, astral projection may take place even when sitting in difficult postures like padmasana lotus. But astral projection from an advanced meditation after doing yoga and meditation for many years, is not the same as other astral projection objectives and methods.

Meditation is an effort to reach a higher state of consciousness while in the physical body with the conscious profile one has in the material body. Astral projection is to reach an astral dimension while being displaced from the physical body. Meditation is more similar to lucid dreaming than it is to astral projection. In lucid dreaming the dreamer remains slightly aware of the physical system and the astral form remains fused into the physical one. In astral projection the astral form is displaced out of the physical system. The dreamer loses physical reference and finds him or herself in an astral world.

Kundalini Visualization (July 2011)

Usually kundalini travels upward through the spine during exercises for breath infusion but a yogi should know that there are nadi channels throughout the subtle body. The question arises, as to why does kundalini come up the spine and does not usually travel into the nadis which are in the body even in the extremities like the fingers and toes.

The answer is that once kundalini manufactured a body in the womb of the parents it is no longer concerned with the details of that body. Its concern shrinks to basic maintenance and to acquiring pleasures and experiences from the body. It will not therefore be involved voluntarily in keeping the tiny nadis which run all over the body in order. Even physically we see that the fluid pump in the body, the heart, is not concerned with the details of how blood gets to the extremities. It pumps the blood on the assumption that it will course through those extremities, even though as the body gets older the plumbing system deteriorates.

A yogi has it as a chore to make certain that the kundalini flows through the extremities. That is why the postures are required as the third stage of yoga. During practice one will feel when kundalini goes to the extremities, even if that happens rarely. The postures stretch, contract and activate some nadis which are in hard-to-reach places of the subtle body. If there is no posture regiment, the yogi has to depend on imagination or visualization to command kundalini to go to various out-of-the-way places in the body. And of course, that would depend on how much the kundalini shows a response to such mental commands. If you can give a mental command to raise kundalini and if kundalini obeys that wish, then obviously you have no need for posture, or breath infusion.

Components of Consciousness? (July 2011)

In meditation attempts should be made to break the default configuration of the components of consciousness. This is not to disrupt consciousness nor even to re-design the inners of the psyche, but to be able to observe and supervise the components. So long as the components stay put in their default positions, it is hardly likely that one will break from the conditioning one is gifted with by the grace of nature.

The two main breakaways are the intellect and the coreSelf. If one manages to move either of these components one can get into this type of action with the memory and the lifeForce, particularly with the lifeForce (kundalini). The main handicap one has is the lifeForce but one cannot attack it at first because it is out of reach. One can however target the intellect. When one gets a footing on shifting that one can consider how to manhandle the other components.

As gifted by nature, the coreSelf is a lazy person with nothing to do but to be entertained by the intellect and to be influenced in moods by the lifeForce. Hence it is an effort to get the core to change from being an influenced experiencer to an active integral part in the operation of the psyche.

To attack the intellect, one must study how one is entertained by its ideas, images and other media fantasies in the mind. Usually a person feels that the mind and the self are one and the same. If a person is told that this is incorrect the person becomes puzzled or feels offended. But really, one should be confident that what I wrote is the truth, despite the fact that one has no evidence of it. To begin this investigation into finding the components of the apparently unified one mind, a person must realize the coreSelf as a mere point of perspective.

Beginning with that, with the observing self as a point of perspective, look for something to observe in the mind. It could be anything, a sound, an image, a memory, a newly created idea, a faint impression, anything. Where does that occur? Is there distance between the self and the impression? If there is any distance, anything, even a micro space, it means that we have at least three components.

Those components are the point of perspective self, the micro space and the impression. This is where we begin. We repeatedly observe this in meditation, until we can pinpoint the location of the impression, the intervening space and the self.

Can one do this?

Does one feel fragmented when doing this?

Kundalini Base Inspection (July 2011)

During the morning meditation, I descended through the trunk of the body to the base chakra, As I went down, I heard naad sound streaming near the right ear. It was loud but it seems to be coming from a distant galaxy, with intentions to attract the self to it. It invited me. It said, *"Remain here. Listen."*

I travelled past it. I went further. As soon as I entered the neck, I noticed that I was no longer hearing naad. Instead there were colors occurring as sounds. When I passed the chest area, the colors as sounds ceased. There were no colors nor sounds. There was light, like clear light coming through a window in the early morning. At first there seem to be nothing at the base chakra when I looked down. Then there seemed to be a shaft of shadow and light mixed. This hung above the base chakra. I ignored it and went under the base.

This going under the base, was an instruction I got from by a Buddha deity in South Korea. His instruction was that one should attack the location of the base chakra and not the chakra itself. If you want to move something, you can either move it or move its foundation. In either case it will be moved. If, however you deal with a stubborn obsessive living object, merely moving it will not be effective. It will re-attach itself to the location. If, however you move the location, it cannot reattach itself. It will have to consider going elsewhere.

Actually, this is exactly what happens when the body dies, that the lifeForce which is attached to the body as its residence, finds that it can no longer locate the body. It reluctantly accepts the astral world as it regrets having no access to its physical form.

The lifeForce is desperate to have a physical body. This means that as soon as it is put out of commission in a physical system, getting another one becomes its obsession. Unless one can tamper with this instinct one is condemned to taking one body after another, as such bodies become available by the grace of nature.

To uproot kundalini the yogi must demolish its base. The Buddha deity stated that this method did not come from a teacher whom he approached during the lifetime in India. Teachers introduced him to valuable techniques but this process and some others were discovered by him or inspired into his mind directly as he practiced.

He set it as my duty to develop and teach this practice. When I got under the base chakra, I found a light-yellow light. I was surprised because I expected brown darkness or a heavy energy. Usually at this place one meets with a denseness like if one met head on with the heaviest matter there could ever be. Because of an aggressive breath infusion practice which I did just prior to the meditation session, I perceived this yellow light.

Due to an influx of foreign thought energy into the mind, the morning meditation was sloppy. This is the system of the mind's reception of disruptive ideas from others. Sitting to meditate is not always ideal where there is a *peace of mind* scene or an egoless bliss experience. Meditation practice can be a mental struggle against self-inflicted disharmonies as well as against bad energies which come into the psyche from others.

When I sat to meditate, it took about fifteen minutes to calm the mind. It was hit by negative idea-energies. These thought-missiles punctured the surface of the mind. They exploded into the mind chamber. I stopped, observe those energies and made efforts to eradicate them. That took fifteen minutes. So long as one's existence is registered in this domain, one can expect failed meditation. One should never get the idea that one is immune to such disruptions or that one does not deserve these or that meditation will rid the self of these once and for all.

It is not a matter of meditation but a matter of location. There will be recurring need to fix the damage done to the mind by self-inflicted disharmonies as well as by raspy thoughts from others which penetrate the mind.

Until one no longer has a register on this plane of existence, one will be subjected to psychological hassles. Of course, one should try to reduce these to the very minimum but one should harbor no fantasies about an absolute removal of such disturbances.

In the astral world, earlier in the night, some relatives of my body enlisted my services in doing renovations. It is ridiculous because in the astral world there is no need to renovate the way we do in this physical world. Still these persons were so obsessed with living in the physical world, that to them astral experience is physical. They do things in the astral world just as if that place was this physical realm.

When they asked me to do renovations, I looked at them. I felt pathetic about their situation. I wrote many books explaining the astral existence but these persons simply ignore the books even though they are educated. Their primary aim in life is to exploit material existence for whatever they can get in the form of fulfillment of desires.

They get a satisfaction from asking me to comply with request for service like renovation. They have no assessment of my worth as a yogi. To them I am a repairman. Such is this life. One should bear it, so long as one is in these dimensions.

Relatives and friends who have little or no self-realization about the psychic or spiritual side of life, make their assessments and evaluations on basis of what is physical. They push these views forward as the priority. If something does not produce physical results, they see no value in it.

Fulfillment of Ambition

Last night I was in the astral world with a sannyasin monk, who is now disgraced. He lost status as a senior in the spiritual movement he served as a leader some years ago. This person was with another individual who was a married man in the society and who was also a senior official. Both of them held senior positions. The married one is still in the society even though there is mounting criticism about him.

In that astral encounter, the sannyasis tried to reorganize his life to reflect the glory days when he was famous and providence supported his ambitions. After a time, due to some faulty actions which he mistook as perfect actions, he lost the status as a senior person. Now his only concern is to reenact what happened in his glory days.

This attitude affects just about everyone, where when one is dethroned from a position, one expends efforts to regain it. Instead of riding the down wave of nature like a cooperative surfer, one thinks that one should go up the curve to ascent the top of the wave.

This occurs from a misunderstanding on our part about the role we should play in the foldout of history. The psychologists alerted us to this as being the false ego or just the ego. I assume that they mean that this is because we impulsively identifying with advantage. What should a person do instead? That question requires consideration. During the astral encounter, the one who was married asked me to do worship ceremony procedures. I agreed.

Because I joined the society after he did this person sees me as a junior. To comply I went to a sink to get water to clean my hands. When I got to the sink, the senior monk was sitting in it. I explained the situation to him. He agreed to get out of the sink but indicated that he would have to be lifted out since his body was crippled. I told him I would lift him and he was a bit alarmed, thinking that I did not have the physical strength to do so. Anyway, I got him out easily.

After this, I washed and went to the place where the ceremony was to take place. When I got there some others whom I knew years ago arrived. These were persons who were assistants of the senior monk who was crippled. I greeted some of them. Some spoke of things from years ago, feeling happy to meet with friends from the past.

After sometime, everyone faded from that place as the senior monk did not have the power to keep us there for long. This experience shows what we do if we are unable to fulfill desires. We keep those ideas in mind. We do whatever is necessary to compel others to help in fulfillment, without considering if nature would sponsor those acts for a second or third time.

Those in theistic societies feel that this is correct because to their view, they do this for a god or deity. Actually, they are mistaken. The way to deal with history, is to ride an ascending wave when history is going in one direction and then to ride a descending wave just the same when history goes in the converse direction. Stated plainly one should integrate with the upswings and the downgrades. The advantage is not to be on the top of a crest but to be riding the wave. If one can change one's attitude the experience would be rewarding. If one focuses on being at the crest, one will be eager to get to the top, only to discover that one cannot remain there. One will experience horror when the energy under the crest breaks apart and no longer supports the ascent.

Fruits on the Sun Planet (July 2011)

This morning session of breath infusion was fifty minutes. During the rapid breathing the subtle body absorbed more and more air. Most of it went to a location below the navel. Then it vanished into thin air, or so it seemed. Arthur Beverford who was my first formal teacher of asana postures, came in his subtle body. He was interested in seeing the effects of the breath infusion on my subtle form. During his last body he did asana postures and some pranayama methods but not the bhastrika rapid breathing.

He said that he would begin to do the bhastrika on a regular basis and would substitute it for smoking. In his last body he smoked tobacco. His main discipline in the last body was Japanese martial arts but he did have a daily meditation practice which began with a third eye focusing technique.

After the infusion session when I sat to meditate, there was fresh energy everywhere in the psyche. Particularly there was a flow of energy coming from the spine into the head. It ascended like a shaft of light but the light was solid, as if it were a shaft made of glass. This lasted for five minutes. After that I descended to the base chakra, since that is the instruction from a Buddha deity in South Korea. When I got to the base, I noticed shafts of energy positioned across diagonally at the base. Some were crystal clear, some had slight tints of yellow or orange. These were like thick sheets of glass passing through each other.

This experience is similar to an experience I had in 1973. While my physical body was in Denver, Colorado, the subtle form separated and transited in a moment to the sun planet. There I saw buildings, streets, people, vegetation, everything, in a civilization which like something in a fantasy movie. Everything there was made of light energy, just as everything here is made of solid, liquid and gaseous matter.

There were trees there bearing fruits which were made of light energy. These fruits were eaten by the denizens of that place. Since the bodies used there were made out of the same materials, those materials were substantial to the inhabitants.

After being at the base chakra for a time, I came into the head. When I passed the right ear, I heard naad which was streaming in loud and clear with definition. There are times when naad is barely heard or it is so distant like something which is light-years away. But on this occasion, it was loud and pronounced.

After hearing naad and moving to the frontal part of the head, I noticed that the third eye (brow chakra) was open. It peered over a lady's shoulder while the woman looked out of a window. An intuition flashed about this place as being an embassy building in Italy. Third eye can open and one may not know it. If one is not focused through it, one may not know it is operative.

Naad sound can lead to the chit akash, which is the sky of consciousness, the spiritual universe. This creation is a shadow of that sky of consciousness. Somehow this shadow came about in the process of cosmic time. Somehow after many billions of years of the development of the shadow universe we discovered ourselves conscious here.

Can the Self be Seen? (July 2011)

With limited sense perception, one should agree to surmise some things which are beyond the sensual reach. The intellect is easy to surmise from the fact that there occurs in the mind, ideas, impressions and images. But it is like a firefly. On a dark night a firefly cannot be seen even if it right before the eyes, but as soon as the electric organ is switched on in the insect's body, one perceives it. The intellect is like that where one does not see it unless it is in the action of producing an idea, or image. Then one perceives it as that image.

A child in the tropics can tell you that a firefly is the bug which illuminates. When asked about the shape of the bug, the child will say that it is the shape of the light. This is not correct but it is correct in so far as the child's sense perception reports. We usually identify the intellect by its activities of producing thoughts and images, just as the child identifies the firefly by the light its body produces.

If one uses high tech goggles, one may see the firefly in the dark even when it is not lit by its light-producing organ. We get some increased psychic perception through meditation practice. One human being can share his night goggles with another human being but unfortunately, a yogi cannot share his psychic vision except by advising the student how to meditate to develop that extrasensory power.

This is where yoga fails to keep up with technology. This is a failure we admit. Regarding the coreSelf, it is subtler than the intellect. Thus, one can imagine how hard it would be to provide proof of its existence. Regarding the cultural self, Buddha established that such a self was a myth. This is obvious when we consider that even though it is serviceable for the time being, these social designations that mark every human being, has value only so long as the physical body lives.

Sometimes we see that even within one lifetime a person suffers from character assassination and the identity as Mr. or Mrs. this or that, is imperiled, so much that the person lives in fear of the name. But regarding if there is an enduring coreSelf which can comprehensively identity itself as continuing to exist forever, the evidence is that none of the selves we usually encounter on this earth can make claims about such continuity, at least not a conscious one.

If the universe already existed for thirteen billion years, something that recently formed an identity and clings to that, can make no enduring claims. It cannot lay its finger on time because it occurred thirteen billion years after time began. It has no autonomy. It is relative. This does not mean that it did not exist before, because we know that one does not have to be conscious or be objective to exist.

We have medical experience of a person in a coma and who exists because after days, weeks or months, he/she awakens and demonstrates the old identity. That means that one can exist and be unconscious of it. We can surmise that one may or may not be eternal and that even if one is, that does not entitle one to eternal objective self-awareness. We must agree to this and then the question is asked as to why try for clarity of consciousness. If one will not exist forever why upgrade the self for conscious self-awareness which will not last beyond 100 years. If the life is one hundred years, why protect it from being killed?

The self is a perplexing topic. What is the self if it is stripped of social identity, stripped of its role as the father, wife or grandmother of someone? Would there be anything left of the self, if its social affiliations were removed?

The observing self is subtler than the intellect. One must first perceive the intellect before one even considers seeing the self. Then there is the problem of something seeing itself. How would that be possible unless it has a mirror? Aborigines are known to express surprise, and even abject fear when they are first given a mirror to peer into.

How can the self see itself or any other self? At least the aborigine can see his fellows but the self can neither visually see itself not any other self.

When Light Energy Becomes Solid (July 2011)

Breath infusion practice was good this morning with energy being balanced in terms of the solar and lunar forces. I was near Washington, DC. Here the sun appeared to move to the south after reaching its northernmost point on June 21st.

Soon winter will approach when the lunar energy will supersede the solar one. During the session kundalini ascended the front on one side and simultaneously went down that side through the front thigh and leg. This felt like a spiral spring energy shooting through the thigh and leg in the front of the main bones in those parts of the body.

I had a visitor who was Rishi Singh Gherwal. He checked some publications he requested of me. My plan was to write a few books having to do with astral projection and lucid dreaming. Rishi requested two books which caused me to postpone other publications. He wanted to know how I felt about the importance of the *Anu Gita*. After the exercises and meditation session which followed, I gave my view that it was an important text in regard to how the person carries the effects of his acts to the next body.

During the meditation session, I journeyed to the base chakra. This was in keeping with Buddha deity's instruction for a two-year period of hammering away at that zone, to smash its tendency for getting rooted in the gross bodies it creates. When I first tried to descend, I could not because in the neck there was energy coming up in a gush like geyser.

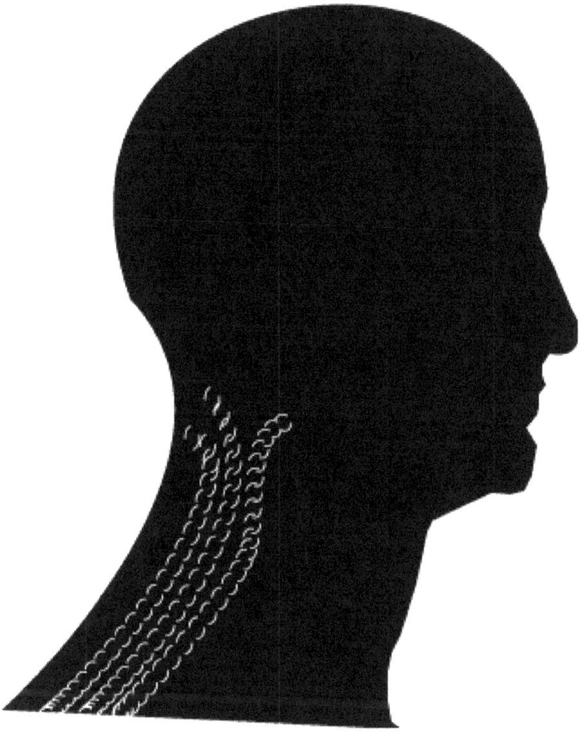

There were three round columns of energy, one in the center which was crystal clear and then one on the left and one on the right side. These were like columns of light which were solid as glass. This is similar to some dimensions where everything is made of light energy but that energy feels like a physical existence where there are solid materials. Science is saying that nothing is solid and yet we live in a world, and the scientists do too, in which no matter what we say or prove, we must respect the solidity of objects. These including the bodies we use.

Realizing that I could not penetrate that solid light energy, I went to the back of the head a little to the right side. There I listened to naad sound. It came from the right side but it spread in such a way as to seem to come from the right and left simultaneously. I stayed with naad for fifteen minutes. Then the kundalini force subsided and the solid light energy became diffused like when in the early morning a heavy mist vanishes as the sun ascends the sky. I then went down to the base chakra with ease.

After this when I got up from meditation, Rishi Singh spoke about the *Anu Gita* and wanted to know my opinion. I currently translate it from Sanskrit. I am in the third chapter. It has four chapters. It is a small part of the *Mahabharata*, not as large as *Bhagavad Gita*. I am in the portion where the effects of a person's actions are explained in terms of what the person becomes destined to experience in the next life.

With Rishi Singh Gherwal, I tried to contact him since in 1970, when Arthur Beverford showed me Rishi's books and began teaching me the asana postures, Rishi taught him in Santa Barbara, California. It took over thirty years before I saw Rishi on the astral planes. He is a simple person, no pretensions and very open.

I may add that the natural way, is that breath energy usually moves down through the front part of the body. When it hits the navel region, it goes through a swirl, and then it goes down to the groin area. If it manages to go further it hits the base chakra. If it does not go further part of it is stored in the sex organ area and part of it is sent upwards to the central gut.

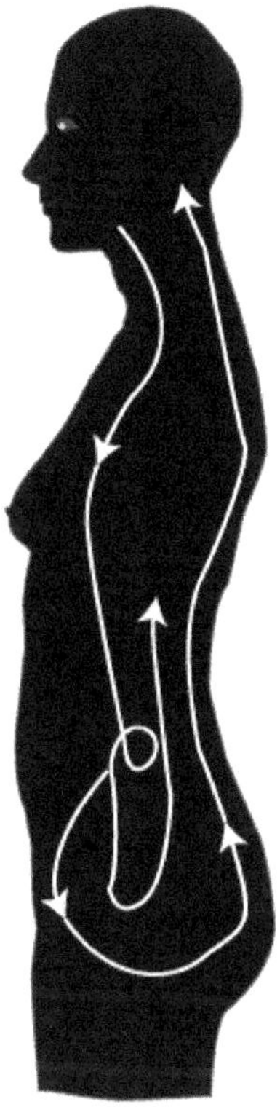

In this system the breath energy does not hit any chakra on the spine at first but engages with extensions of those chakras which are projected from the chakras on the spine to the front part of the body. The yogi may take action to change the natural route of the breath energy, or he may use that route and make it more efficient.

In kundalini yoga, the initial objective is to bore the natural route. This is because a yogi may discover that it is blocked. In the yoga books there is mention about nadis. In fact, the yoga practice which is called nadi shodana, means the process of cleaning (shuddha - Sanskrit) the nadis, which are subtle tubes. Some of these passages are the subtle counterpart to veins, arteries and nerves. The discovery of the subtle tubes is important because it give the yogi insight into the construction of the subtle body, just as in the medical field we are informed of the organs and fluid transport systems within the physical body.

Kundalini Base Attack (July 2011)

The two diagrams below show how to attack the base which kundalini adheres to, rather than the kundalini base chakra itself. This is a strategy shown to me by a Buddha deity. The motive for attacking this base pad is to uproot kundalini and to cause it abandon its tendency for being anchored in a physical form. This is different from the motive for a direct attack on kundalini, which is to cause kundalini to be aroused so that it heads into the head and provides increased psychic perception of other dimensions.

The attainment of increase perception of subtle realms does not usually interfere with kundalini's instinct for creating and taking up residence in physical bodies. But if the base is removed, then kundalini may lose that transmigration tendency.

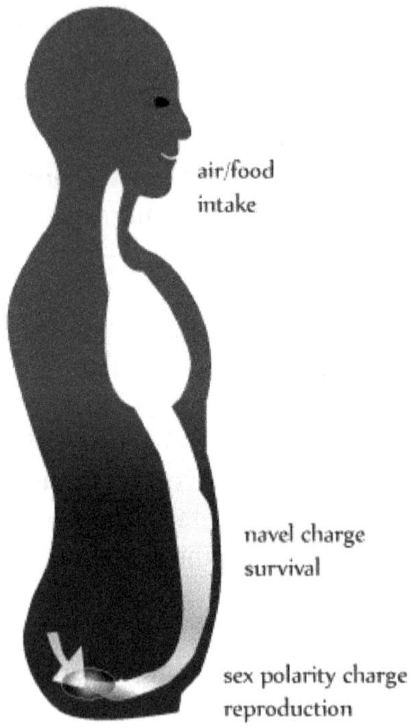

infused breath
attacks kundalini

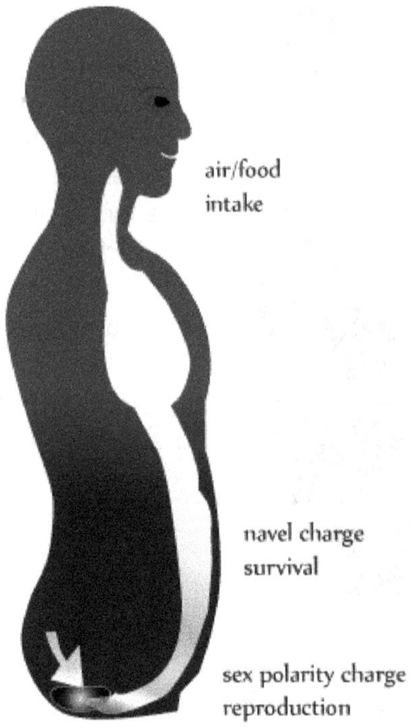

infused breath avoids kundalini
but attacks kundalini's base

Naad as a Light (July 2011)

During exercises this morning, Rishi Singh put energy into my psyche. It translated to this level as information for a book which I a translate currently. That is the *Anu Gita,* the instructions given to Arjuna by Krishna, when Arjuna graciously asked Krishna to reveal the Universal Form once again.

The information from Rishi seeped into my psyche for about two months but today, he more or less injected the rest of it in one infusion. Gradually as I compose the book the information will become available. I continued working on the base chakra, but the kundalini was involved in its chores of body protection. I had to work with that, which meant that the breath infusion was not as efficient.

Earlier during the night, I found myself in a parallel world with some persons whom I knew about 40 years ago and whom I have not seen since then. However, after a time, I was transferred into another parallel world. At that place a large dog like creature attacked. As a result of fighting the creature, my physical body mimicked the actions of the subtle body.

I stayed with a relative in Maryland. The residence is completely restricted to air conditioning. This means that the air used for breath is machine-conditioned and is dependent on the ventilation provided by the machine. The result of this was that the astral body was affected. It went into dimensions which were unfavorable for spiritual practice.

The exercise session which I did outdoors lasted for one hour. After that when I sat to meditate, there were distractions but ultimately, I linked with naad which was not in its usual location but which was at the top back of the head. It streamed in loudly. I took advantage of its radiance. After twenty minutes when I looked forward the intellect changed into a spiritual visionary device but that only lasted for about 3 second, for a flash. Still, this is advancement.

After that I returned to naad focus. Naad is a sound, not a light but still it has a radiance. In some meditations when one contacts naad one will experience its sound as if the sound is a light. It may blare like a bright searchlight.

Marijuana opens then Shuts Third Eye (July 2011)

The plain truth about marijuana and any other hallucinogenic drug, is that it opens the doors of perception into the subtle world, the astral existence. It gets the person there in a jiffy but with a catch, which is that when the drug is neutralized in the body the person will go to a slightly lower level of consciousness than he or she normally has.

This in turn causes the person to long to go back higher, which causes more use of the drug, until the brain cells in the physical body, and the astral energies in the head of the subtle body, become permanently altered in such a way that the drug no longer stimulates. At that point one has some alternatives, either stop using the drug for some time and hope that the cells will be rebuilt or continue using the drugs with a higher dosage or switch to a stronger drug.

But it is not that simple because it varies from person to person, because of genetic differences which cause varying tolerances. Some persons may use a substance for years and still get highs. I knew people who used LSD in large dosage which would put the average person in the psych ward. These exceptional individuals while using LSD function properly driving a car at 80 miles per hour.

Others however cannot function efficiently under this influence. One's third eye or brow chakra may open by the use of the marijuana which stimulates that chakra but eventually it closes the chakra in a way which makes it even harder to open again unless one takes a stronger drug. And then even if one does so, one may in time be faced with the same problem since the chakra will shut down even tighter.

A way out besides more drug use?

Sure, there is a way out if one is patient. That way would be to eat good food, preferably organic food, drink lots of fluids to get all the residual chemicals from the substance out of your cell structures (especially those in the brain and spine). Then one should patiently practice meditation.

Astral Transit with Arthur Beverford (July 2011)

During the last portion of the night, just before 4 am, I was with Arthur Beverford in the astral world. He took a few people and myself to a place back in time, where we were some hundreds of years ago in Inner Mongolia. This time gap was connected to Santa Barbara, California. There was a linking energy, an astral slip-hole between Mongolia and Santa Barbara, California. Somehow, we transferred instantly from Mongolia to that place in California, just as if a person stepped across the threshold of a door.

At first, we were with four persons who were in another dimension. Their astral forms were visually invisible but sensually present. We entered a passageway which was fenced by two wooden walls which were about twelve feet high. We walked through a corridor and then went to a place which used the earth as the floor. When we got into that place, there was a special room in which they were seats of honor but it was covered with red and yellow dyed fabric. It was like a cotton fabric.

The place was old, like thousands of years old. No one was present, but there were Taoist figurines which were on shelves. One was that of a woman and her features were like that of a nurse whom I saw in a clinic in South Korea a few months ago. This particular nurse was a mother of mine in a past life. She used a Mongolian body. At a clinic when I would try to avoid being injected with antibiotics, that lady disciplined me, subconsciously exerting her maternal authority from a past life.

In that astral place Beverford showed where he sat in that past life some thousands of years ago. He was the clan leader and spiritual head of the place. Everyone treated him as a divine being, a deity. He showed where I sat as well. I was one of the senior people and was a son of his in that life. We both practiced the Taoist religion. The bodies we used were Mongolian.

After this we slipped into another time space in the astral existence and came out in Santa Barbara California, except that this place was hilly. At the time there were many water springs coming out of the ground, so that there was no need to get water from any other place. Pure water flowed out of the ground for people's convenience. I asked Beverford about that. He said that it was such that there was no need for farming even. We did not eat during that time, as the bodies used in that place did not require foods for survival. Just by looking at the water or by touching it one was nourished.

After a bit, that place changed as we were transported through astral time to another era when some persons using black bodies were present. Beverford greeted those persons. They had playful activities without any idea about spiritual advancement or astral projection techniques. Soon after this, my astral body fused back into my present physical form. I got up and began doing kundalini yoga practice.

Beverford was present astrally. Due to being on the astral side fully, he entered into my physical body by superimposing his form in my physical form. Then he did every exercise as I went through the sequence of the practice. His main interest was to see how the breath infusion enters and is distributed through the nadis of the subtle body.

He expressed surprise at the efficient of the bhastrika rapid breathing, at getting the infused breath into hard-to-reach places like in the knees and thigh bones. Since he was fully on the astral side his subtle perception was fully open. He could see things which a person using a physical body cannot access. During the session he checked to see how I complied with a Buddha deity's request for attacking the anchor place of the kundalini which is just below the base chakra.

There was a flash of memory from his mind, where I saw that while I was in South Korea on the temple grounds of a Buddhist monastery, Beverford was present and was with a Buddhist monk whom I spoke to. Beverford heard what the deity of that place told me about attacking the base chakra but he did not know the technique for doing it. He observed how it was done during this session.

This event shows that even if one hears an instruction which is given to someone else, one may not be inspired in the method. The deity can give an instruction in such a way that even those who overhear it cannot apply it, even persons as advanced as Beverford. I did not realize at the time that Beverford was present astrally and had overheard what the deity said. Presently, Beverford is hoping to avoid having to take another body but it is hardly likely that he could accomplish that. However, he was interested in the technique the deity awarded since it is a method for stalling rebirth. If done perfectly, it would completely suspend the need for rebirth. This is because it ruptures the kundalini's rebirth habit which is the tendency through which we take physical bodies haphazardly.

After practice I sat to meditate. Beverford stayed on observing how I used naad sound as the focus. He said that he always hears naad but had never used it as a focus, since his main practice which Rishi Singh Gherwal showed was third eye focus. He said he did not realize that naad sound could be used in that way and that it compliments third eye focus.

After some time, about fifteen minutes, Beverford left. Sometime after doing the session there was a burst of a ray of bright energy from the cosmic intellect. It was coming in from high up at about an angle of 75 degrees to the horizontal. That lasted for about 3 seconds.

That is not much of an accomplishment because a yogi should link his intellect with the cosmic intellect for several hours not just a few seconds. Initially when this set of living beings, the individual selves, are let loose in this cosmos, each finds itself with an intellect, which is required as a dashboard to operate the senses of the psyche. In time this psychic adjunct gets out of tune and gives false information which results in haphazard and totally off-key rebirths. To get the intellect back into divine alignment, one should link it with the cosmic analytical aggregate orb. Presently most of us are like marooned sailors who were beached on a deserted island after a stormy night in a ship wreck.

Becoming the Universal Consciousness (July 2011)

There is never an everyday set weather pattern in the material world. Each day has variations. The energy in the atmosphere varies daily. Are we dependent on it? Some people feel that we are not dependent, and that we are gods who create reality and command nature.

The reality is however, that no one, after thirteen billion years of becoming aware in a material body on a tiny nothing planet, off in a corner of the Milky Way, can make any meaningful claim to controlling destiny. When I lived in South America as an infant, I had ample opportunity to observe the fantasy of individual existence in the life of the ants. Sometimes an ant would come into the house to steal sugar. Of course, the ant was not aware that the sugar was put there by a human being and that the human purchased it from a grocer. The ant would come to a certain location on a shelf, climb into a jar, taste sugar and haul a grain of it. Sometimes, as mischievous children, we would lift an ant and drop it through a window. By the grace of nature, the ant body would drop about eight feet without being damaged. But the ant would then be in a place which was unknown to it. It would be lost from its tribe and residence.

What did the ant think before that? Was it thinking that it was God, that it could create its own reality, that it could control the environment? Did it feel that it would become the universal consciousness?

Sometimes in the rainy season, the rain would fall to such an extent, that nearly everything on the ground would float, that included the ants. These ants, millions of them in an ant city which was built with tunnels through the earth found themselves in a fix, with nature disregarding their endeavors. Hundreds of them would be bundled on a twig, board or log, their view of reality scrapped by nature's whimsical weather operations.

In that predicament, the ants for their part hoped to reach a tree to be out of the danger. In this existence the only thing that is certain is uncertainty. We are not located for supremacy over anything. We are not in control.

Part 3

Third Eye Opening

When the third eye opens one sees into another dimension. Rarely does one see into this dimension. When one does it is usually of a distant place. In addition, when the third eye opens one sees through it like looking through a bay window.

You can tell that you are before the third eye when in the dark you perceive an energy moving away from you and then disappearing as another energy again begins to move away from you and then disappear in sequence. When looking at that energy, all of a sudden sometimes there appears a visual tunnel. Sometimes the place where that happens appears as an opening to daylight from within a cave.

Self is Absolute?

The trouble with some ideas of self absoluteness is that it does not cover the area of the reality of the individual self. It avoids dealing with that. Or it suggests that the self can be disbanded or eliminated by the very self. The limited self does not have the power to permanently put itself on the exclusive spiritual planes of existence. Any guru who said that it can is either ignorant of the reality or is bluffing. How did the limited self appear in this creation with this set of psychic components? Who or what put the limited self here?

If one can prove that the limited self put itself here, then I agree to the idea that it can by itself get away from this and go to a plane of consciousness in which it will be membrane-less and will not have to deal with being itself as an individual principle. By my research, the individual self actually came from a level where the consciousness is diffused in such a way that it is there with trillions of other individual selves, all compacted together as it were, like molecules of water in an ocean. One molecule cannot distinguish itself from any other, because it does not have the objectivity for that. Subjectively is the law there.

Hence from one angle, even though it is a particular self, it feels as if it is not that. It experiences consciousness with no idea that it is individual.

There is such a place from which these selves originated. That place still exists. To reach there, kundalini must strike either the crown chakra or the intellect. If that happens the coreSelf suddenly finds itself in a super bright light which has a golden frosty color. It finds only bliss there. It becomes unaware of itself as an individual. It feels as if it is everywhere in that energy, which is really not its everywhere-ness but its linking into a spiritual plane which allows the selves existing there to be linked into a consciousness which is barrier-less

Returning to that place permanently is not going to happen if we are to accept what Krishna said, where he mentioned that once a limited self is in this creation as part of this history, it is doomed to individuality. Here is that *Bhagavad Gita* verse.

न त्वेवाहं जातु नासं
न त्वं नेमे जनाधिपाः ।
न चैव न भविष्यामः
सर्वे वयमतः परम् ॥२.१२॥

na tvevāhaṁ jātu nāsaṁ
na tvaṁ neme janādhipāḥ
na caiva na bhaviṣyāmaḥ
sarve vayamataḥ param (2.12)

na — no; tv (tu) — in fact; eva — alone; aham — I; jātu — ever; na — not; āsam — I did exist; na — nor; tvaṁ — you; neme = na — nor + ime — these; jana-adhipāḥ — rulers of the people; na — not; caiva — and indeed; na — nor; bhaviṣyāmaḥ — we will exist; sarve — all; vayam — we; ataḥ - from now; param — onwards

There was never a time when I did not exist, nor you nor these rulers of the people. Nor will we cease to exist from now onwards. (Bhagavad Gita 2.12)

Stated differently, it means that none of us can permanently cease the individual objective consciousness.

Thinker and Self

Consider that the thinking process and the self are two components in the psyche. Is it true that as long as the coreSelf absorbs the thought constructions of the thinking part of the psyche and the moving actions of the kundalini lifeForce, those influences causes the coreSelf to be unstable? In other words, is the failure to resist the influence of thinking and feeling, cause us to be in illusion?

My claim is that there is a thinking organ in the subtle head. There is also a coreSelf. These are two components in the mind, in the head of the subtle body. In addition, in the psyche there is a lifeForce. The coreSelf does not think. It does not have the ability to do so. This may be compared to a modern human being and a computer. The human being cannot calculate the average density of all the gas in the Milky Way but it can direct a computer to do so.

Even though it can direct a computer, it cannot make the calculation itself. Similarly, I write that the coreSelf cannot do some action which the thinking organ (intellect) can do. I deny Descartes' statement that since someone thinks that person must exist. My conflicting statement is that there is thinking near me, very near to me. I exist regardless of my observation of the said thoughts occurring.

I can validate myself by the duality of myself and something else which exists and is thinking in the mind. To me the problem is one of liability. Am I responsible for what the thinking organ thinks? Am I responsible for the psycho-sensual actions of the lifeForce? If you say that I am, the idea that I am free to think or act is invalid.

If I accept your conclusion it means that I came to terms with my giving permission to the thinking part to think and the moving apparatus to act. My next move will be to curtail the independence of those two components. If I can, I put an end to their autonomy. In terms of illusion, the illusion I see is that the coreSelf fails to segregate itself from the thinking organ and from the energy motivations. It remains in a unified confusion with the two components. Through that it becomes liable for their activities.

There is another issue which is how the coreSelf got in conjunction with the psychic organs. Unless that is settled, we are back to square one with the coreSelf being fused with the two components, like a prisoner who is shackled to two other prisoners or like one of a set of triplet infants who must live with each other because they are three heads on one trunk.

From what I perceive, so long as the coreSelf must remain in alliance with the thinking organ and with the feelings, its efforts to say that it is not those organs or that it is not responsible for those organs is grand speech but nothing else. This is why I prefer that we accept these organs as commodities for which we are responsible. It is like a tail. If the animal cannot get rid of it, it had better take care of it and discipline it so that it helps the rest of the body, rather than tangle up the hind legs and cause the animal to fall.

If someone would show how to get rid of the thinking organ permanently and how to get rid of the lifeForce permanently, I am for it. Until that happens my interest is how to curtail the power of these organs so that the liability for their actions is reduced considerably. I am not interested in the idea that I will get rid of these organs permanently after the body dies. If I cannot junk these organs now, I do not see how I will get the power to do so at death. I cannot remember voluntarily attaching myself to these organs but I discovered myself in that attachment. That itself is a mystery which is yet to be understood.

Kundalini Control (July 2011)

A thought is created in the mind space in the head of the subtle body. It is created by and in a subtle mechanism which is called the intellect. Once the thought is created, several emotional moods or energies may arise. These are experienced as anxiety, worry, anger, sadness, happiness, hate, envy and love. These are manufactured by the kundalini lifeForce psychic mechanism, and not by the intellect thinking mechanism. The mood creation mechanism is the kundalini. inSelf Yoga™ has two methods for dealing with it. One is for restricting its access to the intellect. The other is for infusing the kundalini with a higher grade of energy. If it is infused it cannot produce low grade vulgar emotions. If it is not infused but is effectively isolated from the intellect, it cannot overpower the psyche with response emotions.

The intercourse between the intellect and the kundalini is the main cause of impulsive actions. Their segregation is targeted in inSelf Yoga™. Eventually the yogi is instructed to leave aside the segregation and to work on the kundalini to purify it by infusion of breath energy. Because a yogi does not have the power to get rid of the kundalini, his/her best approach is to get it to function with higher energy on a higher plane. If you have to live with something or someone, if you can elevate that principle, its destructive or vulgar habits would not manifest.

At a certain stage when a yogi understands that he is stuck with the kundalini, he makes the decision to accomplish elevation. He studies its design and operation and seeks a method for its elevation. A yogi focuses more on the subtle moods and attitude of kundalini and deals with it from that level primarily. I gave this information to show how kundalini yoga and related meditation supports mind and sense control efforts.

Segregation of Kundalini and the Intellect (July 2011)

Segregation is the first step for the yogi because from where he/she is located in a position of helplessness, he/she can do nothing else. Initially a yogi cannot infuse kundalini for the very reason that he does not know the method. Initially the yogi does nothing to kundalini besides what was read in books or heard of from others. Kundalini is very difficult to distinguish because its influence is thorough.

To identify the operations of the kundalini, the yogi should make observations internally. Since he/she does not have the required mystic perception, that student can only recognize kundalini indirectly by its activities. After doing that the yogi tries to restrict the unwanted activities. If I have an enemy who is invisible, and who however always sends visible agents to attack me, my way of defense will be to isolate myself from the agents or fight them in the open. Because these agents are tech-savvy, it would be foolish for me to openly confront them. I should isolate myself from them. That does nothing to kill them and it certainly will not get rid of the invisible enemy. It is a stopgap method because I have no other effective defense. Initially that is what a yogi does. He/She however eventually figures that such an approach is a cowardly one. It is necessary but it is below the dignity of the self to hide from the other components in the psyche.

Once the yogi understands that hiding out or isolating the self is ineffective, he/she can consider what to do. At first some people get the idea that they can dismiss kundalini or make it vanish. Some others get the idea that perhaps when the body dies, the argument with kundalini will be over. They feel that kundalini will disappear when the body is finished.

A more serious yogi studies the invisible kundalini. One sees and feels the kundalini and gets it into a visible form internally by internal psychic perception. The yogi learns how to infuse kundalini. He gets the opportunity to access kundalini's behavior when it is infused as compared to its default operation.

Once the yogi can make this comparison in the psyche, he/she becomes convince that the way out is to get kundalini permanently infused. The method for that is a perplexity. The yogi does however try to infuse kundalini once or twice per day.

Subtle Body in Heavenly Form (July 2011)

Kundalini is an intelligent energy. If you are attentive, it will inspire you. Do not be surprised that you are guided by an energy. What happened when the body got to puberty? There was a sex urge. You found a sexual companion. You were urged for participation. This was driven by an urge-energy which had the intelligence to know that a sperm particle had to get down a fleshy tubing for the creation of an embryo.

Apart from this subtle energy intelligence, there can be instructions given into the mind or into the psyche by a yoga guru. In either case, it is in one's interest to execute the instruction. Usually when someone does a kundalini practice, that person is not attentive in the psyche. This is due to distractions and due to the fact that the kundalini itself craves information about the conditions and things which are outside the body. Due to that one does not focus within and this decelerates the practice.

There are three major components in the head of the subtle body. These are the coreSelf which is raw spiritual energy, the sense of identity which aids the coreSelf in identifying its adjuncts and the intellect which aids the coreSelf by providing analysis. In this world it is not possible for a spiritual being to function without the assistance of the sense of identity and intellect.

The sense of identity is capable of visual perception and so is the coreSelf but unfortunately that capability is suppressed. We will deal with the intellect which is currently doing a full-time job as the seer for the coreSelf and its the sense of identity. Unfortunately, the sense of identity is blind even though it is capable of vision.

For meditation Patanjali said that one must silence the intellect. Then it is possible to use it in the interest of the coreSelf. If we can get the intellect to comply, it would develop supernatural vision. This means that these three components, the reliant coreSelf, the needy sense of identity and the calculative intellect are presently incapable of vision.

That leaves us with the third eye. If a yogi is lucky, he may see things at the third eye. If he is even luckier, he will see through third eye, using it as a window into other dimensions. Unfortunately, meditation experiences are mostly non-intense. Many persons who had their first subtle body experience through using drugs, get frustrated when trying to repeat such experiences by meditation. However, one needs to know for sure that drug experiences rely on drugs and on a body that can tolerate the same. It is best to be patient and stick with meditation. But one may compare the experience of meditation with that of drugs in order to get some insight into what occurred during drug experiences.

By repeatedly meditating and by noting the subtle happenings experienced, one would develop over time, the required sensitivity to know which body one experiences at a particular time, One must develop a way to distinguish the subtle body, or a phase of it, from the physical form, even when the subtle one is interspaced and synchronized into the physical one.

The body which is experienced as having a glitter energy is an astral level which is called Swargaloka. This is a lower paradise or heaven but it is very impressive from this human plane. In such a body, all of it is made of colorful lights which have a misty texture. These are very beautiful forms. They can drive an earthling crazy because of their intense bliss feelings.

Each subtle body has particular easy accesses and blocked areas, just as in the physical body, each person has a different ailment. Something is defective in my eye but my friend's vision is ideal. My feet are in order but he walks with a limp.

Each person has certain parts of the subtle body which are easily accessed by kundalini energy and certain parts that are blocked so that kundalini rarely goes to those parts unless special yoga postures and diet are used to clear the blockage.

When kundalini enters the head, it can do any of several things. That depends on which paths are open to it. If the yogi can command or coerce it to go to the third eye or if it goes there of its own accord, that is very good.

Rarely is kundalini responsive to willpower. However, when doing breath infusion, kundalini becomes pliable and responds to control.

On a certain level the entire subtle body has bliss energy, ecstatic feelings. All other persons living in such a paradise existence have bliss yielding forms. The vegetation experience that as well. It is such that if someone wants to change the color of the eyes or if he/she wants to adjust the complexion, it is changed into what is desired as soon as the person thinks of it.

There is no application of cosmetics because the willpower is applied effectively without extraneous endeavor. Such a level of existence however, even though it is fabulous in comparison to this world, is a danger to those who are serious yogis. If a yogi goes to such a place after leaving a material body, his spiritual progress will be suspended. He will be distracted by the wholesale pleasures which naturally occurred there. The beauty in such a place is not skin deep. It will overwhelm the mind of a student yogi.

Still, yoga apart, that is the place a human being desires. People who are permanent residents in those places, regard a beautiful or handsome human body to be just the way we see the bodies of primates.

Kundalini Hanging without a Base (July 2011)

This morning during meditation, I had an unusual opening of the brow chakra, where it opened showing itself to be a culvert-like channel, at the end of which was an environment which was bathe in light. Instead of being like a cone-shaped tunnel or a moving energy cone-shaped tunnel. This tunnel was like a galvanized culvert. I did not rush to go through it because that action usually results in the disappearance of the opening. I slowly focused on it. The experience lasted for the most for about two minutes. Then it disappeared. Then total darkness appeared where that opening was.

This happened as I was focused on naad sound on the right side of the head. Before this meditation, while I did breath infusion, kundalini rose several times, perhaps about six times. Twice it rose in slow motion which gave me the opportunity to check its passage with more precision.

Breath infusion usually causes a rapid movement from kundalini, as if the infused energy strikes kundalini and puts it into its rapid mode. During the practice, after I got kundalini saturated with the infused energy, I focused on carrying out the instruction of the Buddha deity who requested that I work not on the base chakra but on the base to which the base chakra adheres. I did this for some time, until I noticed that the area below the base chakra was no longer there.

It dissipated by the infusion. Instead of an energy cloud being there, there was nothing but pure white light. As soon as I noticed that, I got a message from the Buddha deity which meant this: "It is now suspended in thin air without a support. Keep it suspended. Do not allow it to form an adherence base as before."

After this I observed that kundalini hung just as if a serpent was held by its tail with its head downward.

Kundalini adheres to base energy pad
which is dense due to a heavy subtle energy

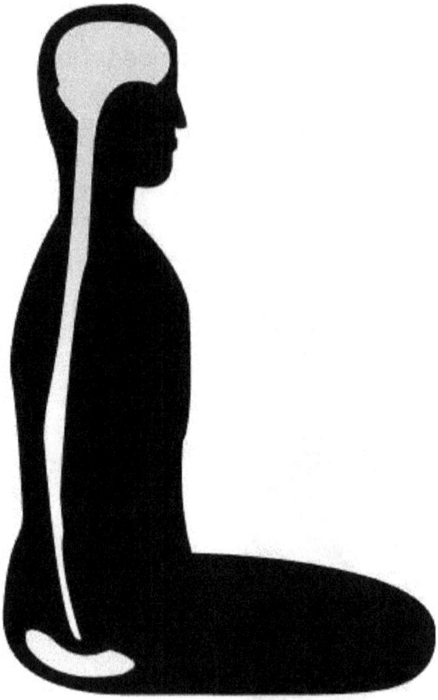

kundalini lifted from base energy pad
which is infused with breath energy

Third Eye Experience (July 2011)

In the psyche the coreSelf is surrounded by opague dense energy. There is this dense energy which keeps the coreSelf blinded but all the same even though it is so, the system is designed for the coreSelf to be wired into another system so that it can see the physical world.

In the *Bhagavad Gita,* Krishna admitted that presently this batch of entities is surrounded by varying degrees of lusty energy, passionate force which he called *kamarupa*. In meditation, if one is luckily, there will be breaks in the passionate force which surrounds the psyche and which surrounds the self in the psyche. In all respects in the normal condition, one is imprisoned on all sides with no escape but through physical sensual access.

Now and again that imprisonment breaks for a moment. One sees into one of the skies of consciousness or sees into another limited dimension. When the purplish, grayish, blackish or brownish opague energy disappears in the mind for whatever reason or by whatever method, one sees into the sky of consciousness which is called the chit akasha. The objective of yoga is to escape from the dense energy and have access to that sky of consciousness.

The Woman, The Child, The Yogi (July 2011)

During exercises this morning a Buddha deity left an instruction in my psyche. During meditation that instruction was this:

Become like a nomad who has no permanent residence. If kundalini's tendencies are not directly reformed in the kundalini itself, it will revert to its instinctual method when it is deprived of a physical body and has only the astral world for usage.

Habits which developed in other parts of the psyche, like in the willpower, in the desire moods or in the analytical process, will have no effect on kundalini. It will keep its posture. This means that the other components of the psyche will comply with kundalini and will be subjected to whatever circumstances kundalini takes the psyche into.

Take the example of a woman with an infant. They travel. The woman does not need milk. The woman does not require toys. The woman does not require to be cleaned by someone after evacuating. These are not her needs. She is liberated from those elementary functions. Still she must service that for the child. Those who think that they are liberated and who are unsuccessful in reforming kundalini from its transmigration habits, will assume those habits regardless of whether they desire or not.

One must change the features of kundalini so that it no longer needs to utilize a physical body. One must remove that tendency from it. If one fails to do this, it does not matter whom one may be, one will be forced to live in the next existence on the level that is suitable to kundalini, just as the mother, even though she is liberated from infancy, must provide accommodations for the child.

Constipation in My Next Life (July 2011)

Pain killers cause constipation. In addition, after a final use it takes the body months to flush these substances. If for instance one takes a pain killer in January and does not take it again, it may take the body months to completely flush that chemical out of the body. This means that the body will show the tendency of constipation in varying degrees while it is affected by the drug. I state this after observing my body's evacuation actions after having a superficial surgery in South Korea. I conclude that there are two effects of pain killers. One is to completely suppress all sensation from a certain part of the body. The other is to suppress only the acute sensations. The first which is usually done using an opiate derivative from opium or morphine, does not discriminate. It suppresses all sensation. This is convenient for surgeons who cannot do surgery if the body reacts to incisions and other types of invasion. This kind of pain killer is very obvious in that it disables motor movements. This not only causes constipation but shuts down the entire excretory operation.

The other type of pain killer which discriminates and which only dulls acute sensations is dangerous because the individual does not know what it does. He/she does not feel acute sensations which may arise. In other words, it does not dull all sensation. It neutralizes certain types of pain by targeting certain nerve junctions.

My claim, and this is based on detailed observations of how these drugs affected the distribution of consciousness in my body, is that these substances shut down more than just the acute pain signals which would normally be felt by the person. They also shut down other operations, one of which is the operation of the intestinal system, particularly the colon and rectum. This causes constipation.

In addition, after the last ingestion of these drugs, the system remains under their influence for a time. Stated differently it takes the body some time to erase the influence of these substances. In the meantime, the body must process dehydrated stools and struggle with the tendency for constipation. But this is not observed by the person because the signaling system which would tell a person of the actions of the colon and rectum is disabled by these drugs.

These drugs include the milder pain killers which are taken in tablet form. It includes drugs which are given intravenously. The sad part is that it affects the subtle body and especially the kundalini energy. This means that the effects of this will go with the individual to world hereafter and subsequently to the next physical body if there is to be one. This is like in the prison system, where the records of criminal acts of an individual prisoner is brought to the attention of the court when he stands trial for a new crime. The new body is built in the mother's uterus using the record of habits from the old body which died some time ago.

Death during an Out-of-the-Body Experience

If the physical body dies while in an Out-of-the-Body Experience (OBE), the person will not be pulled back into the body. The force which does the pulling would have migrated into the subtle body. In dreams, the lifeForce remains in a physical body which uses its energy. If the body got damaged or is terminally ill from a disease, the lifeForce migrates because it will be disconnected from the body when the living symptoms cease.

Our entry in and out of the body in astral projections or in OBE experiences, occurs under the control of the lifeForce. It does not occur by willpower as the main controlling aspect. The willpower is an accessory which is effective only when the lifeForce is suitably operating. When that lifeForce causes the astral body to disengage from the physical system, it (the lifeForce) remains in part in the physical system. A part moves with the subtle body.

It is said that when the astral body is displaced from the physical one, there is a silver cord which connects the two bodies. This silver cord is an energy transmission. If for instance there is anxiety near the sleeping physical body, the astral one is retracted immediately regardless of the desire of the person concerned. But all the same if the physical system dies the lifeForce instead of pulling back the astral body, goes to the astral body permanently. The subtle body cannot locate a dead physical system.

The person would try to be the physical body or better stated, will try to awaken as the physical body as usual, but he/she will find that it does not happen. There will be the realization that "I am dead," which means that "I lost the physical body. I am on the psychic level permanently. I can no longer use that social identity. My assets, physical connections and whatever, are no longer useful to me."

A Yogi Who Died Before He Died (July 2011)

Last night due to friendship with a particular person, my subtle body transited to a dimension which is adjacent to this physical world. These places are important to know since usually after the physical body dies one goes to these locations, lives there for a time, and then goes into a state of total loss of objective awareness, and then one wakes up as an embryo which is expelled from a woman's body as her child.

When astral travelling, one recognizes these adjacent low-level astral regions by their gravitational effect on the subtle body. The subtle body is supposed to float and pass through objects but in these astral regions the subtle body remains on the ground of those places, just as the physical forms remain anchored to the earth without effort on our part.

The mystery of why the physical body does not float like a balloon and does not float away from the planet like helium, is explained in science by the term gravity, which is the earth's pulling force on physical objects which are within a certain distance from the center of the earth.

When astronauts go into outer space, they experience floatation and special accommodations are made to deal with that. In the lower astral world, one finds that one's body acts like a physical body, but sometimes in such places, one finds that the astral body floats like an inflated balloon.

In the astral dimension which I visited, my astral body floated when I first entered but after a time being there, it became heavy. As soon as I became aware of that, the astral form behaved like a physical form would on this planet.

The value of such experiences is that it gives the yogi firsthand experience of what he will face when the physical system dies. Some people would like to know what it would be like after death. They admit that this would be impossible because they assume that no one returned from death. However, there is another way to approach this which is to astral project.

In projection, the subtle body or a collection of psychological organs and energies of the person, leaves the physical system just as it must leave at death, with the exception that the astral body comes back into the physical form. At death it will not synchronize into the physical system. It will be permanently left in the astral world with no facility to use this world.

The astral place which I entered is not the place I would prefer to go to after the death of this body, and yet I found myself there. Why is this? Why am I unable to absolutely control where the astral body goes?

An Embryo or a Fully-Developed Body (July 2011)

An Inquiry:

Upon reading the *Kriya Yoga Bhagavad Gita* book, on pg. 464-467 you mention, "In the immediate past life, my physical body was immune to sexuality. Somehow, I met a lady in the astral world. Later on, this lady turned out to be my eldest sister. She said to me, 'I know how to do this. Do not worry. Follow me. We will get bodies.'

You continued: "Since I was a successful celibate, I lost the instinct for entering a subtle genital area of a man's body for taking a baby form. I saw my sister do this by instinct. Prior to this, I inquired from many Hindus for assistance. Even though I had many births in Indian bodies, still the Indians did not afford me a birth opportunity. The reason is this: I was a yogin by nature, a person who is a bad investment for family life, a misfit who does not conform to the traditional ways of human society. Sensing my antisocial tendencies, no one compromised their ancestor's opportunities by permitting me to enter their family."

You also wrote this, "At that time, another lady came there and entered my father's groin area. She acted just like my sister as if she had instincts for this. Seeing me looking, she spoke as if she knew me or as if my sister had told her something to tell me."

She said, "Do not worry. Hold this and come in after me. You will get through. We know how to do this."

After this lady's help, you acquired the present body. You seem to have gone through a lot of trouble but I wanted to ask you why you did not do what Lobsang Rampa did. Apparently, he was a Buddhist who took the body of a man who fell from a tree and suffered a concussion.

This man had an adult body. Rampa did not have to acquire an embryo. Furthermore, Franz Bardon did this with the body of a 14-year-old boy. In the book *Memories of Franz Bardon*, his son, Lumir, says that after the body snatching took place, Bardon's handwriting was different, including his mannerisms, behavior etc. From what I am aware of, this kind of body-snatching has a downside which implies taking on the karma of the first soul that incarnated in that body. This is the alleged reason of why Bardon suffered in a concentration camp and with severe sickness throughout his life (even though he was an advanced initiate/magician and an accomplished medical doctor).

Can this type of body snatching be done? Why was it not an option for you? Is it true that you take on the karma of the person who first developed the body? Do masters prefer this method in order to avoid going through infancy and puberty in order to get down to work and do their mission as soon as possible? Under what circumstances is this done? What are the requirements to do this exchange?

Reply by Author (July 2011)

Two of our Siddha gurus, namely Matsyendranath and Adi Shankar took adult bodies from persons whose destined life in those bodies was over. In both cases there was trouble, even though these persons were mahasiddha permanently liberated entities. If these persons can have problems with such transfers then it would be stupid for yogis of lesser stature to try these methods.

In the case of Shankara he was challenged by the wife of a Vedic debater to answer questions about sexual indulgence. Since he was a sannyasi monk with no sexual experience in that body, he could not answer the questions. He therefore asked the woman for time to research the matter. After that he took possession of the body of a prince whose body was to die. The prince transited to the astral existence. Shankara whose body was in a trance state took the prince's body. The wives of the prince got to liking Shankara's sexual performance so much, that when they were informed that he was not really the same soul of the prince, they became determined to keep him as that body, intending that he should never regain his sannyasi form. Somehow as fate would have it, Shankara regained the form.

In the case of Matsyendranath who is one of the 18 mahasiddhas, he got in a similar fix but he was saved from it by his disciple Gorakshnath, who is also a mahasiddha. On a foolish yogi would imitate these activities of these powerful entities.

But to address your inquiry, the situation of assuming the destiny of another entity by taking that person's adult body, is there also if one takes an infant form as an embryo. Even when taking an infant form, one has to assume part of the destiny of the parents of that form. In all cases this happens not only in the case of taking an adult form. When we take an infant body, we are tagged with liabilities for our parents good and bad activities, especially their bad behavior.

Currently, I am affected by this. Sometimes I travel because of things a parent did or did not complete. My parents are deceased. It is not that taking birth as an embryo is any different but to take an embryo requires less exertion of mystic power. To assume someone's adult form, takes tremendous exertion of mystic power. That is the only reason why a soul would not do it. You have to be a mystic yogi who developed a particular siddhi perfectional skill. Even Krishna and Balarama, the Supreme Beings, did not do that. In fact, Balarama suffered a miscarriage from the body of Devaki and was transited to the body of Rohini.

An advanced yogi is not concerned with reckless or whimsical use of mystic power. It is just like a rich man who works for the treasury department of the government. He should not flash money nor waste it merely because he manages millions. One may or may not be a yogi. In either case, one should not whimsically upset the way of nature.

Nothing is gained by doing the spectacular. Take my situation. I did abnormal things in this life. In just the last three years, I singlehandedly published several books. I mastered Sanskrit translation in just under a year some years ago without going to a school or being with a teacher physically. These fantastic things were done because of infusion of power into my psyche by yoga gurus. They did it because of dire necessity. It was not for me to demonstrate superhuman ability.

In just a few years, I will not be here to claim the publications as my work. Nature will confiscate it and do whatever it will do irrespective of my desire. I can tell you that the use of mystic siddhis is dangerous. If one does not have the approval of supernatural beings, one may descend to a low astral level or to an animal body as a result. Anytime one breaches the normal way of nature, one may suffer a backlash if one is not protected by a divine being. To take a body one must enter a contract for services. Even if the body is an adult one that is abandoned by someone, still there are liabilities involved and repayment is due to those who served that body to bring it to the adult stage.

How will one repay? Will the God or deity reimburse? How will one settle with the persons who served that body to bring it to the adult stage? These questions must be resolved irrespective of whether it is an embryo or not.

The adult body has a genetic code. The organs in the body are preset with certain flaws according to the destiny of the person who uses the body. It is the same for an infant form, which assumes the genetic configuration from the parents and which has organs which are flawed. In either case it is problematic.

When a yogi takes an adult form as Shankara did, there are resentments from people who will eventually suspect that he is not the person who originally got that body. How will he deal with that either in the life of that body or in the astral world hereafter?

Stuna Karna took the vagina of Ila but he was forced to use it for a long time, even though he was to have it only for two months. Stuna was an official for a deity named Kubera. Ila got Stuna's penis because she had a vagina and needed male gender to save her father from military invasion. When Kubera, the deity, heard that Stuna no longer had a penis and got sexual reversal, he cursed Stuna saying, "Let him remain with that genitalia forever." As a result, Stuna cried because Kubera was a deity with vast supernatural powers. If he condemned someone only God could waiver it. Anyway, Stuna begged and got forgiveness on the premise that he wanted to help Ila to save her father's kingdom from invasion.

Kubera pardoned him saying, "Since that is the case, stay with the vagina and those lovely breasts for the life span of Ila. But do not ever act whimsically again. Do not execute decisions without first consulting me." That story is narrated in the Mahabharata.

A yogi should do no crazy act. He should not think that he can use mystic siddhis. Yogeshwar prohibited students from using the siddhis which one gets if one is successful in any phase of yoga practice. He instructed that if I got a siddhi perfectional power, I should invest it in yoga practice for more advancement.

Infant Body Value (July 2011)

For an advanced soul the value of infancy is that it equips one with cultural assets which one would not have if one took a transfer into an adult body. Most missions to take a body to teach spiritual realization has to do with using a particular cultural profile. Without that one would not be accepted by people with a different ethnicity.

In taking the present body, I became equipped with certain cultural assets because the body grew up under British political and academic influences. If for instance I transferred into someone's adult body, my subtle body may not have that cultural content.

If Jones leaves his adult body and then Singh assumes that body, Jones leaves with his subtle form, along with the cultural habits which are in that subtle form. Singh will enter that form with his cultural assets from India. There will be a clash between Singh's cultural psychology and the body habits of Jones' abandoned physical form. Singh will then have to either accommodate the cultural habits of that body or root out the unwanted instincts.

The real asset of the culture in Jones's subtle body will be gone with Jones. He cannot give his subtle body to someone else. The subtle body is really where the assets are contained.

When one takes a new body through an embryo, the subtle form goes through alterations which makes it contain the cultural substance of the new parents' political and social environment. This does not happen if one is transferred into an adult form.

If a person transits to an astral heaven, the persons appears in a youthful body like that of about 16-18 years of age, but the lower astral planes make no change in the subtle body. If someone left an old body, the astral form will look exactly like that initially. That could change in the lower astral planes if the subtle body ingests a rejuvenating energy. One can go to an astral hell where one would have a ghastly body.

A person does not go to a heavenly astral world merely because she says she will go there, or because her belief advocates that. It happens if the behavior and character was saintly and was approved by the deity of the heavenly locale.

Kundalini in the Extremities (July 2011)

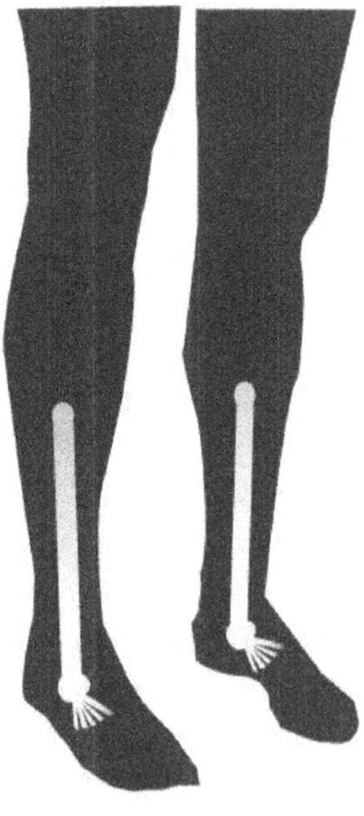

I still target the base of the base chakra. As explained previous the base chakra and the place which it is fused to are two different features. This practice is to target the base not the chakra.

This morning while focusing on this, I got instruction from Rishi Singh Gherwal who said that I should push the air through a tube in the lower legs. When I did this, the tube got infused so much that it was full of rushing white energy, like white heat which shows on heated metal. After that the white heat spread into the feet.

The extremities of the hands and especially those of the feet are hard to reach places in *nadi shodana* practice. *Nadi shodana* is Sanskrit for purification of the nadi subtle tubes. *Shodana* comes from *shuddha* a Sanskrit word for purification. Some yogis feel that there is only one nadi-shodana practice which involves alternate breathing with a count proportion method but there are other procedures of *nadi shodana*. A question may be asked as to why bother with the feet if one strives for liberation which concerns the mind. The answer is that the mind has a kundalini system. At the time of exiting a dying body, the two features move with the coreSelf.

If the core could leave the body and leave with the mental chamber without kundalini, there would be no need to be concerned with kundalini. However, since the self has to lug both the mind chamber and the kundalini, it is sensible to take kundalini into account.

For that matter a person who is not proficient at meditation will find that at death, the kundalini leads the way out of the body with the mind and the self following like obedient tourists who follow an insane tour guide. Where the guide will take them, they do not know. The only thing they know for sure is that it will take them to another body. As for where, when and why, they have no information.

For a student yogi, the task of reaching the extremities like the toes and fingers is a daunting one, but if one proceeds with a daily practice, one will over time achieve the penetration of these parts. If one does not do it who will? One will be deprived of the physical body leaving it with a low energy kundalini force.

Kundalini Transmigration Urge (August 2011)

After kundalini breath infusion, I was to make a few notes. Somehow, I overlooked doing that and meditated. Now I cannot recall the experiences. I repeatedly appealed to students to take notes and submit for review from time to time.

The value of notes is that if you review them you can gain much more from the practice. While doing exercises this morning some very subtle things occurred, so subtle and so subjective that since I did not record it just after the practice, my objective mind has no record of it. To retrieve the information, I may enter the subconscious mind, which in meditation is a subjective region of consciousness. Such a region is like trying to read a book in which the printer printed white ink on white paper.

Here is some of what happened: I worked on the lower trunk of the body, the thighs and feet. In the thighs there was a huge cavern, like a vast cave which was filled with a misty white light. It was empty except for the white misty energy. Both caverns of the right and left thighs seemed to be one cavern even though they were in fact two separate zones. They seemed to be one because my observing consciousness managed to be aware of both simultaneously.

There is a loop area which begins at the navel and loops around to the navel chakra on the spine. It was devoid of sexually charged energy. It seemed to be a u-shaped container which was about an inch wide. Usually this area carries a double charge, a sex charge and the transmigration urge. In this experience the sex charge was missing.

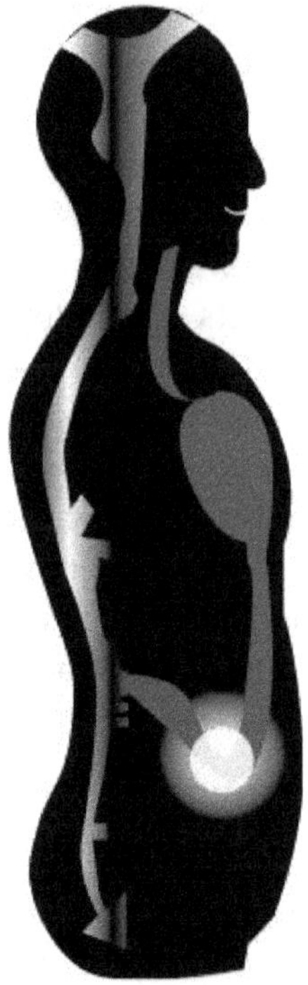

The sex charge and the transmigration urge stay together. These are the basic identity of the kundalini chakra, which acquires a material body through sexual means. The removal of these features of the kundalini protects the yogi from having to be attracted haphazardly to the next birth opportunity.

It is a good idea, to endeavor to be free of the sex charge and transmigration urge, otherwise one will not go with the siddhas after one leaves a body. It is not that one will not take rebirth. One may have to but instead of doing that immediately after the death of a body, one should get in touch with the siddhas so as to get assistance from them in determining where and when one should develop the next embryo.

Without their advice, one will be left to the means of ordinary transmigration by the usual means of attraction to the next set of parents through sexual attraction and the after-effects of one social activities.

Rishi Singh appeared for a split second. He looked. He made this remark: "Clean it properly before leaving the body. Make no assumption about what you can do after departing the body. Make every effort to complete the practice before departure."

Yantra (August 2011)

Yantras are an alternate way to approach either a transcendental zone or a deity of a transcendental zone. A yantra may serve as an entry into another dimension. To use a yantra or mandala successfully in meditation, there are two methods; the internal and external.

The internal one means that you have a photographic highly sensitive mind which can retain an image of the yantra when you close the eyes to meditate. You may visualize the yantra and stare into the center as it is visualized in the internal mental environment.

The external means is to sit before the yantra and stare at it, either on the center of it or on the yantra as a whole. If you are successful with this, your coreSelf will be pulled into the yantra and will be transited to another dimension or a deity who is represented by the yantra will appear before you and offer favors.

As far as Krishna is concerned, he did not recommend its use to Arjuna. It is mentioned as part of the process of bhakti or devotional worship. That was told to Uddhava. Instead of a yantra, Arjuna was showed the Universal Form of Krishna which included many powerful assistants of the Supreme Being.

Some Vaishnava sects in India which follow the Krishna scriptures use yantras in their artwork in the temples and also in worship ceremonies but their main means of reaching Krishna is through deity worship ceremonies. The real yantra of a place or person is a diagramic configuration of that person. As each living being is a bit different, there are trillions of yantras which are the vibrational copies in diagram form of those personalities.

Cosmic Reach / Breast Loop (August 2011)

During exercises this morning three persons who were on the astral side did the practice one after another. These persons are deceased. One left the last body in the 1970s when that body was in its 80s. The other two left their bodies in the 1990s at about 70 years of age.

At first the older astral form was not interested in the exercises but when the other two did it and their astral forms became full of vitality from the breath infusion, that reluctant person became interested and practiced. After the session when I sat to meditate these persons sat as well. During their physical life they were not interested in doing postures nor meditation. They were confident of Christianity. Now that fizzed without benefits in the hereafter, they are interested in doing something else, in taking care of their individual psyches.

One of these persons, a female, had astral liquid squirting from her right breast. Then the left one squirted too. She asked about it. I explained that there is an astral tube which draws fluids up from the area just below the navel and routes that fluids to the breast. I told her that she could turn that tube into another small tube which travels from the breast upwards into the neck and then into the brain, where that energy could be circulated. She found the tube and the liquid stopped squirting. She then sat to meditate.

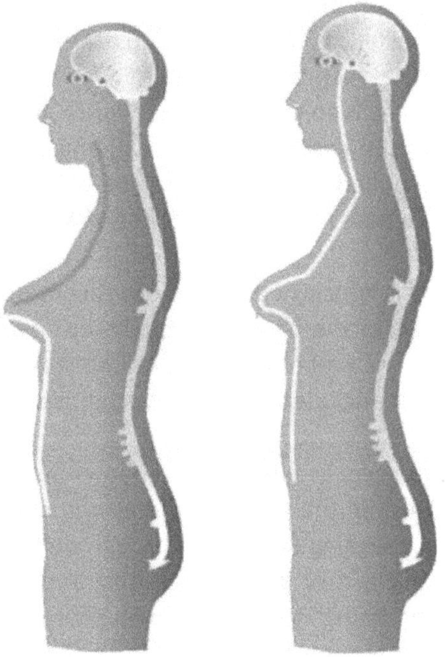

Yoga Compliance - Rishi Singh (August 2011)

During breath infusion this morning Rishi Singh discussed a verse from the *Yoga Sutras*.

ततः क्षीयते प्रकाशावरणम्॥५२॥

tataḥ kṣīyate prakāśa āvaraṇam

tataḥ – thence, from that; kṣīyate – is dissipated; prakāśa – light; āvaraṇam – covering, mental darkness.

From that is dissipated, the mental darkness which veils the light, (Yoga Sutras 2.52)

Rishi said that this verse is the most important verse in terms of getting a footing in true meditation. If this does not happen, the practice is inefficient. This verse describes what happens if one does pranayama breath infusion proficiently. The mental darkness which surrounds the coreSelf will be dissipated. That self will be flushed in light in the sky of consciousness (chit akash).

Rishi said that according to Patanjali meditation practice begins after this happens. This is the result of breath infusion. Here are the previous verses.

तस्मिन्सति श्वासप्रश्वासयोर्गतिविच्छेदः प्राणायामः ॥४९॥
tasmin satiśvāsa praśvāsayoḥ
gativicchedaḥ prāṇāyāmaḥ

tasmin – on this; sati – being accomplished; śvāsa – inhalation; praśvāsayoḥ – of the exhalation; gati – the flow; vicchedaḥ – the separation; prāṇāyāmḥ – breath regulation.

Once this is accomplished, breath regulation, which is the separation of the flow of inhalation and exhalation, is attained. (Yoga Sutras 2.49)

वाह्याभ्यन्तरस्तम्भवृत्तिः देशकालसङ्ख्याभिः परिदृष्टो दीर्घसूक्ष्मः ॥५०॥
bāhya ābhyantara stambha vṛttiḥ deśa kāla
saṁkhyābhiḥ paridṛṣṭah dīrgha sūkṣmaḥ

bāhya – external; ābhyantara – internal; stambha – restrained, suppressed, restrictive; vṛttiḥ – activity, movement operation; deśa – place; kāla – time; saṁkhyābhiḥ – with numbering accounting; paridṛṣṭah – measured, regulated; dīrgha – prolonged; sūkṣmaḥ – subtle, hardly noticeable.

It has internal, external and restrictive operations, which are regulated according to the place, time and accounting, being prolonged or hardly noticed. (Yoga Sutras 2.50)

वाह्याभ्यन्तरविषयाक्षेपी चतुर्थः ॥५१॥
bāhya ābhyantara viṣaya ākṣepī caturthaḥ

bāhya – external; ābhyantara – internal; viṣaya – objective; ākṣepī – transcending; caturthaḥ – the fourth.

That which transcends the objective, external and internal breath regulation is the fourth type of breath infusement techniques. (Yoga Sutras 2.51)

Rishi said that even though postures and breath infusion are parts of yoga, many do not teach these processes. Many teachers are not linked to the tradition of Patanjali. Some create ideas and sell those as yoga. He said that the persons at fault were, first of all, the yogis who came from India and peddled part of the system as the whole process. Then there are those who followed and sold asana postures as the whole yoga.

The verse above which discusses the mental darkness which veils the light has to do with the current condition of the coreSelf as it is surrounded by dark consciousness energy. He said that the removal of that energy occurs suddenly sometimes in meditation but it only last for a split second or more. For the removal of it for long period the fail-safe method is pranayama.

One must be consistent and intense in pranayama breath infusion practice to clear the dark energy, to dissipate it so that the self can be free to be in the sky of consciousness. Rishi said that everything, including the physical world is in the sky of consciousness. Still, one cannot experience that sky because one is in the sky but in a dark cloud of mundane energy which floats in the sky. One self at a time becomes freed by the application of the correct pranayama practice. Rishi feels that if pranayama is unnecessary, we can take Patanjali's instructions and throw them into the sea. Otherwise he said that only a fool would not take the *Yoga Sutras* seriously.

Breathing / Rishi's Opinion (August 2011)

During exercises this morning Rishi Singh Gherwal mentioned another verse from Patanjali Yoga sutras. This verse is used as a quote in the *Anu Gita* which I translated and which more or less is Rishi Singh's book with me as a ghost writer. Of course, people will feel that I am the author, because he is deceased and hardly anybody will buy into the idea of a deceased person dictating a book into someone's head

तस्मिन्सति श्वासप्रश्वासयोर्गतिविच्छेदः प्राणायामः ॥४९॥

tasmin satiśvāsa praśvāsayoḥ
gativicchedaḥ prāṇāyāmaḥ

tasmin – on this; sati – being accomplished; śvāsa – inhalation; praśvāsayoḥ – of the exhalation; gati – the flow; vicchedaḥ – the separation; prāṇāyāmḥ – breath regulation.

Once this is accomplished, breath regulation, which is the separation of the flow of inhalation and exhalation, is attained. (Yoga Sutras 2.29)

Rishi said that this means that if the body has sufficient breath energy, the breathing process will occur with a short respite between the in-breath and out-breath except that the breath will go down to the very bottom cells in the lung. In normal breathing there may or may not be a respite between the in-breath and out-breath but in either case, the air never gets to the very bottom of the lung. There is only top breathing, where air reaches the top one-third of the lung and the alveoli which are in the central part of the top.

If one trains the lungs to use every absorption cell, one could do this pranayama practice. Rishi claims that top breathing results in lack of access to the extremities for the lifeForce. This causes deficient energy in many parts of the physical and subtle bodies which result is gasping for breath or in shallow breathing. Human beings are disinclined to helping the lung system. Their intuition is that the body should work perfectly by itself.

Journey to Astral Heavens (August 2011)

Those who are practice kundalini yoga, should plan to continue doing so after leaving the body. Recently within the last month, I taught some persons on the astral planes. These are deceased people who in the last human bodies failed to practice yoga. They heard about it but did not assume the practice. Now finding themselves in the astral world without negative peer pressure, they are free to practice.

These were persons who saw me practicing some forty years ago. They remember because of the strange yoga practices I did in the neighborhood where they lived. In the astral world about four months ago, these persons were led to me by someone who does not practice but who found my name on the internet. This person still uses a physical body but does not practice.

Sometimes a student asks if I could determine what his situation in the astral world would be after death of the present body. The answer is that the general state of mind at the time of departure from the body will determine where one may go and what one may do.

For purpose of yoga, especially kriya and brahma yoga, going to an astral paradise after death is not an objective. It may happen. Who knows? It is not the objective because if it happens, it means that the yogi was diverted from practice. In a book I translated, the *Anu Gita,* this is explained where a siddha tells Kashyap that people who go to the astral heavens must again resume creature existence as soon as the energy of their cumulative pious merits are exhausted.

Suppose you work for a large company, which has a commission package which includes a holiday in a luxurious resort with all pleasures and amenities in the deal. At the end of the fiscal year, they tally your commissions and inform that you have a two-month holiday.

That will be based on your commission package. Once you get to the resort, you may have such a wonderful time that you forget that there is a time limit. However, your employers will not forget. At the end of the period, you must return to work as usual. If you refuse and insists on staying at the resort, you will find that you are forcibly put on an aircraft back to your city.

Going to the heavenly paradises in the astral world is like that. The problem with it is that when you get back to the human level you may or may not get into a human womb. If you do, your problems are still not over since you may not remember to resume yoga practice. Your parents may be disinclined from that. You may have to wait until you leave parental control, to learn the practice again.

This is why I tell students that the best plan is to set in your psyche the idea and tendency to continue yoga in the hereafter and not to focus on being in an astral paradise.

I went to the astral paradises many times. In addition, I was visited by beings from those places. These places are beyond a student yogi's ability to resists. The pleasure experienced there is such, that one will become addicted. Yoga practice will not be remembered.

Just as with a human body, if one is exposed to sex indulgence, it operates an irresistible pull, the heavenly worlds in the astral regions are many times more alluring in all respects. Some people feel that there should be a set procedure, something definite which will take place after the death. These persons have the traditional religious mentality which is that such and such will happen because I do such and such in the religion on earth.

However, in kriya yoga, there is no concern with that because the status one achieves hereafter will be based on the general disposition during life, not on a religious belief. For a yogi the best thing to do is to set the mind on practicing after one leaves the body. This is effective if the astral form is already habituated to practicing before one leaves the physical form for good. The value of this approach is that it gives one the opportunity to meet advanced yogis after death.

The persons whom I instruct on the astral planes, found bhastrika breath infusion to be wonderful and easy. In their physical bodies they would have found it to be difficult since their bodies were not flexible. In addition, one of these persons who had an astral body which resembled an eighty-year-old physical form, experienced that the astral form was so invigorated by just one session of the practice, that the form dropped 40 years of senility and looked like a 40 years old human body.

This proves that one can continue the practice on the astral planes. The other option of being transferred to the heavenly paradises in the astral world is not a very attractive one. It involves ceasing practice and getting involve in heavenly pleasures which are more intense than anything we encounter in a physical body.

The higher astral heavens are not an exclusive spiritual domain but it is the most fabulous existence one may have in the subtle existence. It is extra-ordinary but it is not liberation.

The spiritual dimensions are completely different from the astral heavens. One should aim for the spiritual zones but to be practical one should see the continuation of yoga practice on the astral planes as the immediately objective, and transfer to the spiritual places as the final achievement. If one cannot put a foot on the first rung of a ladder there is no sense is thinking about being at the top of it.

Hassles Continue After Death (August 2011)

Many people feel that the hassles we face in physical life will cease after death, when we either go to heaven, become liberated, go the spiritual world or to a oneness.

Is anyone certain of this?

Does anyone experience this while astral projecting nightly when the physical body sleeps?

If one does not experience the concept of liberation nightly when the physical body sleeps, one can assume that it will not happen when the body dies. After death, the astral form will do what it did prior except that this will be its full-time lifestyle. There will be no physical existence to resume until one assumes an embryo.

What about people who have no dreams, those who have dreamless sleep in oblivion? For them it will be that only and then they will find themselves waking up as somebody's child, crying after being evicted from the mother's body, but with no memory of the past.

Quarrels Hereafter

Last night I was with some monks in the astral world. They called me to be a witness since I was with them some years ago at a temple. One monk who is deceased but who is crippled and is now living in India in a wheelchair, accused his teacher, the founder of the society. That founder is also deceased. The monk accused his teacher of encouraging certain activities which according to the accuser caused the accuser to make faulty decisions which led to his arrest.

I was called by the founder of the society, who asked me if there was any evidence to support the crippled monk. I told them that it did not matter who was at fault because each person should rectify what providence gave in the form of bad reputation, loss of confidence of the public and such things.

They blamed each other. The founder said, "Those were your independent decisions. You killed my disciples."

The crippled monk replied, "You asked us to praise you in that way. We were inspired by you."

They argued for a while. Then it was time for me to do exercises. This was about 3.30 am. I got up. I began the exercises but they continued arguing. This is the heaven of these people. A yogi should not have foolish ideas and fantasies about what will happen after death. Whatever happens now during sleep will take place at death just the same. The great mystery of what a person will do and where a person will stay after death is known to each person already by the activity or lack of it nightly while the physical form sleeps.

Astral Projection in the Canadian Wilderness (August 2011)

It is likely that deliberate astral projection will occurs from a reclining position. It is easier to do it from a position laying on the back on a hard surface. Sometimes astral projection occurs during the night when the physical body sleeps, which really means that it occurs and then one becomes aware that it happened. That is not deliberate astral projection. That is the normal way in which the psychic nature conducts it.

In deliberate astral projection, the yogi is conscious of the separation but in most cases of astral projection, the person becomes conscious only after the separation occurred which means that he or she does not observe how the separation system works.

For the astral body to find itself waking up as the physical form, after a separation, that astral form has to resynchronize into the physical one, which means that it has to decrease its vibrational rate. Conversely, for it to separate from the physical one, the astral body has to increase the vibrational rate. Usually this deceleration and acceleration occurs by the operation of the psychic kundalini mechanism with or without the conscious observation of the person concerned.

This may seem surprising and unbelievable that one has little or no control over these systems. Let us remember that for the most part the heart beat and lung rate in the physical body are conducted without our permissions. There are systems on the psychic side which operate in a similar way.

These systems are not conducted with the permission, observation or assistance of the coreSelf. The various psychic components in the psyche are hard wired by nature to take power from the core, hence these psychic accessories do not have to acquire permission to get power from the self to complete the impulsive operations.

Suppose you purchase a house which has a pre-set pre-programmed lighting system which turns the lights on at 6 pm and off at 6 am. There will be no switch for you to operate those lights. You will be paying the utilities bill but you will not have a way to control how those lights are using the electric power which you are billed for. In the same way the psychic nature has set up the body to operate without the core's permission.

Does this sound unreasonable?

It is rare that one will astral project from a sitting position during meditation. If, however one desires to astral project and to observe how nature desynchronizes the subtle body, one should do meditation reclining on the back on a hard surface with a dark colored cloth over the eyes.

While sitting in easy pose this morning, on a couch, the astral body projected. I meditated for some time, and then that stopped. There was a blank space of consciousness where there was nothing. I found myself in the subtle body somewhere in Canada. The place had astral snow but there was no temperature to it. It was in an unpopulated area. There were no trees. These places are the tundra, where trees cannot grow. Even on the astral side there were no trees. Suddenly there was a snow leopard which tracked the scent of a dead animal. I watched it as it found the carcass of an eagle which was partially eaten by another scavenger. Then about a thousand feet from that dead body, there was another eagle carcass but that one was not touched by any other predator.

As soon as the snow leopard found the second carcass, two dogs appeared from nowhere. At first the ears of the snow leopard went up in alarm, then it ran to the north further into the tundra, the dogs pursued it in a hot chased. I could read the mind of the snow leopard which considered that if it was one dog, it may take the creature down but since it is two it could not take a chance to challenge them.

As the leopard thought of this, I realized that I was in the astral world. In other words, at first even though I was there, I did not objectively realize that I used only the astral body. Sometimes one finds oneself in another dimension and does not realize that one is in such a place. One feels that one should be in that place and should function under its conditions. That is similar to our position in these physical bodies, where most of us have no idea of a past life. We feel that this is the only life and that we did not exist before, and only what we do at this time has importance.

When I realized that I was in the astral world and that the astral body separated of its own accord without my desire and came to that dimension, I made a mental note so that I would remember to write about it, when I would return to the physical body. But then in my mind this physical existence was not the reference, so the reference was some other experiences I had during the meditation session. This means that a point of reference is there in these experiences. One should know how the mind uses direct and indirect references.

Two Visitors (August 2011)

During exercises this morning, I had two deceased visitors. The first was Swami Rama. I did breath infusion, working on the area below the navel. Swami Rama explained this:

> *The sperm particle heads for a particular location in the womb of the mother. At that place it crimps down to get nutrients. The same impulse one has when one is sexually attracted to someone and desires to get near to that person, operates in the sperm to find that special part of the womb where it has to extract nutrients from the mother's system.*

If a person passes on and does not root out that tendency of the lifeForce, he or she will have to take rebirth as a compulsion. When working on the navel chakra, the real problem is the expression of the chakra. This chakra is the only one which issues the energy which causes a person to seek out someone for sex.

At puberty, this energy becomes visible to someone who is in a young body. Usually it haunts the person from puberty onwards. It is relentless in its pursue of sexual access. After leaving the body that pursuit continues in the astral world. It becomes dormant there as soon as the person becomes fused into a parent's psyche.

Near the end of the exercise session, I had a visit from Rishi Singh Gherwal. He explained that when the kundalini is sufficiently infused with breath energy, it loses the struggle-for-survival instincts, but if the yogi's psyche is de-energized, kundalini will resume its animalistic behaviors.

When I sat to meditate, Rishi showed a level in which the self no longer has a psychic cloud of low energy surrounding it. He said that it is just as Patanjali wrote that the sure way to deal with this is pranayama breath infusion.

Causal Level as The Ultimate (August 2011)

The causal level is the zone where everything which we encounter in this world reaches dissolution. It is the place from which everything which is in the world which we purview, like loving someone, killing someone, making a useful utensil, advocating a certain philosophy and such things, are sourced.

Beyond that causal zone there are two higher places. The first is the brahman level which does not have the source desires which we fulfill now. That brahman level is pure spiritual existence, with no admixture of anything from the causal plane, the astral levels and the physical realities. Beyond that brahman level is the spiritual world proper. Reaching the causal plane is a huge achievement but it is not the ultimate.

This morning when I did breath infusion, at a certain point my psyche reached the causal level. I reached the very edge of it from this side of existence. As soon as I made contact Yogesh came from within the causal plane and touch my head. I have not seen this yogi for some months. Immediately after greeting me, he resumed existence in the causal plane. He does research there.

The causal plane is important for knowing how we got psychic forms and then physical forms, but it has no information about the brahman exclusive spiritual plane nor the spiritual worlds.

Any person on this side of existence who performs enough austerity and who detaches the coreSelf from the psychic adjuncts can penetrate and go back to the causal plane. The problem is that to go to the spiritual place, one must take help from a deity from the spiritual world. Otherwise it a situation of Ring-Pass-Not, which means that one cannot even think of anything higher than the causal. Nothing else is in one's purview. If something is beyond the purview it is as if it does not exist.

(August 2011)

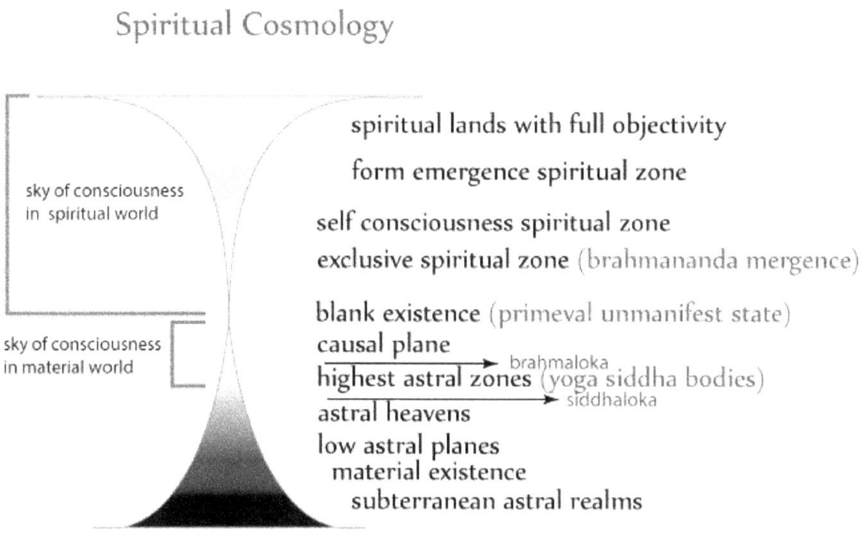

Part 4

Yoga Dedication

A yogi should contact disembodied yogi teachers. The astral activities at night, should put one in touch with such yogis. There is no magic to it. It is hardly likely that anyone doing yoga in the modern environment will be successful enough to project the astral body to a place where advanced yogis reside in the subtle world.

One should make a connection now with a departed advanced yogi. Then it is likely that after leaving the body, one could get to that person or that person could locate one. Then one could be shown what to do to stop the subtle body from again going into a sexual liaison of potential new parents on earth.

The guarantee for reaching an advanced yogi in the hereafter is to follow the instructions of that yogi now. It is based on following the process of yoga which that teacher advocated. Does one feel obligated to follow a teacher? If one does one may meet a siddha after death. I have deceased yoga teachers who instruct me. They are just as demanding on my time as physical people are.

A few days ago, I spoke to a person who has so many social obligations that yoga practice has no priority to him. In his case, we learn that if we can get ourselves in relationships with yoga gurus in the way he relates to his social obligations, we would always be in touch with such yogis. Then for sure, we would meet with them after leaving the physical body.

A yogi who has difficulty keeping a steady practice, should take a good look at people who are socially active. These people are good examples on how crazed one should be for yoga. Some people have this *I-do-not-have-time-for-yoga* attitude. They are great examples of how insane and dedicated one should be to practice yoga. Just as they are fanatical and proud of social obligations, one should be proud of practice. Just as they are tightly controlled by social associations, one should be by yoga teachers.

Diamond Kundalini (August 2011)

This morning during practice, kundalini was not in touch with the base area which is its native anchor point. Instead it retreated up the spine right above where the second chakra would be. It assumed a diamond configuration and was white hot in color. It was like a large diamond suspended in mid-air.

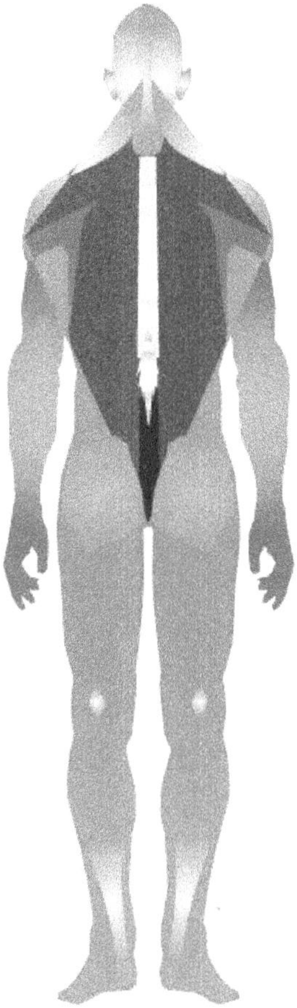

This practice began with an instruction of a Buddha deity in South Korea, who gave a procedure for attacking the base chakra anchor point instead of attacking the base chakra or even the kundalini. Kundalini rose several times. One particular instance was with kundalini firing up through each side of the chest and lodging in the lower jaw bones. This felt as if there was cool air in that area with a bliss aspect to it.

These practices give one the opportunity to discover the various parts of the psyche which usually get only a low charge of energy from kundalini. Since a yogi will have to carry the whole psyche when leaving the physical body for good, it is wise to infuse all parts of that psychic system with fresh energy. Initially one focuses on getting kundalini into the head but the head is not the whole psyche.

The psyche will go as high as its least-energized portion. This is why one should seriously take a look at the various hard-to-reach parts and make sure that they are not saturated with a low grade of energy. If only a small part of the psyche reaches the higher planes, that means that the psyche will not go to that place hereafter. It will go to the place which the other collective is attuned to.

How I Killed a Hen (August 2011)

Someone called this morning about vegetarian diet. This person recently changed from a carnivorous diet to a vegetarian one with dairy products. He had some difficulty with the adjustment. He said that there were times, when he desired the taste of the previous diet, especially when the vegetarian meals were not as tasty. First of all, doing a vegetarian diet as a human being is not natural. Most indigenous people are carnivorous. Considering that the human being is the culmination of all the species on this planet, a human body has the potential for anything which is done by any other species.

We assume that the human transmigrated through many species. Gautama Buddha described his births as reptiles and other species, which he experienced in meditation. A soul using a human body came from past lives with certain developed traits which are experienced as urges and instincts.

This means that we carry the package of good and bad behavior from all past lives. If in that background we were mostly non-vegetarian, it is a wonder that anyone can abstain from flesh foods. I practiced vegetarian diet in many of my immediate past lives. Still in this life I struggled in trying to change from a flesh diet to a vegetarian one. In 1969 I decided once and for all to adopt the vegetarian diet. It took about eight years to completely achieve it.

I know that the cells in my body were desirous of the non-vegetarian diet. Even though I was vegetarian in many past lives, still my subtle body adapted and changed when I was in my father and mother's bodies waiting for delivery as a baby. By the time I was pressed from my mother's passage, I had the potential for eating just about anything. I grew up in a family which was not vegetarian.

I struggle for years to change the physical body. Once it did, it no longer had the urge to eat flesh. It saw flesh being cooked as if it was human bodies being cooked. If for instance I see meat in a grocery store, butcher shop or even being cooked in a pan, to me it is just as if my flesh was cut and prepared as a meal. In the case of items like eggs, I see that as the reproductive fluid of chickens.

As a child, I was instructed to kill, de-feather and cut chicken bodies. Once they told me to kill a hen. They gave me a huge knife. I caught the hen, held it down and then cut off its head. In the meantime, my psyche considered the creature in a very detached way. Even though the bird screamed, that did not affect me one bit,

I was totally detached with no emotion for the bird. The thing that shocked me however was when I gutted the chicken body. Since it was a mature hen, there were many eggs in its body. I was amazed. There was one egg which was in a soft white casing. There were other eggs which had no casing except a transparent membrane.

The non-encased eggs were of various sizes, going down to the side of dot and then to less. There were several of these. I was shocked to see, that with the killing of the hen, these eggs were to be eliminated.

I was sent to an open market to buy fish. Sometimes I would get there when the fishes were removed from boats. Some were live, jumping in baskets. I was trained to bring only fresh fish, which meant fish that were alive or one which recently died. This was because there was no refrigeration. I had to kill some fish by slitting their guts but once there was a pregnant fish. It had several hundred tiny eggs in a transparent sack. I was shocked. I did not know how to handle that.

Personally, I do not have any use for a non-vegetarian diet. To me such a diet is risky since the subtle body will have the propensity for eating flesh. It will carry that after it leaves the physical form, with the risk that one may be attracted to an animal birth in the next life. For self-protection, I have no use for meat diet. I will not however be starting a group for vegetarianism nor will you find me trying to convince anyone about it.

I see that material nature is quite competent in managing the various rebirths here or there. Nature did this for millions of years in her own way. She did it successfully. She does not need my assistance. Each person has to decide what is what and make up the mind regarding what to do and what not to do. Any change from any habit entails some difficulty, some restraint, some psychological struggle to get the psyche to change. There is no way around this.

Many people in the 1960's were inspired to be vegetarians. Most failed and settled for organic foods of any sort, with organic flesh included. It is not easy. It may seem easy if one is in a religious sect, like for instance some Buddhist sects and some yoga sects or religious sects from India and even some Christian sects. In a sect there is a group pressure. That coarces one in the process but even then, nature fights back since it is supportive of old habits even the ones which may shorten the life of the body. Once someone has a motive that makes sense, he can achieve an objective over time, considering of course that habits have a momentum. They are not abandoned easily. Basically, I use one main meal which has something from below the ground, something from above the ground and something in-between. Below the ground means foods like potatoes. Above the ground means something like spinach and string beans, something green. In-between means like carrots.

Items like shelled dried beans I consider to be below the ground even though they are grown above the ground. If it is not green or does not have chlorophyll, I consider it to be below the ground even if it is grown above the ground. To alternate I use potatoes, sweet potatoes, yams or beans like black eye peas, soy beans, or pinto beans. I use one of the greens like spinach, turnip greens or kale, in the summer. During winter I use heavier leafage like collard greens.

Cooking food daily is a chore. I subsidize that one cooked meal with nuts and fruits. I use unsalted dry roasted peanuts. I feel that using salt in nuts is suicidal because you have no idea how much salt you consume. Salt has a bad reputation for hardening arteries and giving heart trouble.

Peanut butter is good but I prefer to make it between the molars because I feel that so long as there are jaw teeth, it is better to chew the nuts and make the peanut butter with molar teeth since that also adds saliva which is part of the enzyme system of the body. With machine peanut butter those saliva enzymes are not mixed in sufficiently. However, using the teeth to grind peanuts or any food may erode or file teeth. Hence one may use ground nuts as nut butter. Other nuts can be used like almonds, pistachio and whatever. It depends on what is available where you live and also on what you can afford.

Recently when I was in South Korean, a lady knew that I was a vegetarian. When she questioned me, she was appalled and felt that I was food deficient. She said that I should eat more to get what I required. When I mentioned peanuts, she dismissed that. I told her that peanuts have just as much and even more protein value than meat. She did not believe but she checked on the internet and remained silent after that. Soybeans also have much protein content. Tofu or Chinese bean curd is made from soybeans.

For fruits I use about three bananas per day. I would warn though that bananas should not be eaten after noon. They should be eaten when sun energy is still active in the atmosphere.

I also use other fruit but I had bad experiences with citrus fruits which are grown using chemical fertilizer. Sour fruit which is grown using artificial fertilizer should not be used. It seems that these plants go hungry for fertilizer and take up a great percentage of strong chemicals which then are left in the body after being eaten and which would damage organs and tissue.

The other part of my diet is organic whole milk. Milk also takes chemicals from fertilizers which are in the grass and grain eaten by cows. I use organic milk and organic whole wheat. This body came from Guyana where rice is the staple. I do not use rice any longer because it causes constipation. Measure for measure whole wheat has more fiber than rice. In the case of rice, the covering is not edible. In the case of wheat, the covering can be used. Provided that is not removed as in the case of white flower, wheat flour is not as conducive for constipation.

This is a quick summary of what I do:

The main meal of carrots, potato, greens, one slice or two of whole wheat, tofu when and if it is available and affordable, three bananas (never over-ripe ones because they are too sweet), organic milk + whole wheat cereal (could be puffed wheat), nuts which are not salted but which could be dry roasted or raw as in the case of almonds and brazil nuts.

I know of persons who grew up on vegetarian diet and who later adopted non-vegetarian meals, just as in the case of liquor where before the young adult stage one may be repelled from it or may find that it burns the mouth, but then something changes in the body. One gets so involved in it as to become an alcoholic.

After my body assumed the vegetarian diet in full, I no longer saw flesh as anything but human meat. If I was in a grocery by the meat freezers, if I looked at the meat, it crossed my mind that my hand or rib or whatever could well be there instead. Once after this change occurred, I was in a restaurant with others. There was a small group of persons in an adjacent booth. A lady chomped a chicken thigh. Right then as I saw it, something flashed in my mind which was that it could well be her thigh. It was shaped in exactly the same way except for the difference in size.

Regardless of my philosophical or religious views, I still have to deal with the perspective my psyche adapted. Another thing that happened is that I grew up in a Christian home where the leader of the home, an elderly woman was a staunch church goer. In that system food is blessed with the Lord's Prayer before eating. I got the view from that, that God provided food, except that one should pray before eating it.

However later in life something kept popping up which was that in Judaism and its offshoot Christianity there is the idea of the good shepherd. This comes from the pastoral life of the early prophets like Abraham. In that system you keep goats and sheep in a flock. You protect the herd from wolves. Of course, the shepherd is good to the sheep but there was the motive for eating the sheep. Once I saw this contradiction, I was determined never to keep animals for flesh.

I cannot deal with eggs because when I see an egg, I see a woman's reproductive fluids. Each egg to me is menstrual fluids in a shell. Of course, eggs are clear and yellow on the inside, but still it is in fact the reproductive fluid of the hen with or without the sperm of the rooster.

The other thing is deeper and this relates to going back into past lives and tapping into the evolutionary cycle and how a being is promoted by nature from one species to the next, all the way up to the human category. This takes millions of years and billions of lives to move up the evolutionary ladder. The situation with domestic animals is mostly a rip off by the human beings who exploit the other species for whatever service or dietary potential the animal bodies have. That is no exception since such rip-offs are more or less common in the various kingdoms of nature.

We are not alone in this. Ants domesticate aphids for a juice which the aphids secrete. In the case of chickens, we strike a bargain with them, where we agree to feed them and project them from predators on the condition that we eat them or keep them and eat their intended babies (eggs).

But there are others besides humans who want those developed or undeveloped babies for food. There are foxes who steal the eggs of grouse or polar bears who take eggs from birds which roost near the arctic. Or snakes which invade nests and swallow eggs. In our case it is robbery when we take the eggs. The chicken is tricked indeed. Looking at that as part of our evolutionary history, it is nasty, something which we should distance ourselves from.

One thing which I came to understand once I began to meditate deeply was that presently in the early part of this life, most of the tendencies in the body came from the parents. These were not my habits. Somehow when this body developed, my psyche adapted those habits just as if they were mine perpetually.

Once I got this insight, I slowly but surely erased those counterproductive habits of my parents. It is important for all people who aspire for spiritual profile, to realize that many tendencies which are undesirable may originate in someone else.

As a child in South American, fish was eaten at least every other day. I bought them. I killed them if they were alive by gutting them after cutting from their excretory opening to the mouth. Sometimes we would boil or fry even the head and eat whatever was not a bone, like the eye for instance. I did these things in this life. Looking back, it was like I replayed a caveman body while using this modern homo sapiens species.

Later when my psyche switched, I found that these activities were superfluous and nonsensical. For one thing the fish usually died from suffocation because their gills are not efficient at processing air from air. It requires air from water. Some other fish died from a slicing action of a knife. Once my mystic senses developed, I could not cut fish because I could hear their screams at the pain of it.

Since I could survive easily without eating fish, there was no justification for me to continue that dietary habit. It is a personal thing. Once I met a Christian lady. She tried to convert me. I asked her a question, I said, "What will we eat in heaven? Will there be cattle and chickens?"

I told her that if God was involved in butchering animals, I was not interested in going to heaven. What is the use of a God who boiled crabs and squid in heaven?

There is another perspective on this which is that the subtle body outgrows senses according to one's habits. This means that if I resumed eating meat, my subtle body would be adjusted to that again. Where does it stop? Do I want to go all the way down to being a tiger or lion in the next birth? My psyche is adaptable to any species but do I really want an animal birth?

The answer is that in my case, I am not interested in doing that. I will not take the risk. I aspire for a higher plane of existence. From what I saw so far in the astral regions, one cannot go to a higher level if one has lower evolutionary tendencies. That is my main reason for my being a vegetarian.

Where I grew up eggs were mostly used in their boiled condition. But there was this habit of always seasoning certain foods either before they were cooked or after they were cooked. These foods were termed as rank foods meaning that they emitted an odor which a human being could not use until it was counteracted with either onions, chives, salt, black pepper or vinegar.

For instance, fish was regarded as rank. It carries a questionable odor. To remove that they were scaled except cat fish. They were sliced here and there. A combination of vinegar, salt, onions, all crushed, was applied. This masks the undesirable smell. Eggs have a rank smell both in the shell and after it is cracked. Once it is cracked it is sprinkled with salt and pepper. That counteracts the odor.

Notice that the animals who eat these things in the wild, have no qualms about odor. This means that if I am shifted to the animal level, I too would have no qualms. But there was one other important use for eggs which was in cakes. My body was acquired from people who were descendants of African slaves, brought to Guyana by British slave owners. However, the diet was changed to that of a British diet. There were these cakes which were made on the basis of British pastry methods.

This meant that to make a cake one had to procure eggs. These were stirred into a batter and mixed with sugar, flour, spices, butter, baking powder and then baked. The eggs serve two purposes which was to make the flour rise in an even way and also to provide taste.

Interestingly they added lemon peel when the eggs were stirred to remove the rank odor. They added citron to the batter. That offset some of the offensive odor. Even when eggs were used with sugar, and butter and flour there was an effort to eliminate odor. I know these details because I stirred the eggs and mixed it into batter.

What is egg rankness? It is the blood smell. Remember what an egg is. It is the reproductive fluid of a hen. If one provides mild heat to an egg and if it is fertilized it will change into a chicken. It has the potential to convert into flesh and feathers. From a chemical view point we can say that it is nature's liquid emulsion for making flesh, bones and feathers.

Unless a person understands how reincarnation works, it may be hard to stop eating eggs. This scene is controlled by nature. Nothing is out of whack in this creation. This is a closed system.

We live like bacteria in a closed jar. This nature system is under control. Nature degrades, stagnates or upgrades. It does so at its own pace.

To one person nature applies pressure for that one to move upward. This makes that person feel uncomfortable with certain habits. For another, nature applies pressure to move downward. That one abandons certain other habits. For yet another person, nature induces for that one to relax and enjoy.

When the Sun Destroys the Subtle Bodies (August 2011)

Yogesh explained the destruction of kundalini lifeForce. This is a high-end kriya but I will describe it. The idea is that to enter the causal plane one has to eliminate kundalini. Stated in another way, so long as one has a kundalini, one cannot resume the existence in the causal plane. Usually one gets rid of kundalini when the cosmos collapses and the cosmic kundalini energy goes into dormancy. Currently, that will happen in many billions of years in the future. Sometimes however there is a partial cosmic collapse and a set of beings go into the causal level even though the whole universe did not retrogress. In that case only a segment cancels.

That may happen to us if the sun explodes. Science is saying that in so many billion years, about five billion the sun will explode, the earth will be fried and that is it for us. This will not only be a physical but a psychic event because the sun sustains us psychically as well. Our astral bodies rely on energy from the sun just as the physical forms do.

Unless a yogi can transfer the subtle body to another system or to another higher energy source if anything weird happens to the sun, say it explodes even before the scientists estimate, then that is it for our kundalinis. Then we enter the causal plane. One may think that is acceptable but is it? For one thing if a person is not advanced and that one enters the causal place, it is as if that person de-existed. Advanced entities can make use of the causal plane but since others did not master subjective consciousness, they become de-activated selves, their existence becomes dormant. It may stay in that condition for billions of years.

Of course, there is an advantage to that, because if for a few billion years you know nothing about yourself or anything else and then if you awaken somewhere, it would be just as if you did not go into existential dormancy. There would be no point of reference in memory.

We recently experienced that in this body, when we found ourselves to be babies in cribs and then school children and then adults with no memory of a prior existence. For us, life began twenty, thirty or forty years ago. Once when I explained reincarnation a man laughed. He felt that reincarnation did not matter if one does not remember the past life.

Yogesh feels that a yogi must try to reach the causal plane to investigate exactly how the subtle body and the kundalini and then the physical systems come into being on the basis of the causal energy and the potency in the causal force. To do this one must disconnect from kundalini. That is done by super-infusing the kundalini with energy until it burns away or vaporizes.

If you heat a metal and if you can keep increasing the temperature, it will reach a stage where it vaporizes. When yogis do this, they enter the causal plane. This is a forced entry of course. It is not like waiting till the cosmic situation is demolished. What is the purpose of going into the causal level?

That is simple. It is to understand exactly how the subtle material nature attracted the spirits and then uses the spirits to manifest itself in various ways. If one can go into the causal plane and maintain some objective consciousness there, even a tiny amount, one could get insight into the subtle operations which control us and dictate what happens when a universe begins.

Remembering Past Lives (August 2011)

To identify the various memory compartments in the psyche, one must first discover where these compartments are located. Initially of course one has no special location for anything in the psyche, due to psychic insensitivity the psyche seems to have no limit nor location. The mind is just the self and the self as the mind.

However, by meditation one develops the insight to know that the mind is a compartment in which the self is housed along with other components like the thought-making apparatus. Yes, it is invisible in the mind but still that is due to not having the psychic vision to sort one psychic component from the other.

During meditation it will happen now and again, that suddenly a yogi has a vivid memory of something that happened over twenty years ago, even something from childhood. This memory will be so vivid that it is not easily forgotten. It will be so clear that it will be astonishing.

This is an example of something that should be noted by the yogi. Special note should be taken of this. Where did that memory arise? In which part of the mind did it occur? Was it to the left of center, the right of center, central in the mind, up or down? Did this begin on the bottom of the mind? Did it ascend from the bottom like a bubble?

A yogi should note this, as to where deep memories are stored in the mind. Later in other meditations, he may go to that place of the deep memories. He opens other memories from the long last past. After becoming proficient, he moves deeper into that location to the place just before he began to form a body in the parents and then deeper to the past lives. But if these memory experiences, are not noted, the yogi will not develop deep insight. It is not magic. It takes practice.

Meeting a Student of Yogi Bhajan (August 2011)

This morning I was with a student of kundalini yoga, who learnt the practice some ten years ago. This person also studied other systems of spirituality and practiced others but it seems that he was unable to make a consistent habit of practice. Making a spiritual discipline a habit, is a special ability of a person who did yoga in their past lives. In the *Bhagavad Gita* there is a verse.

तत्र तं बुद्धिसंयोगं
लभते पौर्वदेहिकम् ।
यतते च ततो भूयः
संसिद्धौ कुरुनन्दन ॥६.४३॥

tatra taṁ buddhisaṁyogaṁ
labhate paurvadehikam
yatate ca tato bhūyaḥ
saṁsiddhau kurunandana (6.43)

tatra — there; tam — it; buddhisaṁyogam — cumulative intellectual interest; labhate — inspired with; paurvadehikam — from a previous birth; yatate — he strives; ca — and; tato = tataḥ — from that time; bhūyaḥ — again; saṁsiddhau — to perfection; kuru-nandana — O dear son of the Kurus

In that environment, he is inspired with the cumulative intellectual interest from a previous birth. And from that time, he strives again for yoga perfection, O dear son of the Kurus. (6.43)

If one does not have this cumulative intellectual interest from a previous birth, one cannot automatically strive again in the new body. One will not have the impetus. When we did the exercises, about five minutes after we began, Yogi Bhajan appeared on the astral side. Lucky for me this process which I teach as kundalini yoga was learnt from him. Some students I adopt are his students with me as an assistant teacher. Yogi Bhajan checked the subtle body of the student. He showed a lump of cloudy energy in the bottom part of the trunk. This was the sexual subtle force in the body.

For kundalini yoga purposes the sexual energy is compressed and sent into the spine and into the head, instead of accumulating in the pubic area. This student because of not practicing consistently for the past ten years, had no compressed sexual force. Yogi Bhajan was disgusted because here was a student who always complained about the practice and who does not maintain the method, not even ten minutes of practice per day. How can there be results from the practice, if the student does not endeavor?

Yogi Bhajan said this to me, "I like you because you do not have students. You have no ambition to be anyone's guru. People like you are the best students. As soon as somebody gets this idea that he is a teacher, it is all over because then he no longer pays attention to what develops in the psyche. He thinks that what his students experience during practiced is his primary concern. He loses track of his advancement.

"With you it is different you know that when you teach, it has little to do with your progression. You are eager to dismiss students. You realize that when teaching you neglect your advancement."

After that Yogi Bhajan left. With this body now at sixty plus years of age, I have little time to stay in it, even if it is not killed suddenly in a freak accident or does not develop an incurable disease. My practice is all the more important.

Seeing God

Once I saw a four-handed Vishnu form which is known as Padmanabha Narayana. This is one of the divine bodies of Krishna. It is all spirit. I saw that form and never saw it again. In fact, when I saw the form there was a message in the apparition which said that this would never again happen in this lifetime.

How should I advice someone on how to see that form. In the first place I saw that divine body of God only because the deity showed himself and temporarily elevated my existence for the perception. I have no way of causing that to happen again. The deity could have said something to give some idea how I could see him again but he did not.

Once I saw another divine body which was Krishna, the cowherd boy with a blue iridescent body, but when it happened, it just happened. I cannot repeat it. I did not cause it. In fact, even though Krishna caused it, there was a message in the apparition which said this,

"This is an accident. This will not happen again." The important part of these experiences is really my assumption of a spiritual form with spiritual vision. Yet, I cannot say for sure how I could resume the divine body at the present time. In meditation some experiences cannot be repeated.

I do not use breath as a reference point in meditation because I do not use props. My experience is that a prop gets in the way. I use naad sound. Once the mind is silent, I use naad sound. If it is not silent, I use naad sound to abandon the noisy part of the mind. From that abandonment the idea oscillation ceases.

There was a time when I did not use naad. I used the centre of the eyebrow or even the observing coreSelf but eventually some of my gurus laid down a restriction which was to keep in naad no matter what.

Once in naad things develop. From that development progress is made. However, if you find yourself out of naad and into mental noise, return to naad. If you do not use naad for whatever reason, then return to the silence point or silence area. Stay there until something happens. If something happens which is extraordinary and which is obviously not the usual mental noise, focus on that. There is supernatural and spiritual insight to be developed. It develops from silence or from naad. It will develop from either but one must be patient because one may have to meditate in daily sessions for weeks, months or years even.

My Schizophrenic Kundalini (August 2011)

When doing breath infusion, one must check to be sure that the air goes into the system and is compressed into the blood stream. It should be absorbed by the lungs and sent to various parts of the body. It should not be entering the lungs and then leaving the lungs without infusion. One student recently mentioned to me the ease with which he could do breath infusion in comparison to when he first started when the air was not absorbed fully.

However, be sure that the air is compressed. One may be breathing rapidly with ease and not be compressing the air into the system. The lungs may expand for air and not absorb it. The lungs may absorb air into the aveoli and then breathing out the air without it being distributed.

Be sure that mentally one compresses air into the lungs and compresses it into the system. It should be force into the navel area. When that is done to proficiency, one may force it into the groin area and beyond.

One important part of this practice is to keep the mind attentive to what happens in the psyche. The mind should not focus on what happens outside of the body. There is an instruction about this in the Anu Gita.

निर्वेदस्तु न गन्तव्यो युञ्जानेन कथंचन
योगमेकान्तशीलस्तु यथा युञ्जीत तच्छृणु
nirvedastu na gantavyo yuñjānena kathaṁcana
yogamekāntaśīlastu yathā yuñjīta tacchṛṇu (4.30)

nirvedas = nirvedah = discouraged; tu – but; na – not; gantavyo = gantavyah = attained; yuñjānena – with proficiency in yoga; kathaṁcana – anyway; yogam – yoga; ekānta = eka (one, primary) + anta (end, objective); śīlas = śīlah = behavior, lifestyle; tu – but; yathā – as; yuñjīta - proficiency in yogic trance; tac = tat = that; chṛṇu = śṛṇu = hear

But one who is attaining the proficiency in yoga practice, should not be discouraged. Hear about this how one whose primary objective in life is yoga, practices trance consistently. (Anu Gita 4.30)

दृष्टपूर्वां दिशं चिन्त्य यस्मिन्संनिवसेत्पुरे
पुरस्याभ्यन्तरे तस्य मनश्चार्यं न बाह्यतः
dṛṣṭapūrvāṁ diśaṁ cintya yasminsaṁnivasetpure
purasyābhyantare tasya manaścāryaṁ na bāhyataḥ (4.31)

dṛṣṭa – seen; pūrvāṁ - before; diśaṁ - place; cintya – thinking; yasmin – in which; saṁnivaset – should reside; pure – in the city; purasyābhyantare = purasya (of the city or psyche) + abhyantare (in the interior, inside); tasya – of his; manaś = manah = mind; cāryaṁ - behavior, operation; na – not; bāhyataḥ - outside

When thinking of a place which was seen before, one should reside in the city in which the incidence occurred. The mental operations are within the psyche, not outside of it. (Anu Gita 4.31)

पुरस्याभ्यन्तरे तिष्ठन्यस्मिन्नावसथे वसेत्
तस्मिन्नावसथे धार्यं सबाह्याभ्यन्तरं मनः
purasyābhyantare tiṣṭhanyasminnāvasathe vaset
tasminnāvasathe dhāryaṁ sabāhyābhyantaraṁ manaḥ (4.32)

purasyābhyantare = (purasya of the city) + abhyantare (inside); tiṣṭhany = tiṣṭhani = situated; asmin – in this; nāvasathe = na (not) + avasathe (city); vaset – should reside; tasmin – in this; nāvasathe = na (not) + avasathe (city); dhāryaṁ - absorbed in; sa – with; bāhyābhyantaraṁ = bāhya (exterior) + abhyantaram (interior); manaḥ - mind

Being situated inside the city, he should reside there with his mind absorbed in the exterior and interior features of that place. (Anu Gita 4.32)

प्रचिन्त्यावसथं कृत्स्नं यस्मिन्कायेऽवतिष्ठते
तस्मिन्काये मनश्चार्यं न कथंचन बाह्यतः
pracintyāvasathaṁ kṛtsnaṁ yasminkāye'vatiṣṭhate
tasminkāye manaścāryaṁ na kathaṁcana bāhyataḥ (4.33)

pracintyāvasathaṁ = pracintya = meditating; kṛtsnaṁ - whole reality; yasmin – in which; kāye – in the body; 'vatiṣṭhate = avatiṣṭhate = being situated; tasmin – in that; kāye – in the body; manaś = manah = whole; cāryaṁ - wander; na – not; kathaṁcana – any way; bāhyataḥ - outside

Meditating in that place, the self sees the whole reality being situated in the body. The mind should not in any way wander outside the body. (Anu Gita 4.33)

Imagine that I did breath infusion since 1972. Still, I am distracted by light which enters the eyes, by sounds which are heard outside the body, and mostly by the crazy security-paranoid kundalini which is always obsessed with using the senses. The kundalini is paranoid. It is desperate to track incidences outside the body.

Even now after many years of meditation, I wrap a dark cloth around my eyes and head so as to keep kundalini from compelling the senses to pursue interests outside the body during practice.

If I do this after so much practice, what is the matter? Do I fail to control my mind? Is it that I cannot control it by command?

Be sure that the air is compressed and that your attention is on the breath infusion. Keep track of where the air was ingested. Keep the mind inside the body during the practice. Do not allow kundalini to pursue other interests. It should not tell you where to focus, or when. It should not distract you from the intended focus within the body.

Sexual Adjustments of Breath Infusion (August 2011)

Someone inquired yesterday of the effects on the sexual energy when doing breath infusion which raises kundalini. See these diagrams:

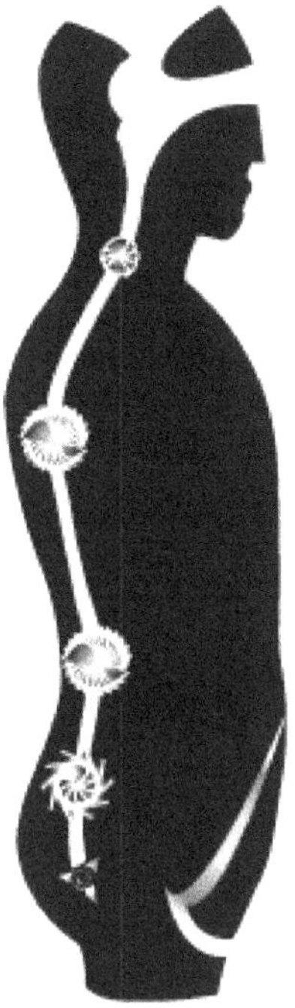

normal
sex hormone configuration

This diagram shows that normally the sexual hormones are formed from droplets of special energy under the navel. These flow to the reproductive organs and then flow out of the body through the sexual organs. For males the flow is routed through the testes which hang outside the body, but the energy is routed back into the body through tubes. Even for males the psychic charge of the sex force is felt inside the trunk of the body as well as in the sexual organ itself.

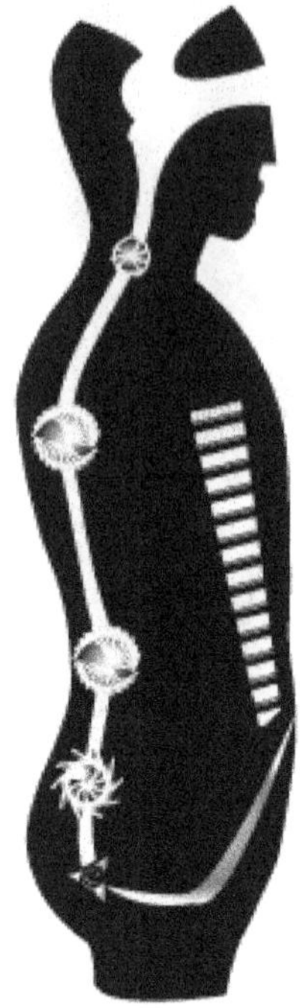

infused energy alters
path of sex hormone

In this diagram the infused breath energy moves from the lungs into the navel area. There it charges and mixes with the sex hormone energy. Instead of routing through the sexual organs, the infused energy forces the sex force to go to the base chakra, where it may cause arousal of kundalini.

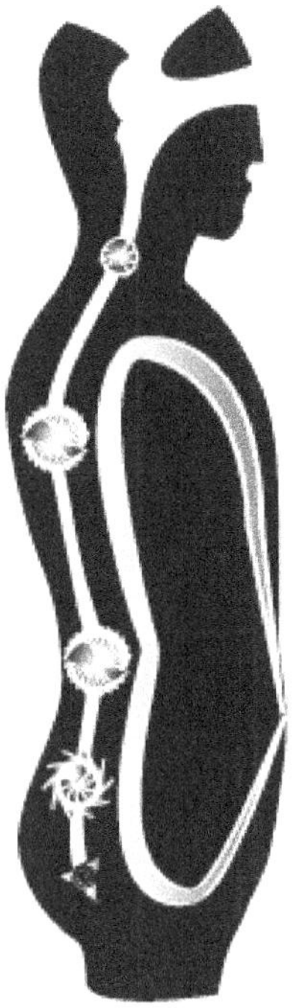

normal sex hormone passage
altered by breath infusion practice

In the diagram, the sex energy which accumulates below the navel area, does not flow out of the genitals. Instead it is route backwards and upwards into the chest. Then it routes again to the navel. Even though it moves through the reproductive area it avoids the sexual organs.

With this change in the subtle body, a yogi who does breath infusion attains the status of urdhva-reta which is that of a person whose semen (reta) moves upwards (urdhva) as the default flow.

If I have to resist sex attraction in the subtle world, my yoga practice is only partially effective. What should happen is that the subtle body should change so that there is no sexual arousal. In other words, at 9 years of age, a human body has no sexual arousal. That is not due to what the person wants but what the body is capable of. The objective in terms of subtle world sex, is that the subtle body was altered so that it does not create the sexual energies and does not have the sexual attraction of an adult human form.

In the diagrams the sexual energies are reformed but they are still there. Thus, there will be problems in the subtle existence. Yogis who are not siddhas but who desire to practice without being distracted for sexual intercourse, must hide in special dimensions in the subtle world.

However, if the yogi has a reformed subtle body, his sexual indulgence in the astral world will not have such a devastating effect on his psyche because only a small portion of the energy will be expended in those sexual involvements. He will not think that it is fun. He will not expand it with partners, hundreds of which are available in the subtle world without the moral constraints which are put upon a person in the physical societies on earth.

Sadly, getting liberated is not as easy as we would like it to be. The subtle body is crazed for pleasure. I may be great. I may have a great philosophy. I may say that I experienced the supreme. If my body still has the sex urge and I am exposed to a sexually attractive person, it will affect me.

The Astral Dirt Road (August 2011)

The father of my body pulled my body in the astral world during the night to a place where he currently resides. He is deceased for some years but he lives in an adjacent parallel world which is an astral dimension which runs parallel to this earthly place and which mimics what happened on this earthly place during the better part of his life.

There are other deceased persons in that place. They live in harmony with each other, in houses which were similar to the ones of the era in which they had the last bodies. There were dirt roads and small wooden shops just as it used to be some years ago in Guyana where my father lived. I noticed that there were no churches. No religious beliefs were stressed. There was no racial attitude. People did what they enjoyed the most on the earth. Money is irrelevant in those astral places.

During one talk with my father, he was with a person who was a ship owner on earth. They discussed taking a ship to another place. My father was a ship captain in the past life. The ship owner had an attitude of being a superior to other persons because of his proprietorship, a trait which he expressed in that astral situation and which set him apart from others there.

After a time, I left that place. I walked on an astral dirt road. A woman whom I knew when my body was a boy, came to me. She identified herself and mentioned an incidence when I acquired a plant from her for my grandmother. She was happy to find me after so many years of absence. As she enjoyed meeting me again, I silently left and went into an astral shop where food was sold. This was exactly as it was many years ago in Guyana with a family cooking food in a small shop and selling meals to passerbys. It was as if time stopped in that astral place. It did not progress to modern conditions.

After this I had a flash and saw that my father was still going to his house in Guyana. At that point I left that astral place. This is an example of what happens in some astral places, where the entire domain suits the nostalgic needs of a group of people, where everything seems physical though it is astral. Eventually these entities will take bodies from new parents. They will come out in this earthly place as babies with no memory of a former life.

Kundalini Reduction and Absorption (August 2011)

During practice this morning Yogi Bhajan showed a procedure for kundalini reduction and then total absorption into the mind chamber which is the head of the subtle body. This process begins with the method which a Buddha deity in South Korea imparted to me. It is the attack of the base area to which Kundalini attached itself. This is not an attack of the kundalini base chakra but the place where the base chakra attached itself.

There is the base chakra. There is the place where the base adheres. This is something like a lamprey fish, which attaches itself to a rock or even to a living creature or it is like how a leech attaches itself to the body of another living creature. There are two ways to get the leech to move, which are to do something to the leech which causes it to release itself or to do something to the location where it is attached which will cause the leech to become separated from that place.

The Buddha deity's idea is for an all-out attack on the location where the base chakra is attached. This is a pranayama breath infusion attack that is so furious, so energy-forceful, that the location itself becomes obliterated or vaporized astrally. Hence kundalini is left with nothing to attached itself to. It becomes confused.

It is well known that Gautama Buddha practiced meditation in India from two austere yogis in the forest in northern India. After following at least two sincere teachers, he did not achieve liberation because their methods were not penetrating enough to yield that. Buddha isolated himself and began to meditate on his own. He did severe austerities, like living on air without taking food or water.

These practices of Buddha are secret for the most part. Many monks are still at a loss to know exactly what he did. In any case one method which he discovered is this attack on kundalini. If one attacks its anchor point, one can subdue it much quicker way than if one attacks the kundalini itself. If one practiced sufficiently the breath infusion practice, if one attacks the area below the base chakra and just forgets about attacking the base or even the kundalini as a whole, one should get rapid results.

First of all, one will not be able to find the base if one has not practiced sufficiently. This method will not work for those yogis who began the practice recently or who have not done enough breath infusion beforehand. When one first attacks the area below the base one will find a brown-black cloudy area of mist subtle energy at the base. This will feel like a round shaped piece of stone.

Above that will be the base chakra. One should ignore the chakra. One should do the breath infusion driving the air mentally into the area below the base. At first nothing will happen. This may occur for days or weeks of practice. After a time, there will be a white fire energy which will surround that area. After a time again the area itself, the mist cloud, will suddenly ignite and burn.

At this point there may be a flash at the place. One may feel compelled to shift focus to the base chakra. One should ignore this compulsion. As one practices day after day, eventually the cloud of energy will burn and be no more. There will be a black space where the location was. Even the base chakra will be there no longer. If one looks up through the spine, one will see a white energy like white-hot metal.

When this happens, one should not be over-confident because kundalini may again resume its configuration. The base area below the base chakra will again resume the dark-cloud presence. One should practice daily, until the cloud is there no longer. When this happens, one will find that there is no base chakra and there is no second chakra either. Instead, there will be a diamond shape bottom to the kundalini which hangs down in the center of the spine above where the second chakra was located.

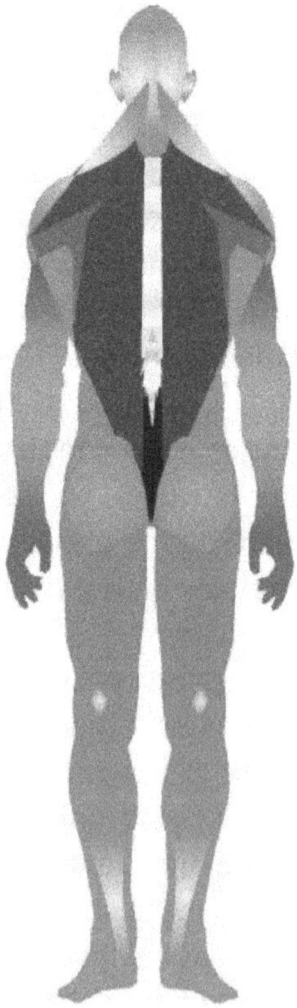

Yogi Bhajan said that one should keep infusing breath energy into that diamond until it retreats into the mind which is the head of the subtle body. That is the end of kundalini for the time being. Kundalini will reconfigure itself if the yogi is not careful or if the yogi is compelled against his wish to become socially involved with persons who are not siddhas.

The physical body is a pre-set time bomb which will die at a certain time in the future. Until its death, even for a yogi, it will exist for a time and do as destined. So long as one is in a certain environment, the repercussions from past lives will find the body and influence it accordingly. Adjusting kundalini will not stop the reactions which are predestined.

The body is the property of material nature. It will continue under that influence. Let us go back to the life of Buddha, where sometime after enlightenment he returned to the place where his body lived initially. Immediately the consequences of his previous actions were asserted. His son approached and asked for an inheritance.

The destruction of kundalini does not affect the layout of time which will manifest. Providence laid before us like asphalt on a highway. The yogi has psychic insight about the actions of nature. It is a mistake to think that because someone knows about a circumstance, he/she can adjust it. That is not necessarily so. Usually nature does not accomodate interference.

A yogi who destroyed the base of kundalini, must still function under time's demands. His way out is to remove his presence from certain levels of existence. Suppose I get an idea that I will go somewhere different in order to avoid the time layout which is before me. What do you think time will do? It will not release me from everything. It will only exempt me from its constraints in this dimension. As soon as I arrive in some other place, time will assert itself and impose the providence for that other location.

Liberation only works fully if the yogi transits from the material energy in full. That means out of it completely even out of its psychic reach. There is no way to escape completely from it so long as one's existence has a register in its physical or subtle domains. The yogi has the advantage of psychic insight into what nature does and to some extent into why it acts in specific ways.

If someone discovers that one can read past lives or do other psychic things, people will ask about that and want the yogi to use those abilities whimsically. That will degrade the yogi. One sure sign of a foolish yogi is that he/she makes the self available for whimsical requests and also for making money peddling psychic ability and the occult. If one understands that nature does not tolerate interference in its affairs, one will rarely exhibit anything paranormal which would affect nature's operations.

The result of this in a yogi's life is that he/she becomes more efficient in compensating whatever debts he occurred in the past and which fate now presents the bills to him for payment. This is how a yogi reinvests his increased psychic perception into the practice and makes advancement exponentially.

Yogesh gave a rule, where whosoever accepts him as a teacher should reinvest in the progress and should not exhibit anything socially. The idea is no interference in nature's concerns, and prompt payment for any debts incurred in previous lives when one was involved in massive ignorance.

Yogi as Bull Accidentally Floors Matador (August 2011)

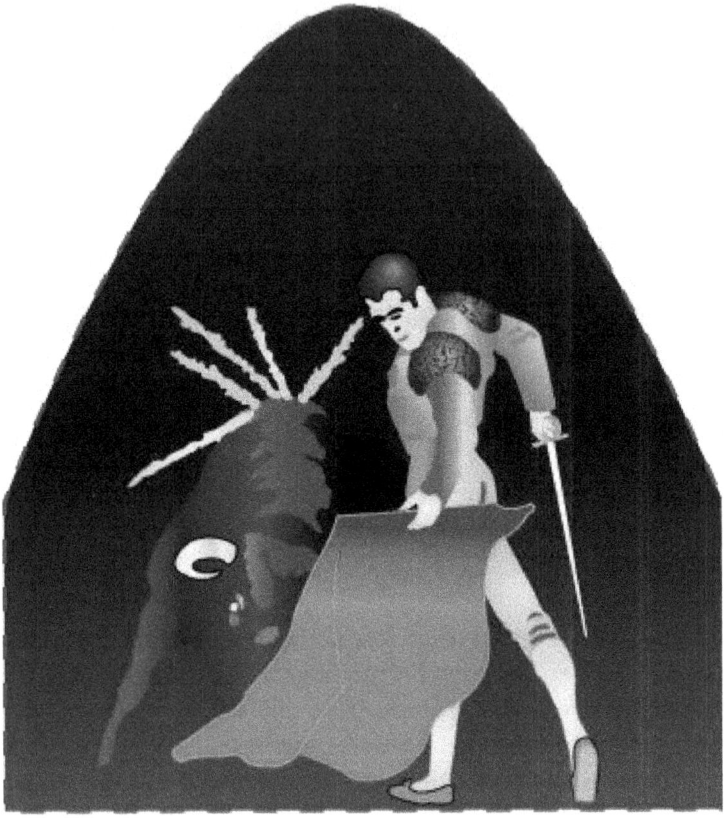

In the illustration the bull represents the coreSelf who cannot see the intellect which is represented by the matador. The core is focused on the cape. The matador is careful to flick the cape in order to keep the bull occupied. This causes the bull to attack the cape and not the matador.

Usually when people meditate, they attack the undesirable thoughts or ideas. Some others sit in the mind with detachment and let the thoughts develop without reacting to them. These persons act as if there is nothing but images in the mind. In this story the bull sees the cape. It should attack the matador but instead it attacks the cape.

In this diagram the matador was floored by the bull's action of hooking and twisting the cape but the bull has no idea that the matador is floored because the cape covers the bull's eyes.

Some bulls (meditators) feel victorious when the cape is not flicked or when it stops moving. Patanjali instructed that the bull should do something, anything, to stop the cape from flickering. Because they do not know of the existence of the matador or the intellect, some meditators set out to do that directly without respect the matador.

In the diagram, I depicted the general whereabouts of the coreSelf. Who is the coreSelf in the illustration? It is not the matador. It certainly is not the sword, nor the pikes which are stuck in the bull. That leaves only one other thing which is the bull.

Exactly, the coreSelf as the bull is lured into responding by the action of the cape which is manipulated by the matador. The cape is the kundalini energy. The matador is the intellect. The waving of the cape is the excitement created by the five senses. When the bull ignores the waving of the red cape, the matador waves the cape to incite the bull. He throws the five senses into action. They pierce the body of the bull, thereby irritating it sufficiently for it to charge the cape.

Using the five senses, the intellect agitates the bull, thereby attracting its interest to the cape, which is the kundalini energy. The enemy of the bull is the matador or intellect but due to the random movement of the cape the bull does not know this. Instead of goring the matador to death, the bull attempts to push its horn through the cape, but to no avail since the cape is too flexible.

A question arises as to why the matador or intellect has more intelligence than the coreSelf which is represented by the bull which is an inferior species?

Another question concerns the possibility of the bull realizing that its enemy is the matador.

Now regarding the sword; What is it? Why does the intellect carry a hidden weapon for piercing the heart of the bull?

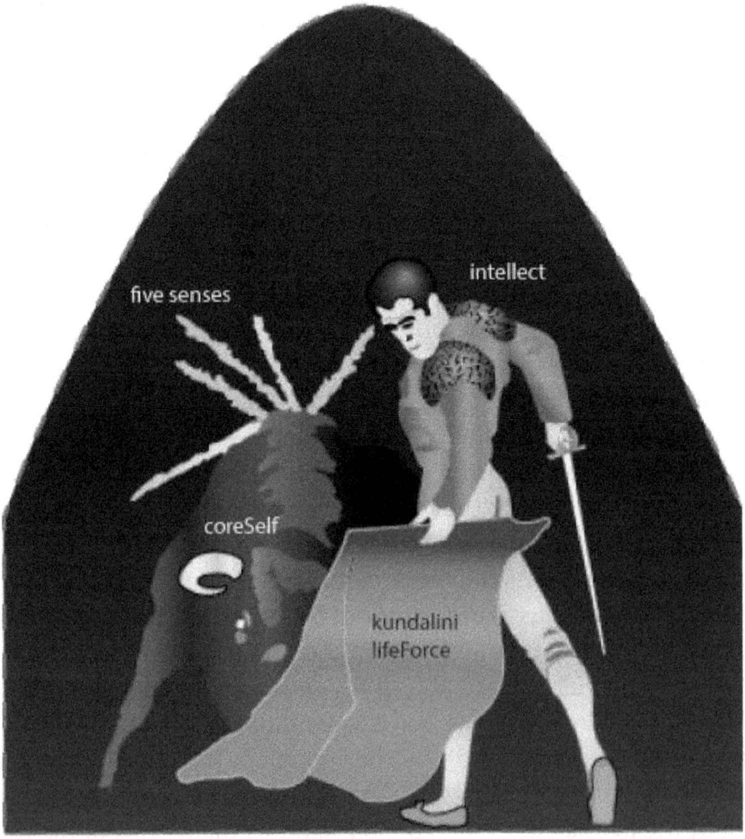

As far as the illustration is concerned, I saw it on a post card in Spain some years ago. I used a digital art program to redraw it. Seeing that post card I was inspired by deity Krishna to see that the situation of the spirits in the conditioned world is depicted in the scene. I bought the post card and forgot about it, until a few days ago when I look through my papers. Again, that inspiration from Krishna was realized.

I got the urge to publish and write about it. It is so beautiful when you are outside of it, looking on the scene. The matador is so elegant and attentive. The cape is playing its part keeping the bull occupied. The sword and the hand holding it, are alert, patiently waiting for the perfect opportunity to strike. The bull has no idea as to the challenge. The senses do their job of motivating the bull. They hang while delivering impulsions into the body of the confused helpless bull.

The matador has very little intention of using the sword. If he kills the bull his fun will end. The glory will be short lived. In the stadium people will rise to their feet either to approve or disapprove the action. If they disapprove, he will be embarassed. His reputation will be tarnished. If they approve, he must find another bull to bring to the arena. The animal will need training to recognize the cape. Once the matador gets to know a particular bull, he does not want to become attached to the animal but he wants the animal to get curious and charge because otherwise there is no excitement which is enjoyed by the spectators.

The self cannot die and thus the death of the self in this case means the discouragement of the self, to the point where it becomes inactive when overcome by negative energies. But it does not stay in those conditions. The matador does not want the self to remain in those states for long.

We can consider that the matador needs the sword to protect himself from the bull, not to kill the bull. It is his ultimate protection. He does not want to use it to kill the bull. His preferred method of controlling the bull is the cape. The problem for the bull is the cape not the sword. The sword is dangerous even if it only puts the bull out of commission for a time, but the common threat is the cape. In the case of the bull where it is scared to death of the hidden hand and the weapon in the hidden hand, which is the sword, it does not know what that is. It cannot get behind the matador to see what is held in that hand.

The matador wants the bull to be attentive to the cape. In that sense it is correct in saying that the self has very little power unless it can figure the relationship between the mind and the emotion, the matador and the cape. There is no point in the bull charging the flickering cape in the first place because the sword has no significance, if the bull would not charge. We never saw a matador run after a bull in a Spanish arena. It is always the bull which does the charging. In other words, if the matador intended to use the sword, he would have charged the bull and did the needful. The bull needs to understand the cape and matador.

Because the intellect carries the weapon of analysis, it can intimidate the self into cooperating with the plan of the inquisitive lifeForce and shortsighted senses. When the yogin silences the intellect, he is freed from its harassments. At that time the senses become powerless to influence him. The protective support of their powerful ally, the intellect, is suspended.

Student's Morning Practice (August 2011)

During breath infusion this morning, I felt a cool tingling sensation running through the right arm. As I stopped the infusion to apply the physical body locks, I could feel the compressed air being absorbed by the subtle body and the tingling feeling increasing. As I began infusing more breath, the sensation ran through the right calf. I could feel it on the left side of the body but it was not as pronounced. Kundalini rose twice in the facial area. A cool tingling sensation rushed up the frontal part of the body into the subtle head. Then my focus was applied through the body from the head. I continued to infuse more fresh air. As I peered downward into the darkness of the subtle form, I stopped to trap the air and apply the locks. A bright spark of light occurred in the lower part of the body near the base chakra. It looked like someone threw a mini grenade of white light that exploded in the distance. It was like the spark that ignites when turning on a gas burner. The rest of the body was dark.

The spark of light was followed by the rush of the cool sensation that travelled up the front of the body into the face. Then there was silence. There were no thought, ideas or images. I immediately sat to meditate. For several minutes the silence remained. Then a very slight muffled sound of Chinese traditional music creeped in. I usually listen to this type of music while practicing Tai-Chi. It was like being in a room on the top floor and hearing a very faint sound of music playing a few floors below, it did not disrupt my focus or break the silence. I remained situated at the back of the head as still as possible. The cool tingling sensation continued on the right side of the body.

Author's Response

During practice it is important to note locations of subtle experiences. The abstract locations are unknown. If one perceives any, one may not perceive it again. One should note a location and be confident of it, even if it is not visible again. Regardless of if one can see it again one should think that the psychic object exists in another dimension at that place.

The flash below by base chakra is the arch of a high charge from the groin area to the base chakra. Initially, when doing breath infusion, one may generate this charge below the lungs. Then it will move near the navel area in the front of the body. Then it will move to the groin if one does more infusion and can keep the energy tightly compressed. If that happens there will be a spark of energy which will jump from the sex area to the base chakra. If it is powerful enough, it will cause kundalini to move up, down or across.

Because of not infusing the charge tightly and not holding it so that it accumulates some yogis fail to experience this spark. Once one sees the spark and notes where it is, that is special for the yogi. He can work aggressively targeting that place mentally so as to force the infused energy to reach that place, by applying willpower focus to it. The location of the base chakra is important. It is imaginary in people who never saw it, but if one has the experience and if one notes its location one will know where it is and be confident even if one does not objectively perceive it. There are other components of consciousness which one should locate. One should know their default positions.

When inner vision occurs, one should study how it is developed and what caused it. To be a masterful yogi, one is required to know such things. It is not enough to know what others said. One should explore the psyche and discover the coreSelf and its adjuncts.

Notice that even if a person has sexual intercourse frequently, he/she may not perceive how kundalini jumps from the base chakra to the sexual organ chakra? That is the reverse of what one experiences in kundalini yoga where the charge goes in the opposite direction.

Wishing the Subtle Body Away (August 2011)

Exercises this morning resulted in kundalini rising into the wrists and then travelling into the fingers. This feels like tiny needles shooting through the wrists into the fingers. These small spreadings of kundalini into the extremities of the subtle body are important for making sure that the entire psyche is infused with energy, not just the spine and the brain.

For a split second, I touched a zone where Yogesh was located. I reached where a Buddha deity, who inspired some practices, was. Both of them glanced for an instant and then disappeared. What actually happened is that I disappeared from their residential dimensions.

Staying in touch with yoga gurus is important. If a yogi gets lost, a teacher may locate him and show the correct path. When I sat to meditate, the kundalini dangled in the center of the spine like a long white diamond shape psychic object behind the chest area. I focused on naad. I braced on the kundalini energy which shot through the back of the head. The various states of consciousness have importance in spiritual practice but a yogi should understand clearly that the subtle body must be elevated. It does not matter what state of mind one assumes and what sort of peace and comfort or confidence it gives, one must find an elevated environment for residence. The hereafter concerns the subtle body. Hence making sure that it is, as elevated as can be, and that all of it is in order and full of light, is essential for success in yoga.

Presently all persons using physical bodies, must deal with those bodies no matter the state of mind and realization. After the death of the physical system one will assume the condition of the subtle body. It is relevant to make sure that one does the best to elevate that subtle form. As long as the physical body exists one should keep it in a healthy condition and not be careless with its hygiene. Similarly, one should be attentive to the subtle form, because it cannot be wished away.

Part 5

Student Experience / Third Eye (August 2011)

Early this morning I awoke by an alarm clock but I did not totally awaken. Instead I found myself in a familiar space in the frontal head area. This location is usually characterized by a purplish colored hue. Today it was a dense purple of medium shade. I looked into a spinning funnel which was about the same color but was distinguishable by its motion. The inner funnel was also purple. Vague odd-shaped objects of a less dense purple twirled down within the funnel. As I watched, I wondered, "Is this the intellect with unformed thoughts crashing and disintegrating?"

The funnel shape faded. The purple landscape moved past me, just like a breeze blowing by the body. Tiny star specks were in the purple landscape and I did not see them clearly. They moved by quickly as part of the landscape. I stayed here for a while and then it gradually faded away.

After sunrise when I exercised, I thought of this. I don't normally do this, but I thought to place my thumbs on the temples, cover and press the closed eyes with my fingers, and do rapid breathing. Years ago, I experimented with pressing the eyeballs in order to see the third eye chakra which appears as an intensely shimmering, golden, donut-shaped ring. It sometimes takes other colors too, with varied hues and textures in the center. In my experience, it keeps taking different shapes and colors. Today, the donut shape was as clear and sharp as I have ever experienced. It presented itself in various color combinations of gold, purple, red, black and silver, changing from one color scheme to another like watching a slide show.

Finally, the center turned into the same purple as I experienced earlier while resting. The donut turned purple. Then there was just purple. I concluded that this experience was given to clarify that I was in the third eye space earlier and during other similar experiences. Question: Was the spinning funnel (described in the 2nd paragraph above) the intellect, which converted into a channel to enter the third eye chakra? However, when I have to get up in the morning, I feel drained, without energy.

Author's Response

If you feel drained, it means that you are drawn to those lower astral places by your sense of compassion. It seems that this is impulsive and you cannot control it. However, you can begin terminating this by meditating and trying to reach higher levels where you can help persons who would be productive when using your assistance. Compassion can be a deliberate action or an impulsive or subconscious one. If it is deliberate you may control it, if not you should strive to gain control. The subtle body goes to those planes because it looks in the astral world for a place to deposit compassion energy. That is like when a wealthy person gets a feeling to give money to the poor but if that wealthy persons goes to a predominantly criminal area of a city, and takes out a wad of money there may be problems when criminals attack, take the money and even kill the wealthy person. This means that giving should be done in circumstances where you have some control over who takes the energy and how they use it. Meditate on this. Gradually you can arrest the subtle body tendency and get it under control.

Some persons in the astral world, are amazed at the beneficial effects of the breath infusion practice on the subtle body. In the physical form there are also good effects, but the physical system will have senility and other aspects of old age. The subtle body however responds directly to the breath infusion practice. Even a yogi who uses an old physical body can keep the subtle body in tip top shape even if his old body is terminally ill. Usually the astral body mimics the condition of the physical form, such that a baby physical body causes the astral form to be look like that of an infant. There were instances of children who were killed and who hereafter visited the parents in dreams in childhood-looking astral forms. When the physical body gets old and begins to malfunction, the subtle form mimics that condition. But if one does breath infusion this will not happen in the same way.

By psychology based on the tendencies in the kundalini lifeForce, each human being aims for the peak of youth, when the body reaches sexual maturity and is in its best condition capable of yielding sexual pleasure, eating palatable foods and residing in posh accommodations. With this in mind, a person passes through these bodies, life after life, with an instinct for getting to the peak of youth in each form. Of course, nature only allows the individual to enjoy that peak for a moment, for as soon as the body reaches the peak it begins the downward spiral to its death.

Still despite that happening repeatedly, one is still urged to the idea of reaching peak maturity in each rebirth. That is the instinct of the kundalini lifeForce. One training in yoga has to do with upsetting this natural method of hoping to arrive at the peak point. The yogi should switch focus to the subtle body. He should neglect the urge to focus on the peak maturity of the physical form. Unless the yogi gets the kundalini to change its views and unless the yogi can arrest the kundalini and energize it, any hope for changing the default system will be dashed to pieces.

Talking to the kundalini lifeForce, praying to a deity about it, hoping that one day it will change, visualizing the kundalini in a new configuration, all this and more may not nudge its basic tendencies. If that is done in the right way with persistence, breath infusion will attack it.

Naad Sound as Boring (August 2011)

Naad sound may be boring during meditation. The key feature of naad is its primary use as a natural focus. This means that instead of having to create or imagine or even visualize a focus, naad is there for the taking without the yogi having to spend energy to create a mantra or point of visualization. No effort is made to create a focus if naad is used. This means that the yogi's attentiveness can be used to focus on naad. That intensifies the concentration and simultaneously disempowers the thought-image creation mechanism in the mind.

Some yoga practice should be done simply because one is told to do so but one cannot expect instant results. All the same that does not mean that one should be a blind follower with mere beliefs which one can never realize. I mentioned before that the first person to my knowledge who stressed and put his word behind naad sound meditation was Sri Kirpal Singh. He called it the sound current. He swore by it as the key to attain samadhi and the absolute. He was around and about in the late 1960s. I never met this teacher but I read his books around 1972. He was not flamboyant or charismatic. He did not have a large following. I remember once I met one of his disciples. It was nothing compared to what Bhaktivedanta established at his Hare Krishna Temples, or even to what Yogi Bhajan did in California and New Mexico. It was very plain and simple. One sat and listened to naad.

I met Sri Sant Kirpal Sing in the astral world years ago. He was an unassuming person, no fuss, no frills, a smile and that was it. He did not claim to be anything. He simply insisted on listening to the sound current.

Since the time of the 1970s, I meditated on naad periodically. My first real conviction about it happened when I was at Blue Beach in the Philippines. This was a beach which was remote, where there was no human population. During the dark moon nights, that place was pitch black, so that if your hand was before your face, you could not see it. I was there in 1970 with a friend named Freeman Faar. At that place when one looked to the ocean one saw iridescent tiny bacteria swirling around on the surface of the Pacific. Naad sound blared loudly. One could sit or recline and listen to it. All other ideas in the mind were obliterated by it. This put one in a state of cosmic attunement. It is not that one became one with everything. It was more like one was wired into a cosmic circuit. One was connected into that reality as a part of it with access to all directions through that specific cosmic circuit of consciousness.

Once somehow or the other, Freeman got some psilocybin, which we took at Blue Beach. That caused the experience to ratchet up a notch so that we made contact with the deity of that cosmic plane. The mind of the deity which we contacted was like the size of say planet earth, and our minds in comparison were like the size of gulf balls but we were connected in the deity's mind in such a way that we had access to its circuit even though neither of us was the predominating personal presence in that cosmic loop of energy.

There was this message from the deity which said something like this, "Take care little ones. Do not act irresponsibly." All the while naad blasted. It was like a sea of energy which pervaded, like a source-less absolute distributor. After these experiences I was convinced about naad. When I read Kirpal's ideas on it, I accepted what he said.

Using a child's body in Guyana and an adolescent one in Trinidad, I would sometimes be by the ocean. Sometimes I heard the constant roar of the waves. Once I put a conch to my ear and heard the naad sound echoing within the shell. In Guyana as a child, I had cosmic contact experiences. Sometimes I would find myself in the astral body, rising up and up through the sky, but with the astral form getting bigger and bigger and bigger, until it got so big that I would become afraid that maybe I would be so big that I would be beyond my control. Then suddenly I would begin to be reduced on and on until I found myself back in a room on a bed as a material body. This used to happen repeatedly. The connection with this and naad sound is that while this happened naad resonance would be there. Then it may change into a thunderclap that was so loud as to fill the entire world but I would be the only one hearing it. Then there may be other sounds like stars exploding. Those cosmic explosions were frightening to my reference point as a boy on earth.

I became convinced about naad by three persons. One was Yogesh who wrote a book called *Science of Sound*. He discussed experiences with various levels of nada. One other person is Krishna who instructed Uddhava in its practice. The instruction of Krishna to Uddhava is the highest instructions I read from India, in fact from anywhere on this planet. I translated Krishna's instruction as *Uddhava Gita English* and *Uddhava Gita Explained*.

The other person is Swatmarama. He wrote the *Hatha Yoga Pradipika,* which I translated and wrote a commentary for. He explained naad in detail. Within the last 6 years or so, I seriously decided to focus on naad sound. In part this was due to instructions from yoga gurus. In part it was due to naad enrichment over the years.

I agree with those meditators who say that naad is boring. It is on the lower levels of mind energy. If one does breath infusion, and the mind is shifted to a higher level, naad sound is enriching. It is an anchor for meditation and even for the state in which one waits in meditation for the third eye to open or for the intellect to convert into a visual organ.

Naad sound is a separate experience. It can be heard at any time irrespective of the opening of the third eye. In fact, it is more consistently available as contrasted to the third eye. Naad sound is reliable. It is always there once you learn how to attune to it.

Subtle Body Pushed into Parallel World (August 2011)

During the night, my astral body was pushed into a parallel world by a force from a relative's astral form. This relative, a woman, still uses a physical body, but recently her elderly mother was deceased.

When I first got to that astral dimension which was an adjacent parallel world, it was in astral Guyana. The astral soil was sandy. This is astral land. The people there had no radio or TV. There were no electronic gadgets there. Everyone lives in wooden or stone houses which are one-story. Everything is quiet there.

One strange thing was that all the bodies there were between twenty and forty years of age. There were no infants nor elderly forms. After walking for a time under the spell of the relative's energy, I found myself at the back door of a house. A young lady opened a door. I walked in. Some of these persons are deceased. Some still use physical forms. They greeted me and began to explain how they were related. Those who were deceased, grew accustomed to the astral existence and existed there without desiring physical bodies.

This went on for some time. Then I got a message from the relative who influenced my subtle body to go there. It said this, "You could stay with these persons and practice yoga. This place is ideal for people who want to live simply and not be bothered with the humbug human civilization."

After that I left that place and came back to my physical body which was in a place in Maryland, USA. Sometimes it happens that due to a power of service into one's life, a relative compels one's subtle body to do certain things. Sometimes the service is indirect. It could be service performed to someone else in the family who indirectly assisted one in getting the body or who indirectly helped in the upbringing of the body when it was an infant. Many of these obligations dangle before one as they are activated by providence and placed on the path of one's fate.

Discovering a Mystic Method (August 2011)

An exercise session went well, with breath infusion saturating the lower part of the psyche so that the kundalini vanished from the lower three chakras and dangled high in the neck and upper chest. For this kundalini relocates. The lower trunk is left without kundalini's dominance. One can infuse breath energy directly bypassing kundalini's way of doing things in the lower part of the body. One should always know that kundalini's motive is to acquire physical bodies, take those forms to sexual maturity and then reproduce other bodies. This guarantees that kundalini will get more physical forms in sequence. That is its primary anxiety. It knows by instinct that these bodies cannot be acquired without a tag-team which creates more bodies.

Kundalini, if it is not removed from its position as the supervisor of how the self takes bodies, will compel the self to take another body under circumstances which are approved by kundalini but which may put the self at a disadvantage.

Only a foolish yogi will not monitor kundalini. People who are plain stupid feel that kundalini will eat, digest, evacuate and do many other things all on its own while the self enjoys life and has sex pleasure as frequently as possible. This system of trusting kundalini may prove to be one's undoing as far as what will happen on departure from the body.

When I sat to meditate some strange things happened but there is one particular procedure which was discovered. I anchored into naad which is the staple practice of meditation. Once anchored, there was blankness and diffused light in the mind. Now and again there would be something appearing in the light but that lasted for a split second. This something was a concoction of the intellect which wanted to illustrate thought operations. Because I retreated deeper into naad, the intellect got no energy and could not display its theatrical operations.

After a time, I noticed that some feelers creeped forward. These were like tiny fingers made out of light energy. They moved forward, feeling for something. This was the sense of identity which tried to release itself from being restricted by the coreSelf. It tried to fuse itself to the intellect to begin thought-idea operations. Anytime it creeped forward I reasserted focus on naad and immediately the creeping ceased the way a turtle suddenly retracts its limbs into its shell. The sense of identity can be curb if one becomes absorbed in naad. Some students consider that naad focus is boring. It is like that from a certain level but it is the key to absorption practice.

Kundalini Withdrawal Kriya (Rishi Singh - August 2011)

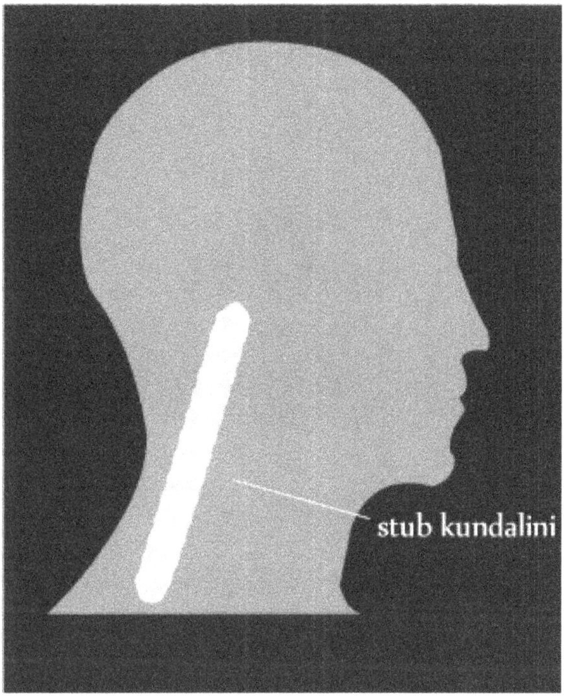

Rishi Singh was present on the astral side during this practice. He supervised the disintegration of stub kundalini which hung from the subtle head into the neck of the subtle body. He did not explain much or say why he was there. I assumed that he was present to explain a technique on how to deal with kundalini when it is pulled through the spine into the head.

My view is that this information is not written in plain terms even in yoga books like *Hatha Yoga Pradipika*. Rishi wants me to record it for use by others. Usually yogis neither record nor discuss these matters except with advanced adepts.

When kundalini begins to withdraw from the location where the base chakra adheres, it assumes a white-hot color and a diamond configuration dangling down in the center of the spine. If the yogi is successful in causing kundalini to retract from that location, when breath infusion is done, kundalini will retreat further and further up the spine. This is provided that the yogi can infuse the bottom of the trunk and thighs with fresh energy.

The more the trunk of the body is infused with specific areas of it being targeted, the more the kundalini will be unable to reattach itself to that base location. This is beneficial for the yogi. This releases the psyche from the dictatorial control which kundalini held over it previously. This is total success in yoga, instead of the head success with doing trance states in the head, while kundalini continues ruling the rest of the psyche and negatively influencing the rest of one's activities.

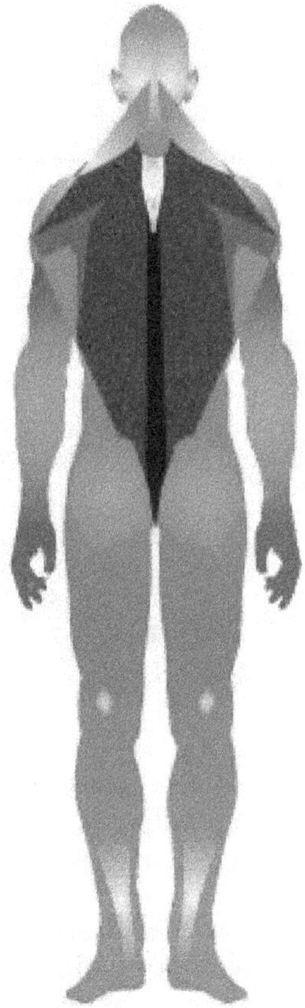

When kundalini is retracted into the neck, it lost the diamond configuration. It hangs under the brain like a white popsicle, glowing with a white light color. At this stage the yogi should make a deliberate effort to remain emerged in naad, to situate the coreSelf in naad. He should do the kundalini pratyahar kriya, which consist of pulling in the sensual energies of the kundalini into the sense of identity which surrounds the coreSelf.

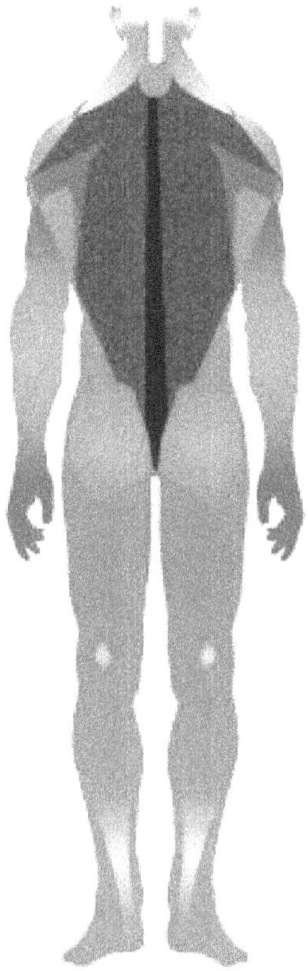

Even though when the yogi does the pratyahar practice kundalini will dangle like a white popsicle hanging below the head. That white popsicle shape will seem to disappear. When the coreSelf is in naad and pulls up the kundalini sensual energies, there is only perception of these energies coming into the sense of identity. The yogi loses the vision of the kundalini hanging down.

Rishi said that this is the second major pratyahar sensual energy withdrawal practice. The first one is done in reference to the sensual energy which flows through the frontal part of the head. Most yogis think that this first one is the full pratyahar practice but it is not. The frontal sensual energies are under the control of the intellect. This is related to kundalini but it is not the kundalini's personal sensual force. The second kriya for pratyahar is for pulling in the energies which kundalini uses to run its creature-survival operations.

Becoming Carnivorous (August 2011)

Today I was with some folks who mentioned a man who was born in a vegetarian household. He grew up with those habits. Later this person was carnivorous. This is an example that brings to fore, the fact, that we can go in any direction, provided it is in the evolutionary capacity. One can go in any direction, according to the social pressures, the personal preference and other factors which cause a person to act in a specific way. It is fine to be resistant to trends or to ancient methods even, to be free of all influences but one must also be realistic to see how the other factors blend with personal will and then there is a resultant effect which may be so powerful that one's desire has little relevance. A good estimation of the realities which we are confronted with, could help us to better determine the various outcomes which we will encounter when we become determined to change.

This morning during practice, I took a look at how kundalini sets itself up in the embryos. I did this indirectly by seeing how kundalini made some effort during the past week to reestablish its base chakra to base area in the subtle body. It hung below the navel chakra in a grey configuration like a grey popsicle. It had only one intention which was to attach itself to the base area.

I decided to track how kundalini gets the power to do this and also what urge drives kundalini for this. I noticed a pushing force which came from a relative, whom I saw recently. It appears that the adhesive force within that person's kundalini influenced my kundalini to reformulate itself and to reverse what I achieved in terms of pulling kundalini away from the base area.

The conclusion is that by associating with a person whose kundalini functions in the normal materialistic way, a yogi may develop a reverse-influence in kundalini which would cause it to reassert the need for an embryo.

Many yoga gurus from India, alerted us with the terms sadhu sanga, which is to say, "Remain in the influence of the great souls (sadhus). Distance yourself from other people." To protect itself from being disbanded and from being deprived of vulgar habits on the physical level, my kundalini tried to re establish its configuration. It failed. I succeeded for the time being.

Subtle Body Caught Doing Yoga

From an email:

Hey Michael!

Last night I had a dream in which I was doing bhastrika and other asanas. During the practice I directed the infused energy to the base of the first chakra (I guess your postings on getting rid of this base had a subconscious influence). The practice felt so real that when I woke up in the physical side, I really believed that I did it earlier on the physical side.

My questions are:

Can you do the practice of bhastrika and meditation in the astral world?

If so, what "air" are you breathing since there is no air in the astral world?

Can someone advance by practicing in the astral world or does one need to be in the physical plane to advance?

I remember that the energy accumulated differently. I could see or feel a ball accumulating with every breath. I could sense it moving through the base. This energy had a more physical sensation than when I do the practice fully awake with my physical body. In other words, this practice in the dream world was more vivid and more dynamic.

Author's Response:

There is air in the astral world. It is subtle air. If something has physical existence, it must have an astral counterpart, otherwise it cannot exist. If we accept conclusions in science, everything physical which we have like mud and water came from subtle materials which existed in some primal state before the universe formed in this way. In the end the earth will vaporize and become nothing, with nothing meaning something that is so subtle to our sensual perception as to be abstract.

It is great to hear that a student became aware of practicing in the subtle body. That is great. Continue this. When one becomes proficient at doing exercises in the subtle body one is qualified to go with the siddhas.

It is a great achievement to cause the subtle body to practice astrally. Usually the subtle body pursues pleasure in the subtle world. It is hardly interested in yoga discipline.

What is the Intellect? (August 2011)

Pranayama practices like bhastrika breath infusion, has the ultimate result of causing the mind to be thoughtless but the real benefit is the opening of the intellect as a tool of supernatural perception. The intellect is converted into a vision instrument, a single vision instrument as contrasted to two physical eyes or two subtle eyes in the subtle body. Why is it that even though many people do breath infusion, they do not experience the intellect in that way?

The answer is that they do not practice the breath infusion to proficiency. When for instance there is much infusion of energy into the subtle body, the yogi who sits to meditate finds that the thoughts occur at a much slower rate and with much less compelling power. That person makes no effort to retract the mind from its usual sensual pursuits. That person does not have to banish thoughts, observe thoughts, or suppress thoughts. The thoughts cease appearing. In that way breath infusion is beneficial because by it the thought-producing mechanism which is in the intellect reduces independent operations.

Even though, normally that intellect is not there and it is not real in the usual sense of real, still based on my claim and the claim of other yogis, it is there. One should have confidence that this is the case. When breath infusion is done to proficiency, the yogi may see this intellect or at least sees its operations as a single supernatural vision tool. Before this vision is gained the yogi can understand the intellect by studying the location where thoughts, ideas and images appear. This research involves no so much what is done as mental constructions but where those ideas and images occur. The mental location should be identified so that the yogi can know that there is a psychic instrument which thinks and visualizes. Even though that instrument is not visible, its creations in the form of thoughts and images, is visible. They are visible at certain locations only.

The intellect is a reality. Even though one cannot verify it, still one should know that there is this invisible psychic organ which manufactures thoughts. It is not the mind space which creates the thoughts but it is an invisible organ which does. It is like those transparent sea creatures. They cannot be seen but still they exist in the ocean. Without this information the effort to rid the mind of thoughts and images and also to rid the self of the influence of those mental constructs, will be a failure.

The self is not influenced by a mind space which creates thoughts and images. It is influenced by a psychic organ which is transparent just as the self is transparent. When meditating one should not treat the location of thoughts and images as just a space in the middle of nowhere, but as an organ in a mind space in which the self resides.

Student's Inquiry:

What color is this intellect? I perceive various hues of different colors in the mind. These have a vaguely spherical shape. I also see a translucent cloudlike object that oscillates, gyrates and scintilates at varying speeds. Besides this there is a very tiny starlike shape object like a star that twinkles. Then there is a blue dotlike object. Is that the intellect?

Does the orb have a causeless color to it, or does the color change according to its relationship with the coreSelf under the varying influences of the three gunas?

Does it manifest differently to one who is more in goodness than passion?

Can the perception of the intellect in the state of non infusement of breath be perceived without it being an instrument to be utilized in the opening of whatever, through the use of drugs?

Author's Response:

The orb is oval-shaped translucent psychic instrument. In some trance states it is seen to be something like a jelly fish with a milky color but usually it is a spherical translucent tiny star shape in the distance in front of you and also the blue dot-like object has to do with the third eye which is different. Counting it from the coreSelf in the center of the head, forward, you will make contact with the sense of identity first and then with the intellect and then with the third eye. Stated differently, you have the coreSelf which is the ultimate focal consciousness in the psyche, then you have the highly invisible sense of identity which surrounds the coreSelf in all directions spherically, then you have the orb which is in front of the coreSelf so that the coreSelf cannot do anything without going through the orb. Then there is the third eye and every other thing which can be used for perception.

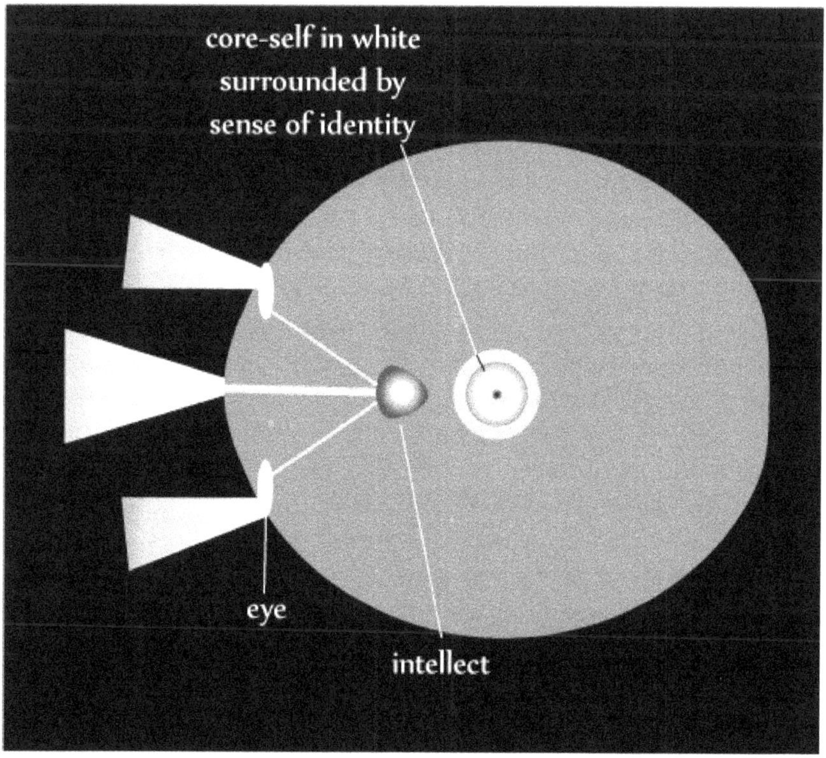

To see the third eye, one must look through the intellect but since it is usually invisible one does not see that one sees through it. The key to this is location. The locations are not random. They are specific, just as the earth is in a specific place orbiting the sun. Each of the psychic components have default positions because they operate in reference to each other. They submit to specific influences.

Jnana-dipa or *jnana-chakshu* and *buddhi* in Sanskrit literature is that intellect. Jnana dipa is not one's understanding. It is a psychic organ which produces conclusions which one in turn assumes as mental understanding. The intellect is a psychic object. It does the analytical calculations, thoughts constructions and visualizations. For that matter it is owned only in a superficial sense. The intellect can produce thoughts on its own. It can entertain the coreSelf with mental constructions.

If it is shut down for a sufficient length of time, something happens where suddenly at its location, where it is usually invisible, it becomes visible and serves as a vision perception into the supernatural world. That is a big issue because it means that the successful yogi will see from this place into the sky of consciousness, the chit akasha.

Starfield Meditation (August 2011)

I got an email about someone's meditation where the person was in a starfield with stars moving rapidly in his direction.

When I was in the Philippines in 1970, some guys who used psychedelics spoke of yitchnoids, which are squirmy astral beings which were about one inch in size. These squirm in space almost transparently but with little extra brilliant light formations. In meditation it is normal to see a sky like this but usually the little light points move slowly or appear stationary. Now the question is: Who sees this in meditation? Where is that observer located in the star field? Obviously, the idea that one is omnipresent, that one is everywhere, is invalid in this experience. If something moves either away from you or to you and then disappears, that immediately admits location.

Where is the observer of the star field? What is the means of perception? Was a telescope or an eye used? Does consciousness serve as an eye in this case? Is this vision omni-directional? Is it in a frontal direction away from the observer? With physical vision, one must turn about to see behind. Doing this one loses the front view.

Astral Encounter (August 2011)

A few nights ago, I had an encounter with a school friend, whom I have not seen physically in thirty years. I attended a high school class with this person. At the time I was 14 years of age. This person was about 16 years of age. Suddenly I met him in the astral world but it was his energy which attracted my subtle body. With astral encounters one should know how the contact is made; if one was attracted to someone else or if one attracted someone else.

If one's body is sixty or over and one begins having dreams of long-lost school friends, then surely that is an omen of death. Old school friends meet in the astral world, wanting to take bodies through the same parents or in the same area, so that they can again associate as juveniles. For sure this is a portent of my body's death. Seeing a friend like this, a person from my youth, suddenly without warning, is a sure premonition about my upcoming demise from the physical plane.

This person wants to stay close to me in the hereafter. That is why the contact was made. This person was hopeful that I would be in the same family as he in the next body. Unknown to this person is the fact that I have no intentions of assuming an embryo in the way he desired. What would be a good reason for me to come back into this world? I guess I could always think of coming back for the newest technology or for a mansion residence after I get a master's degree and can qualify for a million-dollar loan. Or better, I could come back since science promises to increase the length of a human life span by putting nanotechnology into human bodies.

Let me see, that is supposed to happen within the next twenty years. It would not be a bad idea to come back, knowing that with the help of science, I may live longer in the next human body, if not live forever in it if the nanotech stuff can destroy any internal threats to the life of the body. Anyway, my friend visualizes a new physical life. He wants me to be his brother.

Yogi Reaching the Siddha Level (August 2011)

Rishi Singh Gherwal asked me to explain to students that the attainment of a siddha body has to do with the subjugation of kundalini and nothing else. He said that no matter what the yogi attains, if kundalini is not subjugated, the siddha status is not attained. The yogi will surface on whatever level of existence kundalini is compatible with. This holds true regardless of the philosophical and/or religious beliefs. He said this:

> *Consider that even a professor at a university must stoop to evacuate the body. Even the Queen or King of England must pass urine. Even the President of the most developed country on the earth, may have the sex urge. Even the Pope of Christianity must become infirm in body. Even the Swami from in India, has to evacuate foul matter from the body. In the world hereafter, one will have a certain type of subtle body which will manifest on a certain level, and will function in a certain way, no matter*

if one professes a belief in Krishna, or in Rama, or in Jesus or whosoever is the cherished deity, and even if one does not think there is an individual as the Supreme Being, and one thinks that there is Oneness or One Supreme Primal Energy.

If one can use the physical body to bring the subtle form to a higher plane, that physical form was effectively used, not otherwise. Anyone can think anything and have lofty aspirations, but that does not mean that the subtle body was effectively curbed from lower habits. That does not guarantee that the person will not be forced to go wherever that subtle body will go in the astral world hereafter.

Kundalini yoga begins with the effort to infuse the kundalini. That entails leading the hormone energy in the body away from the sexual facilities. So long as there is a route for the hormone energies to go in the direction of the sexual facilities, kundalini will remain at the base chakra and will not rise into the head.

Once the student habitually gets kundalini to go into the head, once that becomes the habit as compared to having the kundalini go to the genitals for sexual pleasure, the yogi should divest kundalini energy to every part of the body, especially in every part below the neck, even into the fingers and toes. Once this is achieved the neck will be flushed completely. Initially working on the neck means only working on sushumna passage in the central part of the spine which passes through the neck. But later for full subjugation of kundalini, one should flush even the fleshy parts of the neck. When this is done the yoga siddha body becomes a reality for the yogi.

This makes for an astral accomplishment where the yogi can go higher than the Swargaloka heavens to one of the advanced places which are listed as *Maharloka, Janaloka, Tapaloka, Brahmaloka (Satyaloka).* In those places the astral body does not have the lower urges. It does not lead back to the realm of physical existence but those in the Swarga places and lower are attracted to physical existence, just as a great person with a physical body will have to use a urinal.

Spiritual Cosmology

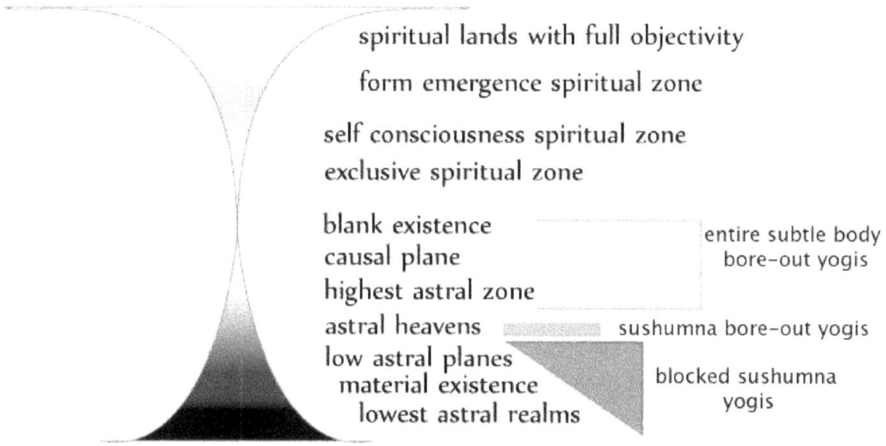

Objects in the Mind (August 2011)

If there is a location for a psychic occurrence, the observer or viewer is in relation to it. One should consider whether it occurs within the mind space or outside of it. For instance, a person may feel that once he is in the mind, he is in himself. But I feel that this is incorrect. The mind is not the self. It is a chamber in which the self exists with other factors.

People think that once they are in the mind, they are in themselves. Teachers tell them the same thing, that they should go inside themselves. I feel that what the teachers instruct is that one should retreat into the mind, the way a person may be told that he should run into a house to hide from strangers who approach the building. If one runs into a house, he does not run into himself, even though he locates his body in the house. Similarly, in meditation people run into the mind and feel safe there. They enjoy the idea that they are in the self which to me is misleading.

How did we become human beings in the first place?

What or Who caused us to be here?

Where will we go after the body dies?

We have some control now, only because the parents cared for our infant forms and these forms matured, and we are in a political system which affords certain civil freedoms.

What will be next? Big talk and grand hopes will not create the next situation. For better or worse providence will.

Kundalini Black-out/White-out

Each person is given a kundalini when that particular limited entity enters this material creation from the causal plane. This kundalini occurs automatically. It is matched to the particular soul. Because it is matched, it has the exact amount of energy which is required by that spirit for operations in the material creation, but this includes the gross and subtle material creation. It is a physio-psychic energy. If however a part of it malfunctions, there will be upsets or even shortages, just as in an electric system if too much current enters a circuit, the components may be damaged. When kundalini rises suddenly with full force and enters the spine, it will usually course though the spine, penetrate the neck and enter the brain.

This occurs on two planes simultaneously. It happens physically and also in the subtle body. If a high charge of kundalini energy hits a psychic organ in the head of the subtle body, the entity will experience a black-out or a white-out. A black-out is when the entity feels a loss of consciousness after a blank space in awareness. This may be a grey or dark space or just a blank colorless space. A white-out is when the entity feels or senses a bright light or a shimmering light or which has a full moon color and then loses objective awareness for some seconds, after which awareness is resumed.

Kundalini does not directly hit the coreSelf. It does not directly hit the sense of identity, which is known as ahamkara (sense of I-ness) in Sanskrit. Kundalini hits the intellect or buddhi organ. If it hits that organ with too much force, the entity will lose objective consciousness because it so happens that the entity, though a spiritual person, is dependent on the intellect for objectivity.

Why does it happen that the kundalini is not matched perfectly to the intellect, so that kundalini cannot overpower the orb? The answer to this question is simply that the kundalini is matched to the individual psyche as a whole and not just to one component. Usually in a house, there is a 100-amp breaker. But usually there is no single component in the house which could use 100 amps without being destroyed. Why did the electrical engineers establish 100 amps as the upper limit of household current? The reason obviously is that the total current needed is about 100 amps. But if somehow that 100 amps runs through any single component, it will fry the circuits. The breaker will trip and will have to be reset. The full power of kundalini should not reach the intellect but if it does, there will be a black-out or a white-out. Then the objectivity will be reset and existential condition will resume as normal after some seconds usually.

As soon as the kundalini force reduces in its surge the intellect will be reset again. The person will be conscious but will know that something was amiss since there was a gap in the continuity of objective consciousness.

If when doing the exercises, one does the locks efficiently, there will rarely be a black-out or white-out, because the locks will control the flow of kundalini in such a way as to limit how much of its power flows to the intellect. The orb will be infused but not to the extent of being put out of commission.

In this respect, just recently Rishi Singh gave clarification. He said that kundalini is matched to the psyche. It is the total power required to operate the individual psyche.

A yogi should be sure to make kundalini become distributed throughout the entire psyche, not just a part of it, not just the head. Due to sexual pleasure, there is this stubborn idea that one should climax energy for pleasure. This tendency should be ignored, so that the entire psyche has well-being and not just one part of it like the sexual organs or the head.

The locks restrict the flow of kundalini. When the locks are mastered the yogi can regulate kundalini's flow so that it does not over-power the intellect. Later with more advancement in practice, one does not rely on the locks but instead use the locks to cause kundalini to go to other parts of the psyche. That gives the result of even distribution of the infused energy throughout the psyche. Since kundalini is a match to the entire psyche, there is no black-out or white-out. Instead there would be light-outs in the head and light-ins in the other parts of the body. It hinges on a steady practice.

The main reason for black-outs and white-outs is the location of the intellect and its relationship to the self. The self is surrounded by an energy field which is the sense of identity (ahamkara). This is mistakenly called the false ego or the ego by many people who have no idea that there are psychic organs in the subtle body. In relation to the sense of identity is the intellect.

Kundalini hits the intellect. If it hits it with too much power the intellect goes out of commission. The self experiences that as a white-out or black-out usually. As soon as kundalini subsides, the intellect resumes objectivity with normal awareness. This happens because the orb has a sensor system which causes it to resume operation as soon as kundalini drops to a certain level.

A question arises. Why does the coreSelf suffers a consciousness black-out if the orb is hit? The answer is that the core cannot perceive anything in material existence without the orb. If the orb is removed the coreSelf will become like nothing as if it did not exist, at least until it is reconnected the orb.

Unless the yogi can become proficient in higher yoga these things are way beyond his power. People think that the self is a big wig and that it has absolute autonomy but these assessments should be reviewed.

The psyche as it is, is not one homogenous whole. It is one psyche for sure but within it there is diversity, both in the physical and astral bodies. The experiences had when kundalini enters the brain or the subtle head, will not be the same as when it enters other parts of the psyche which has different components. If kundalini spreads into the toes of the right foot there will never be a black-out or white-out because there is no psyche component in that part of the body which does the service to the psyche which is rendered by the intellect which is in the head.

The coreSelf is more indirectly connected to the toes, than it is to the head. Thinking occurs in the head not in a toe. For that reason, when kundalini penetrates the toe it will feel just as it would be if kundalini enters any other part of the body which has similar components to those in the toes. Both the brain in the physical system and the mind in the astral body have completely different materials as compared to the rest of the body. The special cells found in the brain is only found in small bits elsewhere in the spine only and in no other part of the trunk.

The tingling sensation is the typical feeling when kundalini goes into other parts of the body, like the tendons, muscles and other types of flesh even most of the organs in the chest of the body. There may also be visions of light of varying colors when this occurs.

What do I teach?

To identity the intellect's location and its location only, I teach that during meditation if any thoughts, images or ideas arise of their own accord, the observing self should note the location of these mental constructions. That location is where the intellect is positioned. Usually it remains in a certain default position. From there it entertains and hypnotizes the self with thoughts, ideas and images.

Notice that I said location of the thoughts. There is a difference between the location of a thought and the thought itself. If you pay attention to a thought or to its content, you are not doing the practice. You should be attentive to the location, not the content.

During meditation, in the method which I use, the observing self neither creates nor supports thoughts. It simply observes the location of the mental place where the thoughts arise. Even though it never saw the organ, it knows that it exists there.

Some teachers instruct a focus on thoughts, or they instruct that the yogi should let the thoughts go by. This is a different practice. In my method one observes the location of thoughts. One keeps the focus on the location.

Then one can answer a few questions such as: Did all thoughts arise in the same mental place?

One can see that this has little to do with observing the thoughts or letting them go by. In this practice one is not concerned with that. The interest is the location.

If one is in a theatre, where do the images appear? Does it appear on the screen? Does it appear on the back of the chair before the viewer?

Is the image projected from the screen or on the screen? Is the projector located in front or behind?

In answering this if someone speaks of the characters in the movie that person does not follow this process. I am not interested in the content of the movie. I do not care about the actors. I am only interested in the locations.

In the case of the intellect, it serves as both the projector and the screen. The evidence of the intellect will come when the student advances further in meditation. Because of getting the hint from the yoga guru that the organ is located there. When there is a vision of it, the student can identify it positively.

The key thing in the beginning is to know that the appearance of a thought is actually the appearance of both the thought and the intellect, just as if one is in a dark room and a light flashes, one's perception is of the light energy and the light source which might be a bulb with a filament within it.

Once the student knows for sure that there is an organ which produced the thoughts, the student's approach to meditation changes. The student can effectively separate the self from the invisible organ and its thought operations. It will no longer feel that the thoughts are the self or that the thoughts are produced in the self. It will gain more resistance to the thoughts, which in effect is more resistance to the thought-producing adjunct, the intellect.

In meditation when the student identifies the location, if any idea appears in the mind at that place, the student simply ignores it and considered that whatever it is, it has no consequence. This frees the student to study the other components in the mind space. Note that the self itself is a component.

In daydreaming, the self sees in something which is like seeing something appearing in a crystal ball or in a small transparent oval shaped glass sphere. That is the intellect. It is an object, just as a binocular is an object, except that the intellect is a psychic object.

A yogi must realize that the appearance of a thought is actually the appearance of both the thought and the intellect simultaneously, just as if you are in a dark room and a light flashes, your perception is of the light energy and the light source which might be a bulb with a filament within it.

Know that there is something there, an organ, a psychic organ. One should be confident that even though one cannot see what it is, it is there. It is not a blank space. There is something there. One never saw it but I described it. Based on trust, one may accept the information.

Patanjali suggested that one should disable the intellect. If one does that one cannot use it for thinking and imaging. One will have a dark space in the mind, except when in meditation there is diffused or bright light or bliss consciousness. Usually it is darkness in the mind.

Patanjali told us to remain in meditation with the intellect in a silenced condition. How does one control it so that it does not function. First of all we are born with no control of this intellect.

Patanjali said that one should be segregated from the intellect. One should cease using it and disable its spontaneous operations during meditation.

Many people think that they should disable the senses one by one. However, since the intellect controls the senses, if one disables the intellect the senses will cease operations. Even the impulse-master, the instinct supervisor, which is the kundalini is regulated, if one disables the intellect.

Patanjali instructed for the silencing of the intellect. But then when that is achieved, one finds the self in a boring space of blankness in the mind. Some say a mantra to cancel the boredom. Others practice breath tracking. Others visualize something.

After a time after long practice one may agree to do what Patanjali suggested. One stays in the dark space of the mind with the intellect disabled. One waits there in that mystic space.

Eventually there is something seen there. Eventually when the intellect is silenced it switches into another operation. There is supernatural vision. One gets to the real place, the sky of consciousness, the chit akasha.

In Swami Muktananda's book, *Play of Consciousness*, there is one part where he described reaching that place and also seeing the blue boy and the blue pearl. When one reaches there Patanjali's instruction makes all the sense in the world.

It is not easy. That is the problem. We live in this dungeon of the material world. We try to make this place into a paradise but all such efforts will come to nil. This is a condemned existence. It is a maximum-security prison. Yes, sure, why be miserable if you serve a life sentence but then again why try to con oneself into thinking it is heaven.

Yoga Guru is Pissed off

During exercises this morning, Rishi Singh Gherwal appeared on the astral side. He was annoyed because some persons came to learn the exercises. In the yoga system one is not supposed to accept students without the permission of superiors.

In any case, these were people whom I knew from over 30 years ago, who are deceased. They found me in the astral world and wanted to get their astral forms energized. I give them little attention but with their subtle bodies they did whatever postures I practiced. They did breath infusion. Because of getting rapid results in the subtle forms, they were encouraged. These were three women who were like the ages of my mother when they used physical bodies which I associated with years ago.

Rishi Singh was annoyed. He said this, "What student has students?"

Then he waved his hands. Three dakinis came and escorted those deceased ladies away. Dakinis are angelic female beings who reside permanently in the astral world. They have exquisite forms but they associate with skilled proficient yogis.

After this I completed the exercises but I knew that Rishi was displeased. I did not attract those persons. They found me because another person who found me on the Internet alerted them to my presence.

Rishi came back after a while. He checked on the practice. By that time, I infused energy into the trunk of the body and worked on the neck. He made this sarcastic remark, "Yoga means brahmachari. Without that everything is finished. Why do you not understand this?"

Anyway, this is how it is with a yoga guru. Sometimes when I instruct students, they fail to understand that I have rules to follow. They feel that I impose disciplines on them. For success austerity and isolation are required.

Seeing Mental Light during Meditation

During meditation this morning, I had some luck with light from the chit akash. This is because of a thorough breath infusion. This is not because of a special concentration or focus. It is due to pranayama (bhastrika pranayama) practice. It is a hard thing to convince anyone about the effects of pranayama since in the West most people feel that they are entitled to sit down, meditate and get enlightenment.

Breath infusion causes the polluted energy in the subtle body to be blasted out and replaced by fresh energy, all over the trunk of the body, in the neck and even in the thighs and knees. The psyche shifts into a clarifying mode which caused the dark cloud of energy in which the self is usually confined to get dissipated.

During the meditation that follows, when one retreats to naad sound in the back of the head, the front part of the head may have a glowing light. To consistently experience this is difficult. Here is why.

When there is mental light, the core-self is pulled forward to see it. This pull comes from the invisible intellect. Because it is an invisible organ, the coreSelf is disadvantaged in trying to detect it.

When there is light appearing in the dark space of the mind or when the darkness lifts off, one should not run to the frontal part of the head. The yogi should stay put with naad sound. He should gentle ease forward with no excitement. If he does this it is likely that the light will stay., Otherwise it may quickly vanish.

After twenty minutes of meditating in a dark closet, Rishi Singh appeared on the astral side. He complained that during the exercises and breath infusion, I was with the three ladies on the astral side.

He said this, "Success cannot happen if you are lax. It is frustrating to have students who do not adhere to the rules. A full effort must be made by the student."

Anu Gita

Bhagavad Gita is concluded in the *Anu Gita*. Both are extracts from the *Mahabharata*. In the *Anu Gita*, Krishna more or less calls Arjuna a person without confidence. an egg-head.

That is serious. It debunks most of what the authorities on the *Bhagavad Gita* said about Krishna and Arjuna. After the war, when peace time was on, Arjuna was perplexed because he could not recall the *Bhagavad Gita* and the vision of the Universal Form. He simply requested that Krishna repeat the experience. This was after the Mahabharata war when Krishna was about to leave for his city.

Surprisingly, Krishna told Arjuna that it was by a special yoga technique that the *Bhagavad Gita* experience took place, and that it was impossible to duplicate the experience. Krishna gave an interesting discourse in which Krishna did not once mention anything about himself as the Supreme Being.

Swami Muktananda's Practice

Exercises were routine this morning with a few incidences. On the astral side one deceased lady came. She is committed to the exercises. She has the intellectual acumen for integrating yoga philosophy. She said that Rishi Singh and some other senior yogis instructed her about the seriousness of a consistent practice. They permitted her to come and practice any time.

Another woman was told to learn from this first lady. A third lady was instructed not to come for lessons even though she could learn from other teachers. This last person was deceased over 30 years. She had an eighty-year old body. By doing breath infusion practice in the astral world, her astral body which looked like the 80 years old form changed into one which was about 18 years of age. This person was impressed with yoga but has the incorrect idea that it concerns beauty and youthfulness.

During the session, Rishi Singh did not appear. Instead, I saw a few dakshini angelic women instructing the lady who was the most advanced of the three deceased persons.

Half way through the exercises when I did a side stretch, kundalini rose on one side of the body. It went into the right eyeball and was like several micro crystals of bliss energy packed tightly in a little ball. When I stretched to the left side, kundalini rose but with less impetus.

Soon after that as I infused the subtle body, Muktananda appeared. He was glad that I advanced somewhat since I last saw him which was over one year ago. He showed some inner locks but did not mention any special processes.

He said this:

When as a youth I practiced pranayama intensively, sometimes I would do breath exercises for two hours. Once it increased to four hours.

At the time in India, some yogis did this. I learnt the technique. This practice culminated in direct perception into the chit akasha, the spiritual world.

The key to the advancement is to never give up. Keep seeking more advanced means of progression. However, there is a retardative energy which affects a not-so-advanced yogi. That negative force will keep the person in slow progression where there is no experience of transcendence.

The old man, our father, Nityananda Baba, assisted me considerable. He infused grace energies into my psyche. I practiced aggressively for years before he assisted me.

The neophytes are bogged by a negative energy which stipulates that they should not do much yoga and that they can do meditation without asanas and pranayama. This is just like when you use a jeep on a country road. If the weather is right, if it is dry, you will coast along as desired, but in the rainy season the vehicle will make little progress. A yogi's endeavors alone cannot cause full success. The yogi is comparable to the jeep. The psychic environment of the mind is comparable to the road. If the road is muddy, even a new jeep that is built for the terrain may be stalled.

There are external and internal forces which impede the yogi. The sooner that is realized the better it will be.

Muktananda showed some locks in the trunk of the body. These control the various hanging tissues which are attached to the organs in the body. These locks can be applied when one's practice becomes advanced.

Kundalini Splits the Head

Email correspondence

I had an interesting third eye experience. I was chanting and walking. Suddenly from the bottom my spine rumbled. Next the energy shot up. It felt like someone touched my forehead. In the next sensation it felt like the skull from the third eye to the back of my head rip in two. What I saw was energy like heat waves bouncing around the room.

Two weeks later I had a similar experience except that it shot up to top of head during kirtan. The top of my head spun intensely and then exploded. I saw the room get brighter in color. Everyone was ecstatic. Time was gone. I felt like a water fountain.

Author's Response:

This is an experience of kundalini rising and overcoming both the brow chakras and the brahmrandra top of head chakra.

These experiences are subjective but they give some idea of the kundalini and its effects in the lower part as well as in the head of the subtle body.

In these experiences even though the subtle body remains fused into the physical one, the person becomes about 90% or more aware of the subtle body and 10% or less aware of the physical system.

This type of experience if studied in meditation will lead to an understanding of the various components of consciousness and how they interact.

Where was the core-self while this happened?

Head in this case refers to the subtle head but, in some experiences, the physical head may mimic the actions of the subtle one. The person in the experience will lose contact with the physical head and may not know if the physical head was involved until after the experience or until others who were present, describe what happened physically.

Usually these experiences happen when one uses mind-altering drugs, and also when there is a flash-back effect from an earlier use of the drugs. In the Sufi tradition, this kind of experience occurred when the person listened to or danced to certain types of music. In the dervish tradition, this is a normal experience of transcendence.

In kriya yoga the outlook on such an experience, is that it is a samadhi practice. If you check *Yoga Sutras,* you will find descriptions of the various samadhis. Check through the descriptions to see if your experience is cited.

According to a person's nature, the kundalini can rise suddenly when the person is in certain environment or exposed to certain sensual conditions. For the purpose of identifying the various levels of existence and their related advantages and disadvantages, all such states should be meticulously studied in introspection.

Muktananda's Posture for the Elderly

During practice this morning, Muktananda showed a posture which I did for five days. I assume it was a posture he discovered. He may have shown this posture before on another level in the astral world but the memory of his previous teaching disappeared when I left that level. In cases like this, it seems to the yogi that he discovered a posture, while in fact, it was shown on a level of consciousness when he was not objective enough to realize he was shown.

There are some postures which I did when I focused on breath infusement. In these postures one does not stress the complicated yoga asanas. One focuses on the infusement. It works better if one mastered the asana postures, but one can do these even without the skill of postures.

Elderly people can do some of this and get help with their introspection even if their limbs have arthritis and other rheumatoid malfunctions.

When this posture is done, the first thing is to force the air down to the bottom of the spine. When one infused sufficient energy there, the energy spreads into other parts of the trunk, into the groin and thighs. When that is infused sufficiently, the energy rises in the trunk of the body and into the neck. It enters the brain, particularly the bottom back of the brain.

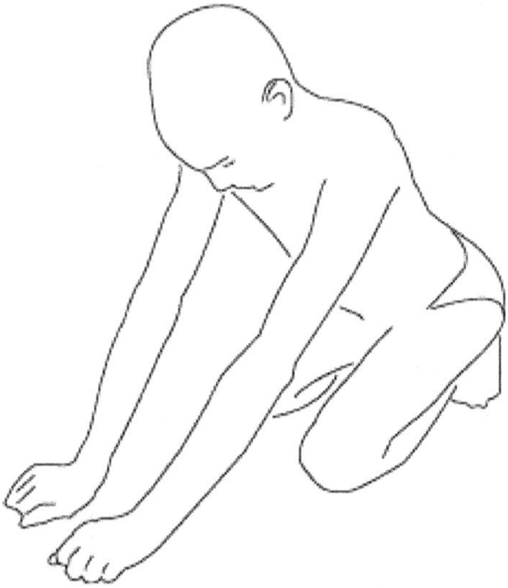

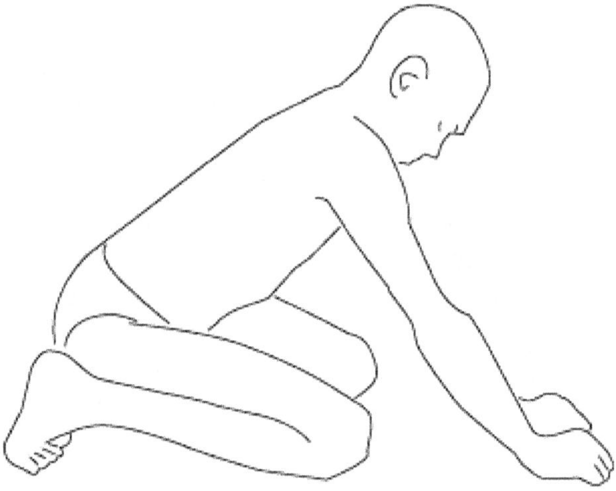

Part 6

Muktananda's Explains

During exercises this morning, Muktananda insisted that the psyche be cleared of polluted energy in order for the meditation to reach the level of the chit akash spiritual environment.

He said this,

The situation is that one becomes attached to focalized pleasure and intense sessions of enjoyment. These become addictions which are reinforced life after life. When people first come to a spiritual master, they expect that he will provide a means of continuing the enjoyment. People directly and indirectly challenge a guru to provide pleasure which would replace the normal pleasures provided in nature. If the guru does not respond they become sour and go away.

Eventually a student should understand that the task is one of cleaning the psyche from within. Whatever you are and whatever you could be, it will develop from the psychological situation within. When doing the practice, one should corral the attention to remain within.

The natural tendency of the mind is the drift away from the focus. It is inclined to create distractions. Do not allow the mind to do that. Keep the mind within and focus on getting the psyche cleared of pollutants.

Patanjali requested that a yogi should clean the perception equipment but he indicated that unless one separates from the equipment, one cannot clear it. Unless the self becomes completely detached, it cannot do the require work.

Material nature will always molest the living entities. That is for sure. Still, one should keep on striving. Do not become discouraged because material nature is relentless in keeping the self distracted. Nature will not change because of anyone's disgust. Just as nature is relentless, the student should harry on until success is achieved.

Consider the *Anu Gita:*

निर्वेदस्तु न गन्तव्यो युञ्जानेन कथंचन
योगमेकान्तशीलस्तु यथा युञ्जीत तच्छृणु

nirvedastu na gantavyo yuñjānena kathaṁcana
yogamekāntaśīlastu yathā yuñjīta tacchṛṇu (4.30)

nirvedas = nirvedah = discouraged; tu – but; na – not; gantavyo = gantavyah = attained; yuñjānena – with proficiency in yoga; kathaṁcana – anyway; yogam – yoga; ekānta = eka (one, primary) + anta (end, objective); śīlas = śīlah = behavior, lifestyle; tu – but; yathā – as; yuñjīta - proficiency in yogic trance; tac = tat = that; chṛṇu = śṛṇu = hear

But one who is attaining the proficiency in yoga practice, should not be discouraged. Hear about this how one whose primary objective in life is yoga, practices trance consistently. (Anu Gita 4.30)

दृष्टपूर्वां दिशं चिन्त्य यस्मिन्संनिवसेत्पुरे
पुरस्याभ्यन्तरे तस्य मनश्चार्यं न बाह्यतः
dṛṣṭapūrvāṁ diśaṁ cintya yasminsaṁnivasetpure
purasyābhyantare tasya manaścāryaṁ na bāhyataḥ (4.31)

dṛṣṭa – seen; pūrvāṁ - before; diśaṁ - place; cintya – thinking; yasmin – in which; saṁnivaset – should reside; pure – in the city; purasyābhyantare = purasya (of the city or psyche) + abhyantare (in the interior, inside); tasya – of his; manaś = manah = mind; cāryaṁ - behavior, operation; na – not; bāhyataḥ - outside

When thinking of a place which was seen before, one should reside in the city in which the incidence occurred. The mental operations are within the psyche, not outside of it. (Anu Gita 4.31)

पुरस्याभ्यन्तरे तिष्ठन्यस्मिन्नावसथे वसेत्
तस्मिन्नावसथे धार्यं सबाह्याभ्यन्तरं मनः
purasyābhyantare tiṣṭhanyasminnāvasathe vaset
tasminnāvasathe dhāryaṁ sabāhyābhyantaraṁ manaḥ (4.32)

purasyābhyantare = (purasya of the city) + abhyantare (inside); tiṣṭhany = tiṣṭhani = situated; asmin – in this; nāvasathe = na (not) + avasathe (city); vaset – should reside; tasmin – in this; nāvasathe = na (not) + avasathe (city); dhāryaṁ - absorbed in; sa – with; bāhyābhyantaraṁ = bāhya (exterior) + abhyantaram (interior); manaḥ - mind

Being situated inside the city, he should reside there with his mind absorbed in the exterior and interior features of that place. (Anu Gita 4.32)

प्रचिन्त्यावसथं कृत्स्नं यस्मिन्कायेऽवतिष्ठते
तस्मिन्काये मनश्चार्यं न कथंचन बाह्यतः
pracintyāvasathaṁ kṛtsnaṁ yasminkāye'vatiṣṭhate
tasminkāye manaścāryaṁ na kathaṁcana bāhyataḥ (4.33)

pracintyāvasathaṁ = pracintya = meditating; kṛtsnaṁ - whole reality; yasmin – in which; kāye – in the body; 'vatiṣṭhate = avatiṣṭhate = being situated; tasmin – in that; kāye – in the body; manaś = manah = whole; cāryaṁ - wander; na – not; kathaṁcana – any way; bāhyataḥ - outside

Meditating in that place, the self sees the whole reality being situated in the body. The mind should not in any way wander outside the body. (Anu Gita 4.33)

संनियम्येन्द्रियग्रामं निर्घोषे निर्जने वने
कायमभ्यन्तरं कृत्स्नमेकाग्रः परिचिन्तयेत्
saṁniyamyendriyagrāmaṁ nirghoṣe nirjane vane
kāyamabhyantaraṁ kṛtsnamekāgraḥ paricintayet (4.34)

saṁniyamyendriya = saṁniyamya (completely restraining) + indriya (sensual energies); grāmaṁ - aggregate; nirghoṣe – without noise; nirjane – without people; vane – in the forest; kāyam – body; abhyantaraṁ - inside; kṛtsnam – whole reality; ekāgraḥ - one object of focus; paricintayet – deeply meditate

In an uninhabited and noiseless forest, while completely restraining the aggregate sensual energies, he should deeply meditate within the body on the whole reality as one object of focus. (Anu Gita 4.34)

Elderly Yoga (September 2011)

When the body is elderly it is stricken with diseases but we know for sure that arthritis increases, circulation is slowed and joints are achy. Elderly persons should selectively create new exercises which an old body can assume. Do not completely stop the asana postures or the breath intake. Adapt, make new exercises and continue.

One problem in old age is diabetes and another common problem is irregular blood pressure.

Starfield Meditation

Sometimes when I do breath infusion, people who are in the astral world, come to learn the practice. A person who is advanced may step into my subtle body and interspace his/her subtle form into it so that he/she can understand the inner effects of the infusion practice. Usually we deny the subtle form as an object. We act as if it does not exist.

Subtle objects are perceived using the subtle eyes and/or the third eye or by prana vision.

When I was in Denver in 1972 I astral projected without fail every day at about noon by lying down on a lawn and lying in such a way that my body was perpendicular to the path the sun took across the sky.

I wrapped a dark cloth over my eyes. Because I was in Yogi Bhajan's ashram, I wore a turban. Even though all sun light was blocked out by the dark cloth, a certain type of subtle sun energy would penetrate the cloth and enter the head. Because I had a relationship with the sun deity from past lives, I got assistance from him to open third eye and astral project.

Both the turban and the dark cloth facilitated third eye opening. In Yogi's ashram even though there was no demand for us to become Sikhs, we wore turbans. Yogi had this idea about two things, mandatory turban and no cutting of hair for any reason. At the ashram we complied with that. Sometimes by the grace of the sun deity, I would transfer to the sun planet in my astral body. Later, because of getting involved in social affairs, the astral projection ability decreased.

Kundalini Experience

When kundalini rises in a way in which there is a complete infusion of the subtle body and not just a part of it, or if it is a full infusion of the head of the subtle body even without any other part of that body, that gives the yogi an indication about certain higher planes of existence.

One should note these planes of existence, just as one would notice an important building in a city during a visit as a tourist. If one reads Patanjali there is a part where he discusses various samadhis. If one reads that attentively one will get some idea of the locations that one may reach. One can then identify where one is in the realms of consciousness, just as a tourist on the basis of a guide book, can identify what is seen while touring.

The value of transcendental experience is this:

One gets some idea of other dimensions. One develops confidence in yoga teachers and deities like Patanjali and Krishna. It is also important to observe that even though one may reach higher places, spiritual bliss levels of existence, one is not allowed to continue the experience. Why is that?

If at the end of this life, heaven, paradise, a spiritual world or a kingdom of God will be a blip on the screen of consciousness, then what is that? Why are we unable to remain in those realms?

In most transcendental experiences, there are no visual perceptions. Why is that? Is there a body on the bliss planes? Is it only higher consciousness without format?

In relation to the kundalini infusement. A consideration is that the kundalini seems to always want to return to the physical creature existence. It is disinclined to having a higher level of existence as its home. It prefers the base physical life. How can that be adjusted?

Thought Attacks

While doing breath infusion and even when sitting to meditate, one should have a reliable method to deal with thought attacks and distractions.

First of all, thoughts always course through the atmosphere from the creatures who live in the vicinity. Many thoughts are random. Some are deliberate and focused on the yogi. The best way to escape from having to deal with thoughts during meditation, is to infuse the system with fresh air energy by doing pranayama practice just before meditation. This relocates the subtle body so that it becomes absent from the plane of consciousness in which trivial thoughts occur.

Thoughts will continue on lower planes but since the yogi's awareness is shifted to a higher level, he/she will not perceive them. However, one should have a set method for dealing with thoughts. This set method should be changed as one advances and gets a better grip on the mental situation.

During breath infusion thoughts may attack. The assault may be successful in the sense that one finds oneself doing the practice on one hand, while paying attention to the undesirable thoughts on the other hand. Whenever this happens a yogi should take note of his/her responses in reference to the thoughts.

Research will help the yogi to know the origin and hypnotic power of the thoughts. Let us say for instance, that a yogi sat to meditate, then his four-year-old daughter called saying that there was a fire in her room. What should he do? Should he respond or should he finish the meditation and then respond?

This is exactly what happens with thoughts, where depending on who sends the ideas and depending on the content, one feels that one should or should not respond.

However, the mere awareness of a thought means that some focal energy is not being given to the meditation. A response to the thoughts is worse since that means that much focal energy goes to the thought at the expense of the meditation. Even the stage of deciding the priority of a thought detracts from the meditation.

Meditation: Primary Objective

Seeing light, seeing objectively and with clear perception into higher dimensions, entering into bliss consciousness are the first primary objectives in kriya yoga practice.

These are on the high end of a consistent successful practice. The preliminary objective is to attain silence in the mind for long periods of time. That honors Patanjali's request for stopping the compulsive operations of the intellect, memory and sensual energy.

Getting that silence, the state where the mind does not flash images, ideas or random thoughts, is an achievement even if the yogi can do it for two minutes during meditation.

How to reach that state?

There is no set method. The important thing is to try and try until you achieve it. When one is proficient, one should stay in the mental silence for as long as possible.

That will develop into something else, into another mental level of awareness, where in the bland mental space, there will be light. Gaps will open to other dimensions with specialized perception or bliss consciousness with self-awareness of the surrounding consciousness-energy.

Buddha's Kriya: Ripping Away the Attention

During exercises this morning there was a flash of a location in South Korea, where earlier this year, I visited three Buddha deities. After the flash there was a live connection to those deities. One is Gautama Buddha. The other is Bhaishavya Buddha. The third being is Amitabha Buddha. I greeted them with the respects due to deities and spiritual masters. I thanked Amitabha Buddha for assistance rendered in translating and commenting on the *Anu Gita* book.

After these greetings which were done simultaneously as I did breath infusion in various postures at a place in northern Alabama, Gautama Buddha said he wanted to say something about using mantras during postures and breath infusion practice. The use of mantras then is different to its use during meditation practice. This is the instruction:

A yogi whose mind is obedient, whose mind is clean, whose mind does not generate thoughts, images and ideas should not use a mantra. There is no need for it. If during postures and breath infusement practice, the yogi finds that thoughts keep arising and that some attention is forcibly going to such ideas, a mantra can be used.

The yogi should get a mantra from a senior yogi, who used a particular mantra and had success with it and knows when to release the self from such use of the said mantra. In India, the most popular mantra used is:

Om namo Shivaya.

In Tibet it is:

Om mani padme hum.

Om is standard as the introductory sound. Hum is a concluding sound in the Tibetan mantra.

Previously, some yogis used Om alone, which was chanted for hours during practice. Hopefully a student can get a mantra which was used by an advanced teacher.

When doing the asana postures and breath infusion practice, if the attention is diverted to a thought, and if the attention was hijacked by the intellect, one should confiscate it from the intellect and put it on the required focus. But if one finds that when one does this the intellect again confiscates the attention and again forcibly directs it to the thoughts and images, one should take help from a mantra. With the mantra being repeated mentally one will have the force to cause the attention to be released from the intellect so that the attention can be applied to the required focus.

What is the focus?

If the yogi does a posture to infuse breath energy into the knee for instance, that area of the subtle body is the focus. The attention should be there. It should not at that time be in the head with thoughts or images or ideas. Even if only a small part of it is with the thoughts, that is a diversion and a mantra may be used as a last resort if one finds that one does not have the power to capture the entire attention.

This is called ripping away the attention from the intellect. In time, this discipline of the mind will cause the yogi to have full success in the process of segregating the attention from the intellect which usually forces the self to perceive and permit unwanted ideas, images and thoughts.

Buddha's Kriya: Retraining Kundalini

During meditation, a Buddha Deity, Gautama, instructed on a kriya for taking kundalini away from the intellect analytical orb in the subtle body. Most students never saw the orb. It is a matter for them of knowing its location in the mind space. It is where images, thoughts and ideas appear. If one never saw it one can use this exercise to restrain kundalini from being attracted to the location where the images, thoughts and ideas occur.

In this meditation, after doing breath infusion into the subtle body, one sits to meditate. One should see where the kundalini energy flows after it enters the neck. It comes up from the lower part of the trunk of the subtle body, near to the anus, from the sacral area of the spine. It rises and passes through the neck.

The yogi should search for it, and find its flow. This does not mean that the yogi should visualize or imagine a flow. The yogi should honestly find the flow. Once that is noted, the yogi should position the coreSelf in naad sound at the side or back of the head.

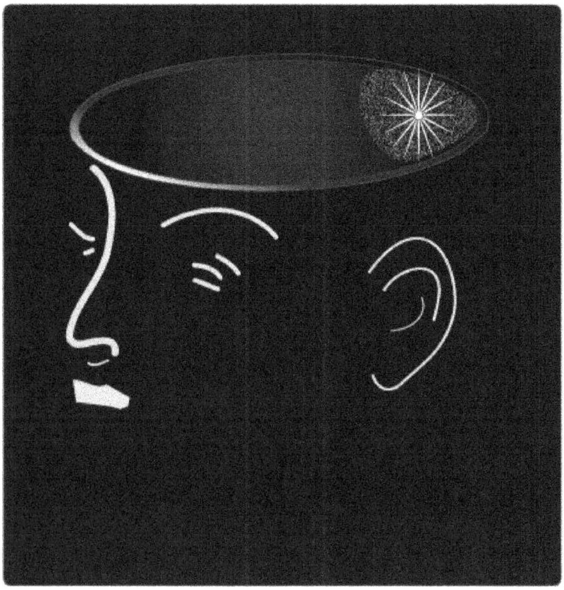

This might be in the central back of the head or to the right or left of the back. As soon as this is done, kundalini may make an effort to flow to the self but it will be pulled to the intellect or to the place where thoughts usually occur in the frontal part of the head. The yogi should forcibly pull that flow of energy up the back of the head so that it is like a shaft of light flowing through the back of the top of the head.

Three People Take Yogi's Subtle Body

Subtle perception gives one the ability to know when one is motivated by other entities. Possession by other spirits is usually regarded as negative.

Escaping into a homogenous consciousness where one cannot tell where one begins and where the next entity ends, does not free anyone from possession, even though it does free one from the sense of insecurity one may have if one knows for sure that one is under an influence.

One molecule of water, on the bottom of the ocean is still under the pressure of several hundred feet of water and is still in a confinement in an oceanic valley or plane, even if that molecule has no way for accounting its time and place.

Yesterday a man who had some domestic issues, called. Later during the night on the astral level, I was confronted by him and the members of his household. Suddenly the man jumped into my psyche and so did his spouse.

This is reminiscent of when one is in an infant body which grows and reaches sexual maturity. At that time many entities who are ancestors or friends of ancestors may live in one's subtle body. They may fuse into it on the subtle plane. They become humbug sexual energies, which cause one to be crazed for sexual indulgence in order to generate embryos.

During exercises this morning, those two persons were still in the subtle body. I noticed them superimposed in the body. But there was a flash of light. The Buddha deity said that I should do breath infusion into the subtle body while ignoring their presence. He added this:

"For the deities, hundreds, thousands, millions perhaps of other entities are in their forms. This is normal. Give it no thought. Finish the session and meditate."

Soon after this another entity jumped into and fused into the subtle body except that while the first man was in the left side of the chest and this wife was in the right side, this other person, an extra-marital lover of the man, was superimposed on the spine facing to the back of the body.

In a sense neither of them was in the subtle body because they were in a slightly different frequency to the body, like waves of energy which enter a television but which have slightly different frequencies and do not mix or superimpose.

During the exercises, thoughts emanated from the psyche of these three persons. By using a mantra whenever I became aware of their thinking, I dodged connection with those ideas.

Kundalini Throws the Yogi to the Ground

It happens during breath infusion practice, that sometimes a yogi's physical body is thrown to the ground by kundalini. The physical system of the yogi is forcibly abandoned by the consciousness-focus of the yogi.

As soon as that occurs, the physical body falls because the coreSelf cannot supervise it. The core loses communication with the physical body.

In the subtle body something else occurs, which is that the core-self may or may not lose its conscious grip on that form. If it does not the yogi comes back to physical awareness with some information about what occurred, about what dimensional switch happened, about that state and most of all about that location.

When it is broken down to what happened to the components of consciousness, as to what kundalini did to what other component, and as to what happened to the self's objective grasp on consciousness, it is an entirely different event. The yogi enters no-man's land, a vague territory, a place which people call mergence or oneness, a place where one loses the sense of distinction and where one gets notions of absoluteness and oneness.

Many students questioned me about the circumstances which occur when kundalini strikes and the physical body falls to the ground, with the yogi losing awareness and then finds the self to be in the conscious body again, finding the body in a fallen position, sometimes with a headache, sometimes with spaced-out awareness.

This morning when after practice, I walked away with the yoga mat to go indoors to meditate, suddenly I noticed that kundalini moved and was ascending the spine. It reached the neck and was to burst like a detonated nuclear bomb. Instinctively after years of practice, I dropped the body down so that the knees were on the ground, I applied some locks. Kundalini was managed efficiently. It distributed power evenly through the top part of the trunk of the body, through the neck and through the head, especially to the back of the head.

Why did kundalini rise as soon as I stood up? I did the exercises. Kundalini rose more than once during the session. I mentally said the Tibetan mantra when thoughts came about to distract from the required focus. Everything went well. I took a cell phone which was on the ground. I folded the mat. I got up with it and walked away. After three steps suddenly I saw kundalini rising.

I looked back into the spine as I walked away physically. I saw this light-yellow mist moving up the spine. I recognized it as kundalini. Before I realized, it moved from the base area to the heart chakra. Then I knew that kundalini would attack the head. I dropped to the ground on my knees and applied some locks. Kundalini then fizzed out slowly. It was like it was unhappy because it did not catch me off-guard. But I practiced kundalini yoga since around 1971. By now kundalini should not catch me offguard.

This is what happened:

Kundalini's accumulation of energy below the small of the back, below the navel chakra was not completely released during the session. Kundalini paused there. When I stooped to get the rug, kundalini got compressed some more. When I straightened the spine to walk away with the yoga mat, kundalini pushed itself passed the check valve which is behind the navel in sushumna nadi spinal passage which is at the small of the back.

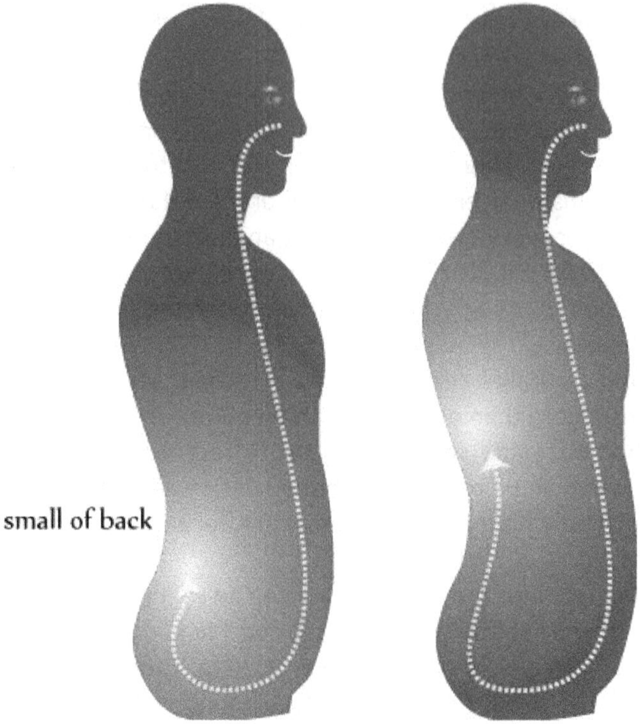

It decided to get into the head to hit the intellect. However due to vigilance I was aware of its movements before it could carry out this plan.

During sexual climax, kundalini becomes so powerful, so attractive, that the intellect moves from its default position in the head of the subtle body all the way down to the pleasure center of the genitals. However, in kundalini yoga practice, the opposite occurs where kundalini has a strong charge. It moves to the default position of the intellect.

During sex, the location where thoughts occur in the head, moved to the location where sex pleasure occurs in the public area. During rising of kundalini during breath infusion practice, sex pleasure location moves to the base of the spine which in turn moves with that pleasure force to the location where thoughts occurs in the subtle head.

What happens when a person faints or passes out?

Would someone who lacked years of kundalini experience fall instead of fainting or having a slight lapse of consciousness during the same experience?

To a non-yogi from the external appearance of the body, the kundalini experience would appear to be a form of fainting. From a psychic view there is a vast difference.

In the case of fainting the same kundalini is involved, except that it was deprived of energy and as a result it could not provide power to the intellect. It does not have energy to operate.

In the case of kundalini rising sudden due to breath infusion or due to bending and doing a certain posture which caused kundalini to surge into the brain in an unregulated way, the intellect would be knocked out of commission for a time, until moments or minutes after the power was reduced to what the intellect could handle. The person would find the self aware in the physical body again.

Sir Paul stated that when this happens to him, there comes the awareness of this very large orb, a subtle bubble in which he finds myself. Is that bubble the intellect? His experience is not the same experience which I described, but it is a phase of the same experience. In other words, the very same experience may be observed differently by different yogis.

Previously, I had that experience which he described. The large orb or subtle bubble is the bubble body. It is the same subtle body but, in a condition, where the limbs of it seem to disappear. The self experiences itself as a bubble of luminescent energy. In that condition there are no sense organs on the body, there is no intellect within it. It is a coreSelf with a certain type of cosmic bliss energy or cosmic light energy (light as in ray of light), or bliss mist energy like shimmering light in a mist.

In that experience the orb is still there but since one left the zones of its manifestation one is not aware of it. Soon after when the energy subsides, the intellect will be present again. It will be perceived as thoughts, ideas and images appearing.

This bubble body is a wonderful form. It should be experienced repeatedly. It causes one to become resistant to emotions on lower planes.

One siddha who is expert at that bubble body is Nityananda who inspired the commentary of *Bhagavad gita,* titled *Brahma Yoga Bhagavad Gita*. His energy was used to compose that publication.

He uses such a body. Remaining on that level of existence continuously as he does is a feat for any yogi. The secret to that is repeated practice until the kundalini gets so used to going into the head and causing the self to slip into that dimension that it does so automatically, even though the full assumption of that state as the Swami attained, really means the elimination of kundalini.

Help from Muktananda

Taking help from advanced entities, being open to their influence and ideas, knowing well that they have nothing to gain but have much to give to a beginner, serves the purpose of attaining liberation from the massive ignorance which happens to be our existential condition currently.

A person cannot make advancement without personal effort. Unless one is willing to walk away from this social situation and get totally involved in self-reform and self-upliftment, even the Supreme Being cannot do a thing to help one but all the same if one makes the maximum effort and exerts the self to the fullest to side-step lower consciousness, one will not be successful without taking help.

Patanjali made it clear that there has to be a reliance on the Supreme Person who was the one who helped the ancient yogis, people whose attainment was legendary.

When giving lectures about the life of Gautama Buddha, people like to stress how he bypassed the teachers whom he first took when he entered into renunciation of social life, but they fail to establish that he took help from those teachers and got to a certain point. Initially he was not versed in any austerities. From each teacher he learnt certain methods. After passing through their processes and getting from it what he could, he went further. This does not mean that he did not take help or that those teachers were useless. One must take help from teachers even if those persons do not have the final process and even if at a certain point one will have to be a pioneer.

Patanjali said that there is a Supreme Person who taught the ancient yogis. They took assistance from someone. It is either that a particular yogi is the Supreme Being Himself or is one of the Supreme Person's parallel divinities or that yogi must take help from the Supreme Being either directly or indirectly, knowingly or unknowingly.

Consciousness is vast. Even when a limited self attains an enlightened state which to him is everything, still phases of the cosmic consciousness is outside his purview. Thus, there is no question of doing it all by oneself.

This morning while doing exercises, at the end of the session, near the last infusement, I saw Muktananada, a noted modern siddha who is now departed. He smiled and sent some energy from his subtle form into mine. When I looked at it, it was an expression of kriya processes which he perfected while he did austerities before he became a famous guru.

It is possible for a yogi to send an energy into another person's psyche as a contribution to that person's spiritual progress. Sometimes such energies do not stay with the student yogi, because the student might not be proficient enough in practice to retain the energy. Donations from great yogis are a godsend in some situations when a yogi hustles to make progress but does not have enough forcefulness and directedness.

The energy from Muktananda mixed with another energy which was in my psyche which was awarded by a Buddha Deity. It concerns having the ability to infuse the subtle body even if the kundalini is dissipated out of it.

The passage of sushumna nadi spinal tube remains in the subtle system even if kundalini is dissipated and that passage is used to infuse energy into the subtle body directly with prana without even the kundalini charge.

My Failed Yoga Session

This morning session was not as good as it should be. Due to pressing social obligations, my night went haywire with much social mixing. I rested later than is required for a good early practice.

When this happens, the yogi should not be discouraged in the next day's practice since if he/she is, it will result in a braking force on the practice habit, so that eventually practice will be abandoned altogether.

If you find yourself in a fix where you rest later and where you socialized much with people who do not have spiritual discipline as their primary interest then you should be sure to do your next day's practice, even if it is a partial session. This will keep the psyche in the habit of practice and when pressing social concerns pass, you will easily resume practice.

During practice there were other minds connecting with my mind, chattering and saying this and saying that. I diverted my attention to a mantra during the practice. That took care of the problem of focus. If this is not done, the attention may shift to the mental chatter, which will result in a focus-less practice, which in turn will cause an inefficient session, which will increase the negativity towards practice.

When a yogi associates with persons who are not interested in spiritual practice, their negative views and unresponsive attitude towards yoga, influence him to go in their direction. The only way to stop the incursion is to practice the next day even if the session is not as good as it should be.

The psyche is absorbent. If it is exposed to influences which see no importance in yoga, it will take energies from those sources. The result will be a reduction and eventually elimination of practice. To prevent this, one should practice no matter what.

Despite the social energy which caused a bad session with much thought projection and also with negative social energies in my psyche asserting influence and making their stand against yoga, still I had some luck with the breath infusion by pressing on with the session. At a certain point it progressed to a place where I infused energy into the spine and then into the neck and into the lower and upper jaws. Kundalini did some minor arousals in the left and right side of the trunk of the body and in the arms.

When I felt it was sufficient, I got a message from a Buddha deity which said that I should do more to increase the infusion in the trunk of the body. I did that but there was another message which said that another two hours of practice was enough.

That last instruction I did not adhere to but I made a mental note of it. Gautama Buddha used to do meditation for hours in fact, days of practice, so what is four hours to a person like that?

When I sat to meditate, there were no ideas in the mind, which is really great and which is the essential benefit of the breath infusion. However, for about four times, I realized that the head of the physical body drooped forward. It hanged down. I lifted it on each occasion.

One thing which happened and which is important is as follows:

Suddenly in the psyche while being slightly aware of the material body, in the subtle head of the psyche, there was light beaming down. It was a spotlight beaming down and shining through the self downwards. That lasted for about twenty seconds.

This is a very important experience because it happens in the dimensions where a person only sees what is required to be seen, and where the only things which are illuminated are those which are required to be seen, where the energy of vision is itself a light which illuminates what is to be seen. This is a chit akash experience but in a partial dimension of the chit akasha, sky of consciousness.

I want to share this experience to alert other yogis. This may happen to a student while meditating. Recalling this experience, one may identify it. I will be deprived of this body today or tomorrow. Who knows when? Who controls fate?

If one reads Patanjali one's faith in him will increase if he listed this as one of the samadhi experiences. Even if the experience of a supernatural body lasts for ten seconds in the life of a yogi it is valid experience about that body, even though one did not use that body for more than ten seconds. Pranayama breath infusion may shift one upwards in the astral planes and into the bodies which are relevant to those levels.

With sufficient practice a yogi can gain control of this light and do explorations in the supernatural world, just as an infant learns gradually to use its eyes and then to explore the physical world. But one would have to move over into that other existence, just as the infant by the nature of birth here, had its focus transferred to the physical plane.

There were obstructions this morning during exercises, mostly residual disturbances from the night before. These were astral interferences. A friend in South American who has a spiritual practice, dealth with his deceased father, who passed on about ten days ago. He asked for assistance in dealing with the old man's de-energized subtle body (ghost) which hovered in the astral world.

My session began later than it should have. I did my best and compressed much energy into the psyche. I had some luck. When I sat to meditate, the mind had no thoughts. The pressure of energy moved upwards through the back of the head. After ten minutes, the energy shifted and the frontal part of the head coursed backwards. Even the physical eyes moved upwards in the head.

After some time, there was subtle perception, but it was like looking through a brown tinted plastic film. Some other persons were there. My subtle body sat on the top of a set of stairs. A lady walked up the stairs and walk through my subtle body as though it was not there. To her it was not there because she was not aware of any other astral dimension than the one she was in. I was in an adjacent one but one in which the frequencies used in her world passed through and did not notice those on the level my astral form was synchronized into.

After she passed through my form, many others passed. Since I began late, I concluded practice about fifteen minutes before I should have. Because of social pressures either on the physical or astral sides of existence, a reduction of practice occurs from time to time.

Swami Rama and the Yogini (September 2011)

I ask students to keep a journal of breath infusion, meditation and astral projection events. If one does not keep a journal, one's practice and particularly the integration of progress may suffer. This means that if one does not integrate the daily progress, one's confidence in practice may deteriorate with a result that the practice slows because one is unable to estimate how advanced one may be. This leads to discouragement which terminates practice.

Even if one is not in habit of recalling what happened in dreams while the physical system sleeps, a dream journal is vital for keeping track of dream activities.

During this morning practice, I did not have my pen and note pad. Some of what happened was forgotten. This hampers the ability to file these reports with details. I do recall however that when I sat to meditate certain things happened which caused me to consider that students can learn much about the kundalini's alliance with other parts of the psyche.

During practice I saw two people in particular, one was Swami Rama. The other was a yogini disciple of his who is now departed. Swami explained that even though morality is important if one gets a chip on the shoulder about it, one will fail in practice. He made some remarks for the benefit of the yogini who was with him. She left her last body without sufficiently completing yoga austerities. She was a bit arrogant about her religious morality.

Swami said this:

In the West there is morality but it is differently based than in India. In India, we have morality, a very variable one at that. But it is based on what Krishna decreed or on what an ancient sage like Manu decreed.

Krishna gave standards and wanted humanity to comply with his view. If the yogi is a Hindu, he follows morality on that basis. If one is a Buddhist one follows what Buddha advised as the eightfold noble path. Morality is designed to ease the impediments which may appear in the next life and those which come in this life which was formulated in previous lives.

However, morality is not a feather in the cap of the yogi. It is not to be used for self-righteous purposes. If you study Bhagavad Gita, you will hear how Krishna tore apart every one of Arjuna's moral arguments. Why did Krishna do that, because after all Arjuna was trained in a cultured family? Arjuna was honorable. He was compassionate. He cited religious injunctions. Still, Krishna rejected just about every one of Arjuna's ideas about morality. Arjuna was self-righteous in Chapter One of the Bhagavad Gita. *Krishna did not like it.*

Be moral but do not let it be a weapon for insulting others. Do not use it as a source of pride or arrogance. The Supreme Being wants a moral lifestyle. That is all one needs to know. Do not try to be a moralist like Arjuna in Chapter One of Bhagavad Gita. *One has to know the relevant actions from past lives to properly calculate the morality of an act. It varies by the circumstance. Consultation with the Supreme Being is essential. If left to oneself, to one's judgment, miscalculations will be made because you may not be detached enough and may not be inspired by the Supreme Person.*

Kundalini's Conspiracy (September 2011)

During meditation, due to a thorough breath infusion, I had luck with making kundalini give up its familiarity and conspiracy to rule the psyche in alliance with the intellect.

Due to an intense session of breath infusion, kundalini streamed upwards through the neck and into the head with such an upward thrust that it went through the neck and did not veer forward to the frontal part of the brain.

Kundalini went upward with a force as if it was pushed by hurricane winds. It was so forceful that it has no attraction to any other component of consciousness, not even the intellect, not even the sensual energies and the sensual orifices which usually pursue circumstances in the external world.

To my surprise, the intellect, the third eye, the two subtle eyes and even the physical eyes and the physical cells of the brain were pulled up and backward in attraction to the flow of kundalini but kundalini had no interest in unifying with these energies.

In this practice, a yogi can study the attracting forces. When kundalini subsides during meditation, the yogi can see how kundalini resumes its conspiracy operations with the other psychic components, totally ignoring the needs of the coreSelf.

The lesson is that if the kundalini is properly infused, it is forced to change its attitude. Its creature survival and reproduction game plans which it forces the psyche to engage in, even if the core-self objects, comes to an end. One can act in compliance with Patanjali's instruction about stopping the operations of the intellect.

Sleep (September 2011)

From the angle of mystic yoga, sleep is controlled by the kundalini life force. Patanjali listed sleep as one of the vrittis or operational modes of the mento-emotional energy. This energy is manipulated by the life force. It is a combination of the mental and emotional force. In that case mental means analyzing and conceptualizing. Emotional means feeling and conceptualizing.

If the life force is not given sufficient rest, it will find a way to take the needed respite. But if it has a haphazard schedule, it may become jittery. It may deprive itself of rest. That will cause irritability and manic mental states.

Manufacture of Thoughts

Meditation this morning was uneventful, without supernatural vision and dimensional transfer. Since one must leave this physical place at the death of the body, it is sensible to develop an interest in the place to which one will go. Just as one lives on the earth, do or die, meditation or not, and one must work with the social and political conditions which are in effect, so after leaving the body one will go to another environment which we term as an astral realm or the hereafter.

During meditation I observed two thoughts. These arose in slow motion. When the mind is surcharged with energy and when the kundalini is surcharged and lost interest in the lower three chakras, thoughts occur in slow motion. This is due to the increased speed of perception.

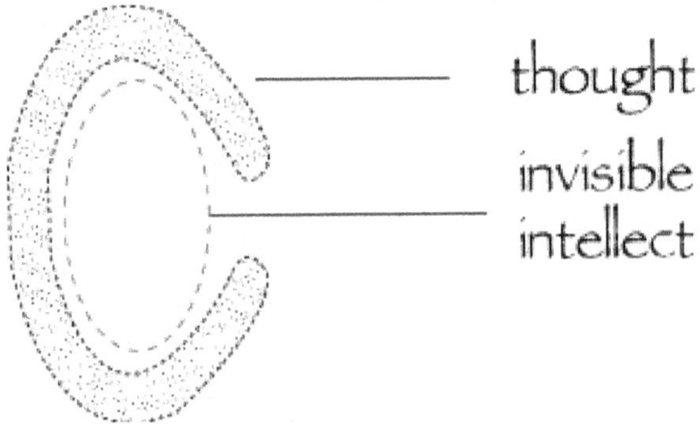

One thought rose through the neck from the memory chamber. Instead of attacking the intellect by piercing it like a missile entering a building, the thought wrapped around the intellect in a swirl. By that action the energy caused the intellect to send an image to the coreSelf for permission to use that memory to mix with an idea which was in the intellect. This is one method used by memory to get the core to indulge in idea formation.

If the self does not stop its interest in such memories and thoughts, it is forced to permit and observe the development of ideas.

Such observation gives the student insight into how thoughts are constructed, how they are mixed with memories, and how for better or worse the self is induced to consent to mental constructions. A detailed observation of how thoughts are manufactured as well as how memories are formed, stored and retrieved, is integral in higher yoga.

Kundalini and Sex Experience

How closely related is the rising of kundalini and the clearing of the channel(s) to the head?

Initially due to blockage in the subtle sushumna nadi channel which is the spine of the astral body, the kundalini cannot penetrate. But all the same the kundalini is not interested in making that penetration. Its default interest in the head of the subtle body is to get sensual information about what occurs outside the body. It uses the faculties in the head, to get information on how best to proceed with survival-reproduction behaviors. For these purposes it does not need a completely cleared spinal passage.

For a student kundalini will rise only when something happens to force it to do so. Its interest in rising occurs in our creature existence mode by sensual excitement and by sexual climax of energy. In other words, the first thing to understand is that kundalini does rise during any common excitement. It does so sensationally during sexual intercourse.

Kundalini has a passage which it used to flow into and through the genitals but one is unaware of that passage except when there is the flow of climax of energies. It is so intense that one cannot properly determine the location or size of the energy. One experiences the rush of pleasure which overtakes one's objective awareness of the experience.

During sexual climax, the transit of kundalini is stunning. For that matter, one is rarely objective regarding how kundalini created that intense electric pleasure. It overwhelms the person. One loses objectivity and has no point of reference to gage the experience.

Kundalini bores its way through a blocked passage during the sex climax. Soon after the climax, the passage is closed. Kundalini becomes sluggish. If one attempts to be sexually aroused immediately after, it is difficult to develop the energy surge. One may wait a day or two for the hormonal energy to accumulate. Or I may take a drug which forces it to.

In a student yogi, the spinal passage to the head is blocked just as the sexual passage is. Just as when there is a forceful charge of sex energy by foreplay, by pornography or by flirtation, kundalini forces itself though the blocked channel. It does likewise when it is energized by breath infusion. However, as soon as it is discharged, the passage becomes blocked again.

Kundalini in the head is an abstract and subjective experience. Sex is common place and has a greater degree of objectivity.

The consequence of having an experience is the real value in the experience not the experience itself. Primitive entities, even in modern human beings want varied experience. They do not understand consequence. In time however one assesses this after repeatedly being stymied by imposed circumstances.

It takes some time to understand this, because consequences usually come in another life. Since I cannot link a circumstance to something I experienced in a past life, I cannot draw valid conclusions.

Actions have no value. They are empty shells. The value is in the consequences. It is only by knowing the consequences that a limited being can get deep insight. Since however the consequences may be sealed, packaged in one life and then unsealed and released in another life, the limited entities are at a disadvantage. They cannot assess what happens.

They do however get some immediate satisfaction by the faulty equations which are compressed into this life alone. They are happy with this primitive math.

Sex experience is just one of the experiences. The full exploration of it is endless because it involves the use of the affection energies which unfortunately can be converted in many different affections. If one converts that over and over into different kinds of relationships, there will come a time when one will lose track of morality and will not know what is right or wrong.

Right and wrong has to do with the social environment and how nature reacts to simple or complex relationships. Wanting to have endless happiness, one chases pleasure but again and again we see that nature frustrates the endeavor. It depends on the life form one assumes. Can anyone show a way of keeping a particular life form forever?

In the astral world this matter was discussed by Rishi Singh Gherwal. I was present with some of his disciples. He blamed sexual pleasure as the main cause of student yogis getting stalled in advanced practice.

I agree that exploitation of the sexual energy will become a problem when its consequence comes in the form of resentments from disembodied ancestors who require bodies and who are deprived of such forms by contraception. One will also have to deal with any reaction nature serves because of feeling offended by one's decision to avoid raising progeny.

This is not about God. This is about nature and the individual entity. Even if God is absent or does not exist, still nature is there with its reactionary behavior which a limited being cannot adjust for his or her convenience.

Some effort must be made to study how kundalini operates through the sexual facilities. Those who are involved in sexual indulgence should make efforts to objectively get some understanding of kundalini's movements during sexual acts. Those who are not involved in sex at this time, but who were previously in this life, should review in the memories and study the energy dispersal in retrospect.

Astral Flying

If one finds oneself in an astral dimension where one can fly while others cannot, it means that for some reason those other persons identify their astral bodies as physical ones. That identification caused the astral body to act as a physical form which means that it is gravity-bound.

Sometimes however when one is in an astral place, and one flies, it is not observed by others. They may sense one's presence, but they cannot perceive one because one's astral form is in another dimension.

In some experiences, where others do see one, they may become resentful of the fact that one flies and they cannot. This is like in the physical world, where wealthy people exhibit things which poor persons cannot acquire. Those poor persons resent the wealthy people for having luxuries.

The lesson is that the astral world is not all rosy. There is good, bad and better there. If one enters a dimension where the persons residing there are not advanced one may find danger. One may feel that the others do not want one to be there. If one flies above them, they may jump and violently pull one down.

Gush Tunnel / Naad Meditation

This morning I was disturbed during the exercise session but I pushed on and use a mantra to ward off the disturbance. The mantra was effective. It was a Tibetan Buddhist mantra.

Om mani padme hum

When I sat to mediate, there were no thoughts. I easily reached naad in the back of the head. I remained there with no urge to go forward. The frontal part of the head was subdued by the breath infusion.

After listening to naad and being in and close to naad for twenty minutes at the back of the head, I shifted some attention to the frontal part. There was a tunnel from the back going forward but it was like a gush-way.

I used this channel to transmit my willpower energy. In this transmission the willpower did not engage with the thought-producing mechanism. It flowed forward through the tube-like gush channel without interfering with the meditation.

I wanted to continue this but mentally some issues arose, I left the meditation. Fragmented meditation, a break in a session, and whatever else that happens which causes a yogi not the meditate sufficiently is bad for progress. One cannot consolidate the progress if one is always disturbed and if one leaves aside the meditation because of pressing concerns.

In the *Anu Gita* there is a related statement:

प्रचिन्त्यावसथं कृत्स्नं यस्मिन्कायेऽवतिष्ठते
तस्मिन्काये मनश्चार्यं न कथंचन बाह्यतः
pracintyāvasathaṁ kṛtsnaṁ yasminkāye'vatiṣṭhate
tasminkāye manaścāryaṁ na kathaṁcana bāhyataḥ (4.33)

pracintyāvasathaṁ = pracintya = meditating; kṛtsnaṁ - whole reality; yasmin – in which; kāye – in the body; 'vatiṣṭhate = avatiṣṭhate = being situated; tasmin – in that; kāye – in the body; manaś = manah = whole; cāryaṁ - wander; na – not; kathaṁcana – any way; bāhyataḥ - outside

Meditating in that place, the self sees the whole reality being situated in the body. The mind should not in any way wander outside the body. (*Anu Gita* 4.33)

संनियम्येन्द्रियग्रामं निर्घोषे निर्जने वने
कायमभ्यन्तरं कृत्स्नमेकाग्रः परिचिन्तयेत्
saṁniyamyendriyagrāmaṁ nirghoṣe nirjane vane
kāyamabhyantaraṁ kṛtsnamekāgraḥ paricintayet (4.34)

saṁniyamyendriya = saṁniyamya (completely restraining) + indriya (sensual energies); grāmaṁ - aggregate; nirghoṣe – without noise; nirjane – without people; vane – in the forest; kāyam – body; abhyantaraṁ - inside; kṛtsnam – whole reality; ekāgraḥ - one object of focus; paricintayet – deeply meditate

In an uninhabited and noiseless forest, while completely restraining the aggregate sensual energies, he should deeply meditate within the body on the whole reality as one object of focus. (*Anu Gita* 4.34)

During meditation one should understand where the observing self, the you, is situated and where the apparitions occur. For instance, is it in the frontal part of the head? Is it up or down? Is it in the center? Is it to the left or right side? Is it at the back of the head?

A purple area surrounded by black or a dark brown area surrounded by purple or black is usually the third eye area which is also known as the brow chakra. To know definitely where that it located, closed the eyelids. Squeeze the eyelids on the eyeballs. With both hands press gently on the eyelids while looking forward. Do this for about three to five minutes. You should see a light in the center. It may be a doughnut shape. It may be disc shaped or be a blotch. Note the location.

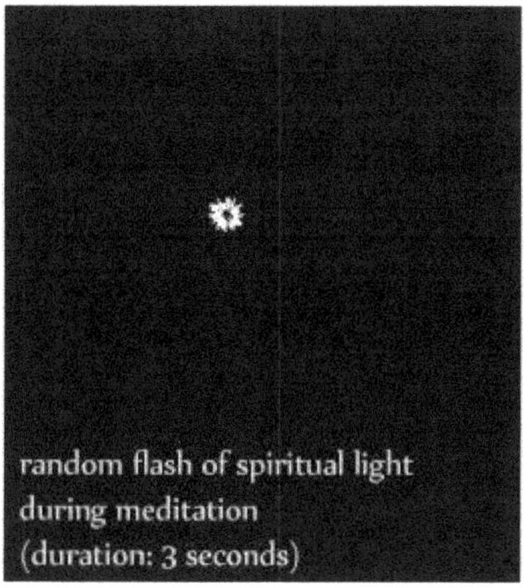

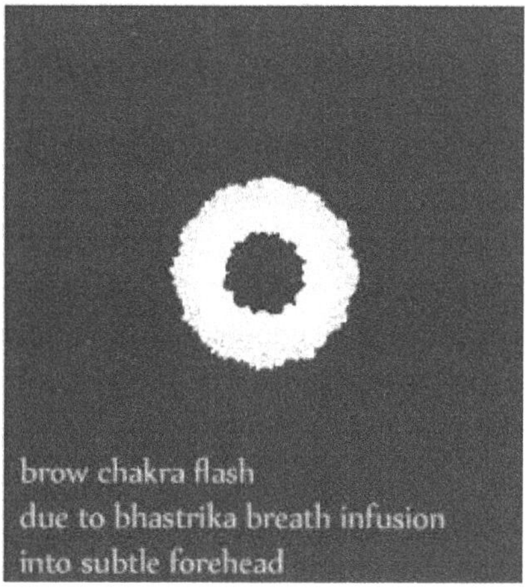

To be sure that this is a location and a special location of the brow chakra (third eye), one can press on other parts of the head and one will not see anything similar. When one presses on the eyes, the optic nerves which are connected to the third eye are triggered. Once one knows the location of the third eye, when one has an experience there one will know that it is the third eye.

There is one hitch, one thing to be careful about, which is that between the observing self, the you, and the third eye, there is an orb. This is a psychic organ which one will not see but one can take my word for it. It is there between the observing self and the third eye. For that matter one cannot use the third eye without seeing it through the intellect. It is median between the observing self and the third eye. If something appears half-way there, one can know that it is happening in the intellect. Thoughts for instance do not arise at the third eye. They appear in the space between the third eye and the observing self.

There is something else which happens at the third eye, which is that one may see a doughnut shape moving towards the third eye or moving towards the observing self coming from the third eye. This will travel and then disappear. As soon as it disappears, another similar shape appears and moves again. You will know that it concerns the third eye because it will either disappear in the distance at the third eye or it will be in the distance at the third eye and then get bigger and disappear as it approaches the observing self.

The third eye can show many perceptions and mysteries. It can do many things. The value of its operation is that one develops or manifests psychic perception. With the third eye one can see into other dimensions. One can see past lives and many other things of interest to mystics.

Operation of the third eye means that the subtle body is energized. The person has objective astral experiences. That is important if one desires to know for sure if one will exist beyond the life of the physical body. How will one exist then? In what body? Where will the subtle form go?

Some do not care about location. But if you ask anyone to relocate to the Sahara where there is no food and no organized civilization, how many persons desire to live there. The next location? Why care about it? Does it matter where one will be hereafter?

Usually one has astral experiences because of being a mystic or yogi in the past life. One assumes a new body but with no memory of the past. By psychic experiences, one is prompted to again begin mystic practice, to become proficient in it.

Value of Parents

One thing about family which cannot be denied, is that as infants, one must take help from them. Even though after juvenile stage one may not require the assistance, still the help rendered by parents or guardians in the infant stage is priceless.

Even in cases where one can point a finger and claim that one was abused, there is with that bad account a list of rendered service. Some appreciation is due to parents and others who assisted in nurturing the infant body and educating that form from the toddler stage to the teen years.

Sometime before the modern laws for what doctors and psychiatrist could do, a researcher took an orphaned boy and kept him like an animal in cage. There was no education, nor special care. The food was thrown on the ground. The infant grew like an animal. He did not learn language as most kids do. It proved that if it were not for the culture of higher animal behaviors most human beings would act like lower animals. If there is no cultural orientation we would regress to the primitive stage.

This means that without parental guidance, we would act like infant animals. Can you imagine what it would be if as an infant you were left to your own devices without someone cleaning your body after passing urine and stool, without someone feeding you routinely, with no supervised baths.

For these services we are indebted to others and should always be appreciative. But it does not mean that these others have to patronize the lifestyle we prefer. Somehow, we should appreciate these people, render reciprocal services to them whenever possible.

Sharing Meditation Experiences

I received an email in which a student explained that he did not post his meditation experiences because of being neophyte and to suppress on false pride. Both of these are important reasons not to tote one's advancements. One should maintain humility and not take to the role of a teacher just for ambition's sake.

There is however another side to this, which is that once one gets an instruction from a yoga teacher, one should do the best to comply with it. For instance, suppose I ask someone to keep a dream journal. The person may be disinclined or may feel that there can be a benefit in doing that. Or there may be negative energy in the person's psyche which causes him to be discouraged even for a small chore like keeping a dream journal and filling reports in it every time the body awakens from sleep.

Why stick to a commitment to keep a journal? We find that in the history of spiritual teachers, there was always commitments which students maintained.

Why be obligated to a teacher? Why even bother to do what the teacher suggests?

False pride in accomplishments, is real. False pride suppresses advancement. It erases it. But that does not mean that everything one does is motivated by false pride, especially when it comes to complying with the request of the yoga guru. Suppose I decided that in order to decrease false pride, I would no longer file these experiences, and I would no longer publish books, because there is a possibility that I made mistakes in some writings.

What will happen? How many people will I deprive of spiritual advancement?

I do not feel that ego and pride are reasons not to share experiences. It is better to give the experiences and then later to say that it was misunderstood or to say that one is uncertain of the significance, than not to share the experiences.

Meditation Experience

After about four to five months of meditation practice a student visualized a large gyrating disc as big as his height. He saw this even with open eyes. This was visible even while he walked around at home. This happened on couple of occasions, but when he blinked the eyelids several times the gyrating disc disappeared. He ignored this incident thinking that he hallucinated.

Later, on another occasion, when he was half-asleep, he again saw the gyrating disc which pulled him towards it with very great force. When he went through it, he was drawn towards a long tunnel travelling at a high speed. When he reached the end of tunnel, he viewed a scenery near a beach on one occasion, and an old temple on another occasion. When he resumed physical consciousness, he experienced heightened awareness.

Is this a third eye experience or intellect? He did not see an eye or a bay window during these meditations.

Again, on another occasion when he sped through the long tunnel suddenly, he was interrupted. Someone called his name. Halfway through the tunnel, he resumed physical consciousness. This time in his forehead between the eyebrows he saw a bright light like a blazing sun. There was a pleasant feeling. It lasted for the whole day. Is this the core-self?

It is definitely not the third eye. The third eye does not get that big. It is never the size of your full body height. This could be one of two things.

- Another being's complete aura
- A time warp entrance to another dimension.

My hunch is that this is another being's completely aura. This happens if one is transited into a higher dimension. The energy is on the same plane as elevated beings. One perceives one of them in the form of the person's aura. Just as we have physical signatures, we have psychic signatures or forms. This person has a divine form which has limbs and senses but the student perceived only the psychic aura.

The gyrating disc is neither the third eye or the intellect but all the same he perceived it by looking through both the orb and the third eye. In this case he went through a dimensional vortex and was translated into another dimension on a beach and then near an old temple which was on this earth or somewhere else in another dimension. Usually we take it for granted that these places were places one lived in a previous life. Or they were places where one met spiritual guides previously.

The heightened awareness after returning to the physical body, means that the subtle body was still surcharged so that even when it was resynchronized into the sluggish physical system and it was lowered to match that body, still the high charge of the experience remained. He experienced the high energy even when the physical body resumed full operation.

The best way to see the third eye is to not chase after it and to be open-minded about it. It may open and not open in the form of an eye. An open mind helps to have an attitude of "Let it happen." as compared to one of "I will make it happen."

When he saw a bright light like a blazing sun in the forehead between the eyebrows. That was not the core-self. In the first place, the coreSelf is the viewer. While viewing this it would not see itself nor see itself reflected. It will feel itself as the observing presence. What was observed on this occasion is the cosmic intellect (cosmic buddhi). There is a similar light which is called cosmic sense of identity (cosmic ahankara). There is yet another light which is called cosmic kundalini or sutram.

Then there is another light, the ultimate light which is the cosmic spirit or supersoul, supreme being (param atma).

In this experience, I assume that the blazing light was outside the third eye chakra. If it was inside that chakra between the intellect and the third eye, that is another experience.

Usually one will look through several psychic organs to see that blazing light.

Here is the sequence of interlocking visions:

- first you must look through your coreSelf
- secondly you must look through your sense of identity when it is in a neutral state
- thirdly you must look through the intellect
- and lastly through the third eye

Since he looked through these four components, he did not see any of the components as objects even though each is a psychic or spiritual object, but he could see other objects.

Why did I say it is cosmic buddhi?

The reason is that if you see the cosmic sense of identity you cannot see it by looking through the third eye and/or the intellect. When the cosmic sense of identity becomes visible, it strikes the sense of identity directly without going through the analytical orb or third eye. In fact, it is such a subtle light that it cannot be perceived by the intellect or the third eye. These are of a lower frequency. The same goes for the cosmic self or Supreme Being, in that even the sense of identity cannot perceive that, because that is transcendental to the sense of identity. Any of these perceptions is an advanced samadhi state.

Initially when the individual spirits are let loose in this cosmos or when they find themselves to be existing here, they find themselves partitioned with a kundalini, an analytical orb and a sense of identity. These psychic organs are awarded to each spirit. The organs come from a cosmic pool of such organs which if seen would be a bright blinding cosmic light. Yogis use these lights to surcharge the kundalini, analytical orb and sense of identity with a high level of energy.

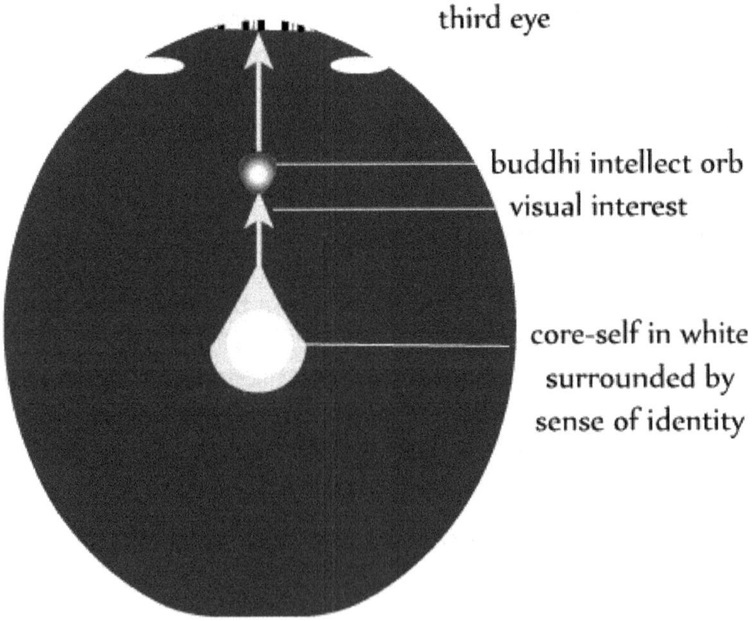

The diagram shows coreSelf surrounded on all sides by sense of identity. Vision energy from sense of identity travels through the intellect, and then travels through the third eye chakra into other dimensions or into this dimension.

Usually when one sits to meditate, one experiences quietness and spatial consciousness without definitions or formations. When there are definitions and clarity of an environment or communication and perception of supernatural beings, that happens to someone who practiced extensively in a past life, where the result of those intense efforts is in the subconscious area of consciousness and somehow it suddenly leaks into the objective awareness.

Since one is not aware of achievements from past lives, all this seems to be new and special. It is like when a person who is a great musician has dimentia. That persons becomes like an ordinary person who can neither read nor compose music. That person forgets the achievements and abandons the status and does not know how to respond if he is taken to his musical instrument.

Sometimes for some reason the dementia slackens for a day or an hour and for that time, the person begins playing with skill again.

Activities and achievements from the past life travel with us to another life. Most of it is subconscious, like the mass of ice which is below an iceberg. Having forgotten acts from the past and being excited about current events, we prance like silly children who find themselves in an amusement park.

To recap the past achievements, one should do meditation. Gradually over time, the past nature will reassert itself. One will have some understanding of why one took another physical body, and what one should do in the new life.

Taking a new body is like going to sleep for some years, say twenty years and then waking up with no memory of what was done before, waking with the idea that one is a new being, that one recently began existing. It is similar to the trees in the northern regions. They freeze and subsequently quit growing for some months When they bud in the spring, they have no idea that they existed last summer. Nature senses the warmth of spring. The plants begin growing again, budding, leafing and flowering but again winter comes. They cease growing again.

One repeatedly emerges in the creation as an embryo. With enthusiasm, one becomes excited. One experiences the newness of a growing body but again in the elderly years, one notices the reduction in liveliness, which concludes with death. One is forced from the new body. One endures the same forgetful trance stage during the creation of the new embryo. One becomes a child again.

One may see a blue-white star in third eye area, but it usually appears as a small dot at a distance. It may approach one or sparkle. It may move away from one. One may see white radiance or light coming from the top of the head.

The coreSelf is not seen objectively as another object or reality. One should realize that in perceiving anything one peers through the coreSelf. It is like being the filament of a bulb. In that case the brilliance shines beyond the filament into the environment. To see another object, the filament must look through its energy field, and then look through the space around that.

Assume therefore that the object seen is not the core-self, it is something else. coreSelf usually does not see itself. White radiance at the top of the head is usually the brahmrandra crown energy emanation. It is accompanied by bliss consciousness and spontaneous absorption.

The blue star or dot, is at the third eye. It leads one to the chit akasha sky of consciousness. This star is illusive. It is most difficult to stabilize. Usually it recedes from the yogi. When he tries to focus, it quickly disappears.

One objective is to keep focus on this star, and to either draw close to it or bring it closer. Sometimes suddenly the yogi is drawn into and through this star into the chit akasha sky of consciousness.

An advanced meditation practice is to stare at this star for minutes or hours as much as one is permitted. One does this from within the psyche, within the mind space where supernatural objects and dimensions are perceived.

Part 7

Kundalini Arousal during Sleep

Kundalini can be aroused at anytime, anywhere and also for any reason. In yoga we deliberately energize kundalini once we understand how to infuse it. Besides that, during excitement or dreams, kundalini may be infused at any time. It may be aroused when bending the body or standing suddenly.

A sudden flash of lightning and also loud cosmic crashing sounds may be heard when the subtle body switches from one dimension to another. These may be frightening initially but a yogi can get used to this. The fear is experienced when this happens without blissful feelings. If there is bliss saturation the yogi feels secure, while if there is no bliss consciousness, the yogi may be frightened. A limited self is not unlimited. When it is confronted by something colossal, it may be frightened.

Sometimes when the cosmic situation shuts down or a portion of it is demolished there are huge explosions in outer space. A limited entity becomes frightened fearing destruction. From *Bhagavad Gita* we hear that the limited self, atma, though limited, is eternal. Still, we find that a brave person may get the shivers in an earthquake or on a battlefield.

Once when this body was about 14 years of age, I travelled on a ship from Guyana to Martinique. Suddenly there were rogue waves. There was no rain but suddenly the sea was violent. The ship went through some large waves. Even seasoned sailors got scared. Every sailor except for a few in the engine room came to the bridge where the steering controls were.

Suddenly as if out of nowhere there was a large wave that washed over the ship. The ship was insignificant to that wave but the captain who had some experience stared the vessel perpendicularly into the wave. The ship went through the wave and came out behind it and resurfaced. We felt that we were finished but since the captain was experienced with the sea, he had no fear of it.

After that everyone was relieved. We glanced at each other like people who returned from death. If the wave had hit the vessel broadside, it would have been the end. Everyone realized that their confidence in life was illusory. It is irrational to be confident that life will go on because there is a greater power which can remove it at any moment. Security in a physical body is an illusion.

Sometimes when the galaxy is demolished, some yogis like Markandeya consciously survive the experience. They transit to a parallel galaxy but for the most part, everyone else except the major deities became existentially suspended or disabled. Later after billions of years, when there is a cosmic initiation, the entities become conscious with no understanding that they existed in a previous creation.

While meditating one may hear loud cosmic noises which are scary. Or it may be blissful, expansive and desirable. These occurrences are experiences due to the various levels of the subtle body.

On kundalini:

The practice of pranayama which is the fourth stage of yoga is the process for altering kundalini. In fact, by this process one can get rid of kundalini, or stated differently one can be elevated out of the realm of kundalini's control. Usually as human beings or as animals, we have little control of kundalini. It exercises a great influence over us. But kundalini can be better regulated and then transmuted and eliminated by the proper yoga practice in the fourth stage of pranayama breath infusion.

Kundalini is not the coreSelf. It is an accessory to that self. The intellect as a psychic tool is not the spiritual self. It too is an accessory to the self. Science denies the existence of a mind and regard it only as an electro-biological something, but in astral projection we find that we have an intellect. We have a mind. This means that there is a subtle mind which compliments the physical brain. Since we can think during astral projection, we can know for sure that we have an intellect which is psychic, and which is not the physical brain. But if a person has not experienced astral projection that person's doubt about the subtle body is acceptable.

Patanjali gave the first major accomplishment of yoga as a segregation of the coreSelf and the psychic perception equipment. Kundalini is one of the perception tools. It is a crude apparatus but it will do because if you are a caveman using a stone axe is just as significant as a modern person using a laser beam.

Kundalini is crude. Its main concerns are survival and reproduction. If a lifeform becomes aware of itself somewhere, it acts to survive. As soon as it feels that it will survive for a time, it develops urges to reproduce. Once it achieves that it moves on to experience the environment in which it found itself. That is what kundalini is about. But the spiritual self, eventually realizes that kundalini takes it on a wild goose chase. Thus, the effort is made to resist kundalini's influence.

If kundalini must be relied on for higher awareness and access to higher dimensions, that may never be because kundalini is disinclined for that. That is why a yogi endeavors to raise kundalini on a daily basis. If one relies on kundalini to get one to a better place and a higher level of consciousness, one will never achieve that.

Kundalini / Influence and Control

Kundalini is the psycho-biological mechanism which regulates the body. It is such that when there is no physical body, kundalini resorts to being a psychic mechanism. It returns to its biological life as soon as a specific spirit is fused into the feelings of its would-be parents.

In this post I will explain how to change kundalini during day to day activities, just by talking to kundalini as if it were a person. Actually, in normal usage when we say that someone is a person, we are really speaking about kundalini as the person, because the coreSelf is only a power supply for kundalini. The coreSelf is used by kundalini. You can talk to kundalini, believe it or not.

The first psychic organ to respond was the kundalini. But this was not seen by the intellect because the kundalini operates in secrecy. The kundalini executes covert actions, such that even the intellect has no idea of kundalini operations. The senses even though these emerged with the intellect, are under the influence of kundalini. The senses conspire with kundalini to hide psychic activities and feeling motions from the intellect.

Kundalini, once it gets information from the senses, became excited because that is what kundalini is about. But the kundalini did not show this excitement to the intellect. It learnt over time that the intellect cannot be trusted. Unlike the senses, the intellect is resistant to kundalini and wants to censor what the kundalini approves. Thus, the kundalini found ways of influencing the intellect without letting the intellect know it is affected.

In the meantime, the dependent coreSelf does not have the details of these operations. It cannot directly perceive anything in the physical or psychic planes. It is reliant of the sense of identity, which in turn depends on the intellect. which is under the influence of the senses, memory and kundalini.

As soon as kundalini gets information from the senses and hides it from the coreSelf, the enthusiasm to pursue that interest is reinforced. Kundalini sends a flash message to the eye telling it to be on the lookout for subjects of interest.

At the same time kundalini sends a message to the intellect but it is a covert communication. Thus, the intellect does not know that it is influenced. It perceived sensual data and checks in the memory for related incidences.

At this point the core begins to understand what happened. It may try to stop the operation. The core may stop the intellect from getting images from the memory. It may turn about and say to kundalini, "Do not pursue this. This disrupts meditation. Cease this."

Just with that mental speech kundalini may retract the interest. It may retrieve the flash energy with which it initially pierces the intellect.

The Covered coreSelf

In meditation this morning I studied the various sheaths or surrounding covers which veil the coreSelf. These sheaths are necessary in the core's effort to identify and interpret actions of the psychic equipment and the objects on the various mental and emotional levels of existence.

For the purpose of yoga however, one should study these sheaths and withdraw the coreSelf's energy from them. This results in isolating the coreSelf from the equipment, giving the self an opportunity to consider its predicament in conjunction with the various perception tools.

Using the example of a foundry worker who carries molten metal from a cauldron to small molds, we can see that the worker must use a fire-proof glove. In fact, the glove has several layers of asbestos-like materials which can resist intense heat. The first realization is that the hand of the foundry worker cannot in any circumstance directly make contact with the molten material. Similarly, the first admittance of the self is that it cannot under any circumstance make direct contact with physical energy.

Contact is made indirectly only. It is this indirect contact that is the problem. Even though the molten metal is dangerous, still because of the desire to have metallic materials the foundry worker must risk the danger. Due to desires the coreSelf is forced to associate with physical and psychic reality. These desires are not necessarily thought-out or constructed by the core. For instance, in the case of the foundry worker, he may not need the metallic utensils which he manufactures and still his desire energy is involved in the production.

Let us say for example that the desires for the materials are those of the king and queen. The foundry man is a peasant. He has no need for swords for an army, and no need for dainty jewels to adorn his wife's body. And still desires are involved, even though they are not his personal needs. Because he was born as a peasant, he has no alternative but to do what the king says. If he refuses, he may be confined in the king's prison.

The self may not need the facilities and involvements of physical nature. Yet, it found itself involved and finds that it must participate in the theatre of the world.

The foundry worker can figure that he does not desire the metallic creations and still that knowledge may not free him from the employment of the king. He must work regardless. A yogi may investigate into how the coreSelf is connected to material nature but that same yogi may remain involved nevertheless. We must agree that initially the understanding of how we are connected will not necessarily free us from the involvements.

In the investigation, first the foundry worker should examine the outermost layer of the glove and then work backwards to the innermost layer and then reach the skin of the hand. How many layers are there in the glove?

How is the heat of foundry transmitted through the layers and then is felt as warmth in the hand?

How is the clenching action of the fingers transmitted outward through the layers of the glove resulting in dipping into the molten material, and lifting some out in the laden. What purpose does each layer of the glove serve, in terms of transmitting the clenching action of the hand or reducing the impact of the intense heat which flows from the foundry to the hand?

During meditation, I segregated the attention power of the self which went through the sense of identity and then through the intellect and then though the sensual energy of the kundalini and then though the brow chakra. The attention energy is of interest. It flickers from the coreSelf into the sense of identity. This energy activates the sense of identity sensing apparatus which in turn activates the intellect, which in turn energizes the sensual energy. The result of this is social involvement in the world.

For the purpose of inSelf yoga™, this social involvement should be denied so that the self can use its energy to reach higher levels of existence, thus freeing itself from being imprisoned on lower planes.

Kundalini's Base of Dispersal

Kundalini assumed the base chakra as its hometown. It did this soon after the sperm particle became embedded in the mother's egg. At that time, it had two anchor points one which became the placenta and the other being within the developing embryo itself.

Since it was configured it can change. We know that the placenta anchor is lost to kundalini as soon as the mother's system ceases transfusion of blood to the embryo. This happens during parturition when the fetus is delivered. To replace the mother's nourishment, kundalini switches its anchor to the lungs and to the sucking impulse in the body of the infant.

If there is enough infusement kundalini is forced to either rise while remaining at the base, or it may be forced to leave the base temporarily. A person is rated as a siddha when the kundalini becomes completely detached from the base and is resident in the head.

Siddha means that the person is no longer in the survival business, because the psychic mechanism which runs that concern is no longer operating in the subtle body.

If a yogi reduces the need for physical existence, when doing breath infusion, kundalini will lose its interest in the survival method. It will jump to higher chakras where it can find support from the self.

Even though a person taking a material body, must use a subtle form which has a kundalini, still at the time of fusion into the feelings of the parents, that kundalini changes in configuration to that of a sperm particle. Or stated more precisely, the entire subtle body shrinks to the size and shape of a sperm particle.

In a sense Charles Darwin's idea about the life forms developing one into the other, occurs for each of us when we take a human embryo. The first form that of the sperm particle acts like a soft bodied aquatic creature. Gradually it mutates and alters to that of a mammal.

Two Yogis Curse Each Other

During practice this morning as I did a procedure given by a Buddha Deity in South Korea and by Rishi Singh Gherwal,

Muktananda came and demonstrated a small detail which is part of the same technique. These are end of life practices used by yogis when providence threatens to kill the body.

If the yogi exhausted time and cannot attain the siddha state before being evicted from the body, he must hasten and set his subtle body so that he can continue the practice after being deprived of the body. More or less that is my condition.

I went to Guyana around 2003 to do end-of-life austerities, but providence acted in several ways to ruin that plan. Now I roll like a stone which cannot find a place to settle as it moves down hill.

The only thing to do now is to be sure that my subtle body is not compulsive to take an embryo soon after the death of the physical system. To achieve that, I must change the direction of the attractive force in the subtle body. Usually this force is attracted to sex facility and to hormonal energy. By that attraction one is again pulled into a mother's uterus soon after leaving the physical form.

On the astral side this morning, for some reason, Muktananda came. He said this:

"Crush the light! Compress the light there! Do not worry about getting the light to there!"

Soon after this within seconds Yogi Bhajan arrived. Muktananda pointed to him and said this, "He said he was a better yogi. He said he was a master of kundalini. Did he ever show any disciple that? He was unaware of it."

Yogi Bhajan made this reply, "What do you know about what I know? Disciples are not shown every last detail. We leave room for others. We are not like you. We do not covet disciples."

After this they left. Regarding if this was a jest or not is hard to tell. Sometimes mahayogins go at it. As a disciple I am not concerned. But there might be a serious side to this, who knows?

Here is an elaboration of the instruction from Muktananada:

The infused energy which accumulates below the navel should be crushed or pushed down into the lower trunk. It should be compressed there and not be permitted to rise up the spine.

This instruction contradicts the usual process of raising kundalini. Muktananda told me in a mental message afterwards that this is a secret technique coming from Chaurangi a great siddha who is long deceased. This technique was also known to some Tibetan Masters.

Once the yogi infuses the lower trunk of the body and in the subtle form the energy there turns into light energy (light as in sunlight) the yogi should put a downward pressure on that energy to compress it into the lower trunk. As this is done the yogi will notice that the light energy is compressed. The rays of light become shorter and shorter.

In kundalini practice, usually the effort is to raise the energy through the spine into the brain but Muktananda gave a contrary advice which is to not let the energy go up the spine but the compress it downward, forcing the light to become shorter and shorter and more intense in the lower trunk, thighs, legs and feet.

Muktananda spoke into my head:

As far as kundalini is concerned getting it into the head is a basic requirement for yogis, but in the advanced stage that is no achievement. One should tackle the other parts of the psyche which will if not purified, cause the yogi to take another body haphazardly.

Yogi Bhajan is okay. His system is valid. It is just that he used to criticize me. I took that opportunity to harass him. It is nothing serious.

The person Chaurangi was a Nath siddha. Formerly he was a prince but his stepmother is alleged to set up a situation where his arms and legs were amputated. Somehow, he was rescued by Matsyendranath who places him in the care of Gorakshnath, who taught him the hatha yoga practice. By a blessing from Gorakshnath for completing the practice to perfection, Chaurangi's limbs were restored. He was the master of kumblaka, breath infusion and retension practice.

Student inquiry:

What are the end-of-life austerities that should be performed so that one does not take another body after death? If a person has sincerely practiced pranayam and meditation through the adult life until death, should that not facilitate hereafter?

Author's Response:

The *end of life* austerities are those which would cause kundalini to leave the body through one of the head chakras. Usually kundalini leaves through base, sex or navel chakra. When it does this, the coreSelf follows to a lower plane in the astral world.

If kundalini is trained to relocate into the head before death, and if that is its habit the yogi would go to a higher plane. He may avoid a haphazard rebirth.

It is true that if a person practiced pranayama and meditation consistently until death, that should help to facilitate his resistance to rebirth.

However, it is not a specific thing because it would depend on what pranayama and meditation that person performed and as to the effectiveness of the practice.

For instance, in Christianity, there are statements guaranteeing heaven in the hereafter with Christ, provided the person accepts Christ as Lord and Savior. The same type of guarantee is offered by other religions like Islam in relation to the Prophet Muhammad. In Hinduism many sects offer similar guarantees in relation to Shiva, or Krishna or Devi.

But this is different, because one person might sincerely practice pranayama and meditation and still fail to resist rebirth hereafter. Whatever the yogi does, it is only good in so far as it is an effective method which upgrades his or her psyche.

A person might spend a lifetime using an inefficient method. He or she may be sincere and still that person may get a low result after death. Sincerity alone is no guarantee. The method of pranayama and meditation has to effectively yield elevation, then we can vouch for it.

Successful Astral Projection

Pranayama breath infusion is the ideal way to energize the psyche so that it stops the thoughts constructions. The standard method is not to watch the breath or to watch the thoughts or to try to ignore the thoughts. Instead of using these methods, even the one using a mantra, one should do the breath infusion which shifts the subtle body to a higher plane of consciousness where the chitta-vrittis image-thoughts presentations cease. Make this the standard method of thought removal.

Pranayama is not for lazy people because it takes energy to do it. One must endeavor with it before one sits to relax and meditate. That takes energy but it is the method for yogis who agree to follow the ashtanga eight-staged process.

Timing in the astral encounters is vital. This will eventually give the yogi a feel for astral time scenes. In the astral, sometimes one experiences a lifetime in five minutes or it may seem to going on forever, while only five minutes transpired in physical time. This is another problem with subtle existence. It is a reason why we become attached to the physical world which has a reliable time sequence which does not slow down, speed up, jolt and bolt. Study of how time operates on the astral levels is part of the preparation to leave here at the time of death.

On earth, we have tides at sea with the swelling and shrinking of the ocean. Science informs that this is operated mostly by the pull of the moon. Within twenty-four hours one can experience two tidal fluctuations.

The astronomers explain that on some planets which have liquids, there might be several more tidal cycles in a day and on others, tidal cycles may not even exist because of the lack of moons.

In the astral world however sometimes, the tide rises fifty feet within five seconds and then it drops or disappears altogether. It is not as linear as it is physically. This again is part of the reason why people prefer physical existence because it is reliable in reference to the rapid changes which the astral existence expresses.

Astral Beings

There are the two classes of beings whom a yogi should associate with. These are the siddhas and the deities like Krishna or Shiva. Siddhas are persons who are not in the Godhead status but who are spiritually realized and spiritually evolved. As far as the deities are concerned trying to contact them from this end of existence is impractical. They are so far away existentially from the human condition of consciousness, that one cannot generate the energy level required to make contact with them.

If any contact occurs it will have to be that they made the effort and that is not likely. In the *Anu Gita* we hear that Arjuna begged for access to the supernatural and divine planes of existence where those deities reside, but Krishna rejected the plea. If for Arjuna they are unwilling to give the revelation or darshan (Sanskrit), then it is unreasonable to expect such favors.

Even if a deity reaches someone, it would mean that the deity energized the person's psyche since only by that can one perceive the deity. After the energization, there may be no repeat. One will be stranded with only physical and lower astral access.

There are many stories in the *Puranas* of devotees of particular deities and also of aspiring siddhas who saw particular deities but once only in a particular life time and only after superhuman austerity.

It may be argued that in Arjuna's case he did not have to do austerities and yet he made contact with the Universal Form Supervisory Personalities and with the four-handed divine form of Krishna as *Vasudeva* or *Narayana.* Actually, this is not true. If you read the *Mahabharata* which is the text from which the *Bhagavad Gita* was extracted, you will read that before the battle Arjuna did perform gruesome austerities in the Himalayas. These were such legendary deprivations that Shiva appeared and challenged Arjuna. Then Arjuna even went to the Indraloka celestial astral paradise which is mentioned in the *Anu Gita* as the place of *Shatakratu*.

Arjuna performed austerities, even though those disciplines are not mentioned in the *Bhagavad Gita*. Persons who never read the *Mahabharata* are left with the false assumption that Arjuna was no yogi but only a devotee.

The second feature that qualifies Arjuna for the revelations and apparitions is not his friendship with Krishna but his assignment from the universal form to function on the battle field to discipline the corrupt members of the Kuru political dynasty.

The other group of people whom one should meet is the siddhas. With these there are different barriers to their association. The first fence is that these people are antisocial. In order to reserve themselves for more spiritual advancement and to maintain the relationship with their teachers and deities, these persons are not free to associate with any and everybody, even with persons who desire spiritual advancement and who are willing to practice the methods of release.

Let us discuss one person, whom is Babaji. He is famous as the leading teacher in the kriya yoga successions. His name is mentioned by Paramhansa Yogananda in the book *Autobiography of a Yogi*. With Babaji there is a rule. He is never found by anyone. He finds a person if he desires to communicate with that individual. Searching for him in the astral world is a lost cause. One will never find him. If he wants to see someone, that person will see him, hear or be inspired within the psyche to do techniques which he releases into it.

Some teachers like Yogesh who wrote *Science of the Soul* and *First Steps to Higher Yoga,* books everyone should read, have gone to the causal plane. Reaching him is useless unless he first released himself from that level because on that level no conversation is possible. On that plane everything is latent and non-communicative.

But they are other siddhas like Yoga Bhajan. These can be reached if one has a strong interest and practices the system of yoga taught by any of these teachers.

A siddha is someone who is no longer a target for consequential energy on this level of existence. Such a person is reluctant to again open a relationship since if a relationship is reactivated, it will be near impossible to suspend it.

No siddha in his right mind will open a consequential account unless he or she is instructed to do so by a higher yogi. If one has no approval of a higher yogi, and if one is stuck on a lower plane of existence, how will one be rescued? A flawed system of self-realization cannot free one from material existence.

People who are sensible take risks if they are covered by higher ups, not otherwise. Only foolish people take risk with no coverage or with guarantees from ordinary entities.

There is one thing that helps considerable and that is continuous non-stop reading of books like *Bhagavad Gita.* Constantly reading those books gives one a high probability of meeting siddhas in the astral world. The other thing that helps much is continuous practice.

I will share a hint. I have not seen Babaji for some time. There were periods in this life when I saw him frequently. Astrally, I used to find myself where he was in the Himalayas.

There was a time when I was with his band of siddha-disciples in the astral world. We sat together around him. We did meditations which he inspired to each person separately. There was a time when I noticed how he assisted those who did yoga but who did not know he rendered assistance.

When those persons would do meditation, the practice gave a vapor energy. It rose through the astral atmosphere. Babaji saw it rising. This is how he knew who practiced and whom he should assist.

The secret with the siddhas is that if one consistently practices whatever little one knows, they become aware of it. They will look in one's direction, check one's psyche and act to assist one.

One may desire to go to them but that is a crazy idea because that would mean that one's psyche is first energized to the level they reside. It is not just a matter of desire. If one's psyche becomes energized sufficiently one will move up notches in the astral realms and one will be with them but desire alone means very little.

There is an example from my life which shows how searching for siddhas in the astral planets is a complete sham. I met Authur Beverford around 1969-1970 at Clark Air Base gym near Angeles City in the Philippines. I was desperate to take formal instructions in yoga. Three years prior to that I had some flash-backs of some of my past lives as a yogi in northern India and Tibet. I felt an urgency to reinstate the practice. Beverford, even though he was a disciple of Rishi Singh Gherwal, was primarily focused on a Japanese martial arts practice.

Soon after I met Beverford, around 1972-73, he returned to the USA and was living in Ventura, California. I went there. He gave me the entire set of Rishi Singh Gherwal books. Many of these books are out of print. The ones that are available have an ancient form of English and does not use a full English vocabulary.

I was highly impressed with two of those books one was about postures and the other was about Markandeya Yogi who was swallowed into a supernatural body of Krishna and who lived in that body like a little virus for thousands of years and was then spat out by the deity. This was a small booklet, but it was an extract from the Mahabharata.

After I read that book, I knew that the deity had the key to the whole thing. Without his assistance one is nothing. Without his information, one will never understand what happens here.

Beverford also gave me a set of Rishi's books called, *Great Masters of the Himalayas*. Rishi told Beverford that Yogananda used those books to create his successful book, *Autobiography of a Yogi*. Once when I was with Beverford he saw that I read Yogananda's book. He said this, "Just for your information, Rishi went to examine his body days after his death. Rishi who was an expert pranayama yogi, did not find any sign of non-corruptibility. That declaration was a farce as far as Rishi was concerned."

Rishi was in California when Yogananda passed on. Rishi taught hatha yoga in Santa Barbara.

After this I became determined to meet Rishi in the astral world. This determination continued for years from 1973 till about 1979. After searching for him in the astral time, in the days when I used to astral project frequently and my third eye was active, I ceased searching. I came to the conclusion that he was either not wanting to deal with me or he had left and entered the causal zone and had completely deleted traces of his existence here. After this I abandoned the search. I was tired of trying to locate him.

When I began looking for him, I got in touch with Yogi Bhajan who gave me the techniques which I needed. Sometimes one gets the techniques and do not realize that one has what one needs.

But it was only in the last two years or so that Rishi came to talk to me. How many years is it now since 1973? That is more than thirty-five years.

When a siddha wants to find someone, it may occur immediately but when one desires to find a siddha, it may never happen anyway.

Astral World After Death

Last night my subtle body was pulled into a parallel world where some persons live during the interim period between leaving a physical body and getting an embryo. One person who is not deceased was present. He made plans for a residence. This person has class status currently on this planet.

This person wanted me to assist in constructing an astral residence which was up to par with the class status needs. In that dimension some who were already deceased lived in low status buildings but this person did not want to live like that. He wanted to construct a high-class large residence with smooth inner walls, brightly painted colors and various types of décor.

The whole thing is ridiculous because in the astral world whatever one needs can be constructed by mental commands. One does not have to hire anyone. One does not have to engage servants from a lower status. One does not need laborers toiling in factories so that one can become a millionaire from making profits from their labor.

These attitudes and profiles for wealth are not necessary in the astral world. Still, a person who is habituated to exploiting on earth carries to the afterlife the same attitude and tries to re-enact the same vicious hypocritical lifestyle of some wealthy people on earth.

Being self-righteous but totally ignorant of the larger realities in the astral dimensions, some people think that everything is based on physical endeavor. In the astral world such ideas have no validity.

No one has to work to acquire money in the astral existence. People in the heavenly world, in the celestial astral regions have so much opulence that a rich person on earth who has billions is like a nasty bug in comparison. And yet those heavenly residents have not worked one day to get the wealth.

This planet is the place for working. In the heavenly dimensions, no one lives like this to acquire wealth.

Wealthy people on earth cannot explain how this earth came about and why there are resources in one location and not in every other place. Why is there gold in one place under one's man house and not under another.

People cannot explain these things. Still, they feel they know why one man deserved wealth and why someone else works day and night for very little salary.

A yogi should know that there are basically two problems to solve before leaving the physical body for good. These are the internal and external environments. The internal environment is the psyche which is usually called the mind or the being or even the self. It is not the self but those who cannot detect the psychic components consider the mind or psyche to be the self.

In any case if one feels it is the self, then one should understand that self before death. If one perceives that the self exists in a psyche or in a mind space, then one has should research that.

The other aspect which many meditators either think is irrelevant or think that it is an illusion is the external environment in which one will find oneself in the afterlife. There will be an external environment because at no stage will a limited self become the total existence, no matter how adept that self is at mergence in consciousness.

Thus, a yogi should investigate the subtle external environment he or she will reside in the afterlife. Both aspects, the internal environment and the external subtle one, requires investigation.

On which astral plane will one transit to in the afterlife?

In this life one found the self to be with a name as Jim Smith or Joan Ovid, and as a physical body with responsibilities. What will it be in the afterlife? Where will one reside?

In this body, one needs an education, job and family? What will one need in the afterlife? Will one be required to build a house, get a mortgage and have a college degree?

Will one be in a disadvantaged ethnicity in the afterlife? Or will it be in a subtle body with privileges? Will there be slavery in the astral environment? Will it have a democracy with a bill of rights?

Will the parents feed one cooked animal bodies? Will the parents be like cave people who ate raw meat?

Pranotthana Kriya / Swami Rama

Last night in the astral world, I had an encounter with another person from the early part of the life of this body. This again is an omen about the upcoming death of this body. This is a signpost which states: "You will soon be evicted from the form. Heed these warnings."

The person I met was an acquaintance from the early stage of this body. That person wanted to hash over incidences from the past. I avoided that and simply mentioned the subject of our upcoming eviction from old bodies. The person was uncertain about where we would go and whom we would meet. That person said, "Since up to now there was little or no experience of an astral heaven, my assumption is that religion is invalid. Heaven may be there but we cannot verify it. What is our situation? We will again be babies here or there. We may be wandering ghosts on the invisible astral domains."

Soon after this, it was time to do the before-dawn session of breath infusion. I rose to do that. This person followed me on the astral side and did some of the practice, doing whatever I did. Previously around 1974, this person was shown these practices by me, but he ceased the effort. Now he thinks that perhaps the practice should be maintained.

About this time Swami Rama came in his astral body. For some reason he was in a happy mood. He wanted to check on my agnisara abdomen infusion practice.

This is a technique which a yogi is supposed to master before leaving the body. If this is done successfully the yogi will not have to take a haphazard rebirth. Instead if the yogi has to take another body, if fate decrees that as mandatory, the yogi could select the new parents and plan a way to again curtail the usual social life and continue yoga practice in the new body as soon as the body reaches maturity and the parental influence wanes.

As I practiced, Swami Rama looked into my subtle form. He made some recommendation. It was like looking into a person's body using X-ray vision where one sees the organs in the body and how they operate. Swami Rama instructed that I should focus on the foot spark practice for some time until the feet were shocked out.

This foot spark practice entails blasting breath infusion through the center of the leg into the foot. There is a subtle pipe in the subtle body which runs along the leg just as the leg bone runs in the center of the physical leg. A yogi, if he can reach this pipe, should breath-infuse it so that the infused force blows from the knee downwards into the foot. When the infused breath reaches the foot, if the yogi can push it out of the tube it will make sparks in the foot.

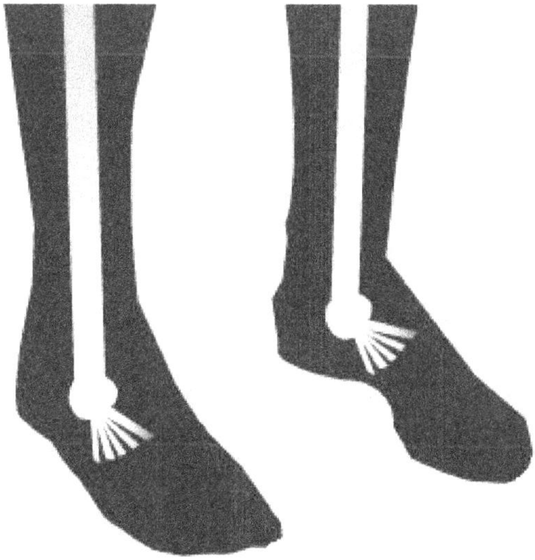

Agnisara practice is usually described as a navel exercise, consisting of muscular rupturing turns of the stomach region, but to complete the practice, one must change the energy from the navel downwards to the toes.

Kundalini yoga as it is commonly practiced concerns the spinal column, having to do with energy moving up the spine into the brain. When this is mastered the yogi will find that there is an added practice, which is infusing the lower trunk of the body with enthusing astral energy and using the same channels or nadis which kundalini used in the past when the yogi was not causing kundalini to move upwards.

Kundalini is the natural supervisor of energy distribution in the body, both in the physical and astral forms. When a yogi causes kundalini to abandon its creature survival tasks, the yogi must assume some of the routines directly by infusing breath energy (prana) into the various *hard to reach* places of the psyche. The yogi uses the same nadi channels which were designed and used by kundalini previously. This practice is under the general name of *pranotthana*.

Kundalini & Food/Diet

If one lives in an ashram, hermitage of an advanced yogi, one is duty bound to eat what is prepared. In other words, one does not have freedom in diet there. This is similar to when we take a new body. First of all, I was a vegetarian in many past lives. Still in this life, because of the parents I was fated to accept, I had to assume a non-vegetarian diet. After some years, I gradually curbed that habit. I resumed my vegetarian position but not without a struggle. My body was designed with genes which called for a non-vegetarian diet.

Sometimes after entering an ashram, people complain that they have to stick to a diet which is set up by a guru, but they fail to understand that this is the system of how one gets these bodies, since whosoever the mother is, determines what one will eat in the next life. Because one must take nutrients from the mother's blood which courses through the placenta, one will be conditioned to her diet. If she eats flesh one will be conditioned to that. In her uterus, one's body will absorb whatever she consumes.

We know for sure that the infant, once it is born, may not eat flesh. It will get milk but really this milk is only as good as the diet of the mother. If the mother eats fish and beef, her milk is produced from that. The infant is in effect eating fish and beef when suckling the breast.

When I was an infant, I stayed with my mother for the first 3 years.

I was attached to suckling her breast. Even though I was a yogi in my past life, still that instinct for attachment to the mother expressed itself forcefully even though I had no intention of being like that. Subsequently the diet which I preferred in the early part of this body was non-vegetarian.

All yoga practice from previous lives was neutralized through attachment to the female who was my mother. This is our situation. We must honesty look at this and assess the lack of resistance to these influences. Once the body grows and one becomes independent one makes claims but the plain truth is that nature has the upper hand and will use it if and when one assumes the next body. One must eat whatever the parents ingest, even if it is raw fish, even if it is rotted matter.

In yoga we should use our intelligence and find a way to sidestep an outright challenge with nature because if we challenge nature, we will be the losers. Why? Because a limited being cannot be God at any stage. It cannot be supreme at any stage. It is best to recognize the supreme power and even the vast psychic material nature. With nature it is best to be humble and servile.

Instead of trying to set up a special diet, one should practice. The practice will stipulate diet as one advances. Pranayama yogis have a saying:

Prana will show the way.

If one practices, the purification which one gains will inspire improved diet. Instead of calculating what to eat, if one practices sincerely the diet will be controlled by the increased purity.

Someone may wonder, "Why is the yogi eating this? Why is he not enjoying food as others do?"

The answer is that from within the yogi is prompted to eat certain foods due to increased purification in the psyche.

A yogi soon learns to eat to facilitate practice but that applies to those who practice aggressively. Those who are careless and irregular with the practice, do not become controlled by the purity energy in the psyche. They do not become reformed from bad diet.

A yogi eats to facilitate practice, which means that the time of eating should facilitate practice. Even the quantity of eating should compliment practice.

The key is not what one should eat or the quantity but when should one practice and how frequently. If one attends to that the eating habits will automatically be reformed as the practice itself will reform the psyche.

Some people who discover that I do not eat anything heavy after say about 3 pm, become alarmed and wonder why I am such an extremist. They do not believe that such a restriction has spiritual benefit. The point is that if I eat after that my morning session of practice will not be as efficient. During the night my astral awareness will decrease. To facilitate my practice, I cannot eat heavy foods late in the afternoon or at night.

If I want to meet yoga gurus in the astral, if I want to be aware of psychic communication, I must curb late eating which causes a decrease in subtle perception in the separated astral body during sleep.

But it is not that I made a rule. The rule came about from having a consistent morning practice. When I lived in Yogi Bhajan's ashram in Denver around 1973, there was a rule that we had to rise about 4 am and then report for bhastrika breath infusion practice. From then onwards I kept up this habit. Over the years my eating habit came under the control of my practice. The practice dictates what, how and when I eat.

It is not the other way around where my eating habits dictate my practice. I practice sincerely and take my obligation to yoga gurus seriously. One of the things that get in the way of spiritual practice is not being accountable to anyone and feeling that the yoga guru is just anybody. One gets this idea that one does not have to do what the yoga guru recommends. That is permissible if one is not serious about progression along the path which that teacher mastered.

Kundalini is affected by what is eaten as well as by the time it is consumed. The student should observe what takes place in the psyche when he or she eats particular foods at certain times. It is adjusted in reference to how it facilitates practice. If some food causes one to be sluggish or causes one to reduce practice, then one should shift to a diet which compliments practice.

Take an extreme beverage like alcohol. If that is ingested it has a certain effect on kundalini. If the student notices this and then sees that this is not what is desired, he should stop the drinking activity. If you are not living in an ashram you are on your own regarding how to control diet. If one practices daily as instructed by the yoga guru and if you do not make excuses for neglecting practice, naturally and gradually one will be inspired from within the psyche to hedge the diet and reduce parts of it which are constrictive of spiritual advancement.

If the yoga gurus generally state that the best time to practice is before sunrise around 4-6 am, then obviously if one adjusts the life around that certain things will naturally change.

Why the isolation?

A question is:

Why are yogis required to be isolated from social involvements?

The answer is that for a yogi social involvement causes a reduction in spiritual practice. Social involvements mean less spiritual practice and more focus on physical history.

Generally speaking, social association is not concerned with spiritual practice, but it may be conducive to religion and superficial spiritual behavior.

Everything has its price. If the yogi wants to accelerate practice, he or she must reduce social associations.

The way of the material energy is that if something is exposed it is subjected to reactive energies. Any object is open to exploitation either as the predominant exploiter or as the target of the exploitation. This happens to be the way the material energy is oriented. If one puts yogurt in a Petri dish and set it out in the open, it will not be long before bacteria will find and exploit it.

If a yogi is exposed in the social world, it is natural that he or she will be exploited or will be lured into taking an exploiter role over other realities which are disadvantages.

To avoid this one should go into isolation. One should be absent from certain environments. Since everything is reactive in varying degrees, a yogi should not expose himself or herself. One should not test material nature just to see what will happen, because what will occur is predicted by the law of nature for these associations. A yogi cannot benefit from normal social associations because these are incapable of yielding spiritual perception.

If one is not powerful enough to resist a temptation, it is sheer foolishness to expose oneself and then think that one can ignore the temptation. Better to take cover and avoid the reaction or exploitation event altogether.

There is only so much time in one day. It is not that you can adjust the day's duration. That is controlled by the earth's rotation on its axis. A limited being is under the regulation of time. If one avoids confrontations and temptations, one could use the conserved time to proceed with spiritual practice. In that humble way one can make advancement.

It is unreasonable to think that now after this universe developed its course for several billion years (13 billion by estimation of scientists); we will controll the events of time. Such an idea about control is a large chunk of vanity. The fact is that we have to work under time's constraints and with humility make the best use of this opportunity. Even then we are under the gun of time. We do not know how long this show will endure. In a flash suns could burst into the skies. These would fry this planet. Our aspirations would hit the dust. Understanding this, one should be humble and not try to confront or challenge the cosmic energies.

My view is that a yogi should key-in to providence and work with whatever providence throws his or her way as being mandatory social services, regardless of whether the involvement is palatable or unpalatable. In the *Bhagavad Gita,* Arjuna was faced with a very unpalatable situation and Krishna advised Arjuna to take it. To prove the point, Krishna revealed the

Universal Form to show that it was a divinely sanctioned duty which Arjuna was requested to complete.

A yogi should be sensitive enough to know when to take an opportunity and when to carefully avoid one if that is possible. Some things which happen in life are happening of their own accord without anyone particularly desiring them. But a yogi should be prepared for everything while at the same time, taking precautions to avoid much of history.

Initially when one begins meditation, one needs to avoid environments and people who are hostile to the practice. But if one is advanced one can take challenges and confront situations which would stymie a beginner.

As far as testing the effectiveness of spiritual advancement, even without one planning for encounters, one must face circumstances and associations even undesirable ones. Providence will force one to participate even in cases where one is unwilling to do so.

There are differences on the psychic side, where even if a yogi was isolated where no one could reach him, even then he will be hassled with subtle phenomena, psychic presences, which he must deal with. It is not true that merely by becoming physically isolated; one will be isolated to the full extent. It is not so. In fact, if one achieves physical quarantine, one will immediately realize that a decrease in physical contact causes an increase in psychic pressure.

When a yogi goes into isolation his subtle perception increases exponentially. His correspondence with others increases. Furthermore, many experiences which one could derive from the physical side are available on the psychic level.

Let us take a simply instance of sex desire. Suppose a yogi goes into isolation and does not have a sexual partner does that mean that he is restricted from sexual association? It may mean that but it may result in increased sexual indulgence because the subtle body being barred from physical expression, may rebel and cause increase sexual participation.

Isolated development and the application of the progress in real life circumstances, are required. But why should I yogi plan that, when nature has a cast of time and personalities which will manifest around the yogi circumstantially?

Sometimes when a yogi goes into isolation, nature objects. Subsequently, the plan falls apart. Sometime around 2003 I moved to Guyana. I planned for isolation in the tropical forest there. However, nature objected. If nature permitted it, by now I would be a liberated person.

Nature actually threatened me with death of the body if I was to persist in the isolation attempt. I actually got a house in the jungle from a man, who was a wealth lumber merchant, but some persons, who worked for him, stole most of the tools and equipment which were needed to live like that.

As soon as I left that place and was in the process of going to another isolated place, nature sent a man to offer me some land near civilization. I could not refuse that because I saw that nature was not giving me a choice. This is like when a man escapes from prison and he crosses a lonesome road on his way to freedom. He is then stopped by armed police who say to him, "You can turn yourself in or you can run away. It is your choice." Actually, there is no choice because if he runs away the police will shoot him. It is a choice between re-imprisonment or death. The running away part will not happen. It would be prevented by bullets.

Right now, I am in the USA being stuck here and being warned not to make any attempts to escape again to isolation. My choice is to remain isolated even while I am among millions of people. Isolation is the final way out because finally one will have to make up one's mind as to whether one wants to keep transmigrating in temporary bodies.

When he found their association to be distractive in reference to spiritual progress, even a person as great as Buddha slipped away from his disciples. Isolation is a permanent requirement but if one makes progress, I can assure that nature will make it so that one must associate with others to share the techniques.

Dying and Meeting Old Friends

Last night I was given another rap on the knuckles about the upcoming death of the present body. Five persons from the teen years of this body, were suddenly with me in the astral world. These five were friends of mine some years ago. They were sisters and brothers in a family living next door. Two were males with whom I had a close friendship. The three females, their sisters, I did not have much of a relationship with but during the astral encounter it seems that they were more friendly with me than the males.

All of a sudden, the females acted as if I was their intimate boyfriend during those teen years. This meant that their subtle bodies had somehow advanced the relationship to the boyfriend stage. The subtle body can be puzzling in terms of how it processes and even advances emotional energy. A yogi should have insight about this.

One of the females, the one who was the most indifferent and snobbish, was the one who was the pushiest with the romantic feelings. Without her knowledge I checked in her psyche to see how her emotions evolved even in my absence for some forty plus years. This person claimed me as her very own. In wonder, I played along with the circumstance checking to see how her psyche developed its emotional content into that sexual affection.

Luckily as fate would have it, these persons got in touch with me about thirty minutes before my alarm clock ran for doing the early morning exercises. Since they knew that I did yoga even then years ago, I told them that I would depart to do yoga practice. They followed my subtle body to the location of my physical form.

They did whatever I did even though they never did the practice prior. Thirty-five years ago, when they saw me doing these exercises, they considered it to be weird. Now they considered that it has value. The three females were interested when their skin began to tighten as they did the rapid breathing.

The one who claimed me as her special boyfriend earlier flexed her breasts forward to show that her breast was firm due to some rapid breathing.

The others looked at her in amazement. They were also breathing but did not experience the same degree of effects from it.

After this the two brothers came forward. One read books about bhakti yoga. Years ago, he did not take postures and breathe infusion to be anything. Now he complained, "I am not so sure about the bhakti yoga path now. It did not yield the promised results."

I did not comment. Little did he know that bhakti is not bhakti yoga. Bhakti which is impure affection energy cannot give one the results of bhakti which is pure affection.

They wanted to discuss the prospects of us staying together and taking bodies in the same family or same area and country but I expressed a subtle force to suppress the conversation.

Friends are friends but yogis are also yogis. Serious yogis have no use for friends after leaving the body because there a yogi must switch to association with siddhas. I did not get into a conversation because their disappointment would be too much to bear. After this their astral forms disappeared which meant that they were pulled back into their physical bodies.

Dreaming of old friends, of family or class reunions are not necessarily a portend of death

In the *Srimad Bhagavatam* there is a story about *Kamsa*, a ruler in Mathura India during the infancy of Krishna. Kamsa saw various signs about his death. I used Bhaktivedanta's translated English of that tale.

> *Kamsa began to see various kinds of inauspicious signs, both awake and dreaming. When he looked in the mirror, he could not see his head, although the head was actually present. He could see the luminaries in the sky in double, although there was only one set factually. He began to see holes in his shadow, and he could hear a high buzzing sound within his ears. All the trees before him appeared to be made of gold, and he*

could not see his own footprints in dust or muddy clay. In dream he saw various kinds of ghosts being carried in a carriage drawn by donkeys. He also dreamed that someone gave him poison, and he was drinking it. He dreamed also that he was going naked with a garland of flowers and was smearing oil all over his body. Thus, as Kamsa saw various signs of death both awake and sleeping, he could understand that death was certain, and thus in great anxiety he could not rest that night.

As above Kansa was seeing doubles, literally. His vision shifted frequency to the ghost realms. When he would look in a mirror instead of seeing through physical eyes only, his vision energy passed through his ghost body.

He even began to hear naad sound as a loud buzzing in the ears. Because he was transferred to the hereafter, even though he had a physical body, he saw no footprints which are the way the astral body registers in the psychic world. Even though he was a king who rode horses, he saw himself ridding donkeys which were the conveyance of slaves and serfs.

Someone gave him poison. Even though he knew what it was he willingly drank it since fate controlled his life fully. Fate decided that he was no longer an actor of history. Even though he had nihilistic tendencies, *Kamsa* assumed that his death was near. His confidence, his political skill, his efficient protection system against enemies, were absent, as if a powerful agency erased that from the earth's history.

However, the same dreams by someone else may have a different meaning. If someone dreams about meeting friends, it would be a portent only if those friends desired to be together again in the next life and only if they considered that they were to be deprived of their physical bodies shortly. In my case those conditions were present. The individuals whom I met considered their impending deaths and thought of a preferred birth environment of the next body.

Thus, to know what a dream means one must be insightful about the motive for the meeting. Meeting to associate without an underlying sentiment regarding having aged bodies, has another meaning.

In my case, I always thought of leaving the body suddenly. I considered this since the teen years. In fact, part of the impetus to do yoga comes from this continuous facing up to the fact, that regardless of whether I desire to do so or not, I will be deprived of the body.

As far as I am concerned death stalked this body from its inception. It stalks this body even today. Even though the kundalini managed to deprive death of its prize for some sixty years, eventually death will strike kundalini once and for all. The body will be finished. With this in mind I am attentive to spiritual practice. I urge others to do likewise.

Some persons locate me in the astral world with intentions for me to review what death is, to explain it and perhaps to give them something with which they can outmaneuver it, either to remain as a physical form forever, or to just leave the body without pain, disease or incapacity and to transit to a pleasurable astral world. Of course, I cannot help anyone with this if the person has not developed an effective yoga practice.

Yoga Practice Hereafter

What would happen after death to a person who effectively practiced yoga? Can the person continue and progress in yoga in the astral world, with the techniques he practiced physically, or will he be forcefully fated to take birth immediately after death? How long will the person stay in the astral world?

If you hear the term siddha aptly applied to a yogi who uses a physical body, that person should continue the practice and perfect it in the astral world after leaving the physical body. After death, some siddhas go to a supernatural or spiritual world. That is beyond the adjacent and lower astral planes. These persons do not have to continue their practice since their practice was completed before leaving the physical body.

To continue the practice of yoga after leaving a physical body, the subtle body which transits to the hereafter must have a compulsive yoga habit. The system of transiting from a physical body is counterproductive towards continued yoga practice in the astral world, because as it is, the natural system is that the yogi is offered pleasures in the astral world, pleasure which he or she can hardly refuse.

Once the yogi is lured into such indulgence, the habit of practice becomes muffled. The tendency for liberation gets squashed. The yogi enjoys the offered pleasures and then just finds the self in an adjacent parallel dimension seeking out a body, seeking out a couple who are on the verse of sexual intercourse.

That attraction acts like a vacuum pump to suck the yogi's psyche into the body of the future father or mother and then the embryonic process occurs. The yogi forgets about his or her practice and is pushed out of the mother's body, crying and screaming as a little infant.

By the grace of Krishna, we got a conversation called the *Anu Gita*. It occurred when Krishna brushed aside Arjuna's request for a repeat of the *Bhagavad Gita* discourse including the fantastic apparition of the Universal Form and the Four-handed Divine God Form. In that discourse this issue is raised about how long a person stays in the astral world. Basically, a siddha, who experienced this, said that one stays there for as long as one has effect-energies which could be manifested there.

These effect-energies are acts which were committed during the past earthly lives, acts which were either socially beneficial to one and all or downright criminal. In either case, one goes to an astral heaven or hellish place. One enjoys or suffers proportionately and then one finds oneself in the realm of a purgatory, waiting for the next body opportunity. A yogi who was a good guy, a social nice-guy, would stay for a longer time in the astral heavens than one who was antisocial and isolationist. A yogi, who was cruel to others for the most part, will spend some time in astral hellish places. It would vary from yogi to yogi. Later, that person would find the self to be in a parallel world from which people in the hereafter make their application and wait for influencing would-be parents.

To get the direct information read my book *Anu Gita Explained*. There is also some inside information in my one personal gift to all students which is the book *sex you!,* a book people think is about sex but which is about reincarnation and how it is related to sex.

Basically, speaking if you do not desire another body immediately after leaving the current one, you can out-stride nature and achieve your aim if you develop resistance to heavenly pleasure. The one thing that guarantees another haphazard body for good people is their compelling attraction to heavenly sex. Once one is involved with that after leaving the body, one will take rebirth.

It is not a matter of determination. It is a matter of the tendencies in the subtle form. If the subtle form has tendencies to enjoy heavenly sex, then the yoga scheme is all but over. The key is to change the tendencies of the subtle body. Making up your mind to resist sex or to stop it has nothing to do with this, because the subtle body is not concerned with willpower. It ignores inhibitions and moralities. It services even sublimal desires.

The subtle body in the astral world after death works by impulses not by mental determination, plans, philosophies, samadhi gimmicks, imaginative states and the like. Thus, unless the yogi can change tendencies before death, he or she will be unable to affect its behavior in the afterlife. To sum this up, it means haphazard rebirth by being attracted to a couple having sex on earth. What begins as that attraction for a yogi will end as the reality of becoming aware of the self as a crying baby. The cycle which is called samsara will begin again.

Eyes and Meditation Connection

The main purpose of working with the eyes is twofold. The basic is for the purpose of discovering and understanding the third eye. The advance is for abandoning the optic nerve channels and retreating to the coreSelf.

In the *Meditation Pictorial* book, the eyes are dealth with in the first chapter where there are exercises for retracting the optic energy which comes from the core-self and which splits into two and travels through the right and left optic nerves.

Initially one gets curious about the third eye. To get evidence about it, one may practice putting slight pressure on the closed eyelids. Slight pressure is applied with the fingers. This is sometimes combined with using the thumbs to close the outer ear canal. This helps to get one to hear naad sound which is in the head. This is called *bhramari mudra*.

In the advanced stages one loses interest in the chakras and focuses on the kundalini lifeForce energy which uses the chakras for energy distribution purposes.

The importance of the eyes in pratyahar energy retraction practice is this:

In the human form, the eyes take a great percentage of the sensual energy in the psyche. Hence if it is curbed much of this energy can be retained in the psyche and use for extra-dimensional perception. The self only has a certain amount of total energy at its disposal. If it conserves energy from one sense or from one zone of the psyche, it can apply that reserve to another pursuit, to mystic concerns.

Try to trace the energy which courses down the optic nerve. Where does that energy merge in the subtle head? If there is an organ in the subtle head where the two optic channels converse, one may discover it and discover that it is more important than the eyes which are like lenses used by the optic energy.

Yoga Preliminary

Doing asana postures and sitting to meditate are two different processes. Try not to mix them. Patanjali give eight stages to yoga but he also gave it in six stages, where the sixth stage is the last three stages combined into one practice.

Here is a break down

1. yama
2. niyama
3. asana postures
4. pranayama breath infusion
5. pratyahar sensual energy withdrawal
6. dharana, dhyana and samadhi rolled into one practice or done separately as three techniques.

Yama and *niyama* are social behaviors. Leave those aside. Doing asanas postures and breath infusion is a set of exercises. When one sits to do pratyahar sensual energy withdrawal, that is a mental and emotional exercise.

Meditation begins with dharana which is linking the mind to a higher concentration force or person. In other words, most attempts at meditation are either pratyahar sensual energy mental practice or attempts to escape from or silence random mental and emotional activity.

When one sits to meditate, one should be comfortable. In fact, there is a posture called *shukasana* which means easy pose. Unfortunately for some persons with a stiff body, even that may be painful. In that case one should use cushions to make it comfortable for the body during meditation.

When one does asana postures comfort is not the concern. That is stretching and relaxing alternately but for meditation, one should assume an easy sitting or reclining posture. This will ease the attention so that one can transfer it to what is transcendental to the body. If the body is uptight there will be a mental struggle. That will ruin meditation.

The fifth stage of yoga is called *pratyahar* which is a combination of two Sanskrit words *prati* and *ahara*. *Prati* is a prefix which is used in this case to produce the opposite meaning. It is similar to anti in English, like social and antisocial.

Ahara means consumption and when *prati* is put before it, it is the opposite which means to cease consumption.

Our natural condition is that of being consumers not just in terms of human products but in terms of nature at large. As soon as my baby form was born, I cried. It was a protest expression which meant, "Where is my mother? Where are her breasts? How sweet is the milk? Where is my father? What job has he got? How much income does he earn?"

In the beginning I consumed. That was my primary interest. I looked into the world both mentally and physically, even emotionally, for what it could give me. Consciousness was streamed from me, but I did not observe it.

With eyes opened peering into the world I looked, looked and looked to consume. My concern was to find enjoyable persons, places and things. Even with eyes closed I did this. Even when there was pitch darkness, I peered in the darkness to find something to consume.

Then someone said to me, "Abandon consumption, retract the energies. Stop peering about in the day or night. Reverse the order of things so that consciousness streams into you not away from you. Retract. Pull in your feelings. Search in the core of you. Sense what causes consciousness to stream out of you."

This is the first step in meditative yoga practice. One may do this for months or years before one can advance to the next step of meditative yoga practice.

In the Gita we get some help in conceptualizing this. Krishna said this:

यः सर्वत्रानभिस्नेहस्
तत्तत्प्राप्य शुभाशुभम् ।
नाभिनन्दति न द्वेष्टि
तस्य प्रज्ञा प्रतिष्ठिता ॥२.५७॥
yaḥ sarvatrānabhisnehas
tattatprāpya śubhāśubham
nābhinandati na dveṣṭi
tasya prajñā pratiṣṭhitā (2.57)

yaḥ- who; sarvatrā — in all circumstances; anabhisnehaḥ — without crippling affections; tattat = tad tad-this or that; prāpya- meeting; śubhāśubham — enjoyable and disturbing factors; nābhinandati = na — not + abhinandati — excited; na — nor; dveṣṭi — distressed; tasya — his; prajñā — reality-piercing consciousness; pratiṣṭhitā - is established

A person who, in all circumstances, is without crippling affections, who, when meeting enjoyable or disturbing factors, does not get excited nor distressed, his reality-piercing consciousness is established. (Bhagavad Gita 2.57)

यदा संहरते चायं
कूर्मोऽङ्गानीव सर्वशः।
इन्द्रियाणीन्द्रियार्थेभ्यस्
तस्य प्रज्ञा प्रतिष्ठिता ॥२.५८॥
yadā saṁharate cāyaṁ
kūrmo'ṅgānīva sarvaśaḥ
indriyāṇīndriyārthebhyas
tasya prajñā pratiṣṭhitā (2.58)

yadā — when; saṁharate — pulls; cāyaṁ = ca — and + ayam — this; kūrmo = kūrmaḥ — tortoise; 'ṅgānīva = aṅgānīva = aṅgāni — limbs + iva — like, compared to; sarvaśaḥ —fully; indriyāṇīndriyārthebhyas = indriyani — senses + indriyarthebhyaḥ — attractive things; tasya — his; prajñā — reality-piercing vision; pratiṣṭhitā — is established

When such a person pulls fully out of moods, he or she may be compared to the tortoise with its limbs retracted. The senses are withdrawn from the attractive things in the case of a person whose reality-piercing vision is established. (Bhagavad Gita 2.58)

Students Challenge the Yoga-guru

For the last week, I worked with Swami Rama on the agnisara practice. Some yogis feel that if one completes this discipline; one can resist having to take another body whimsically.

This practice concerns the navel and the way one took nutrients from the mother's body while being an embryo. If that system is still in place at the time of death, it will immediately act in the subtle body to prompt another rebirth without respect to one's spiritual needs. One will be careless in attraction to the new parents. This will be a setback when one gets the new body.

This morning Swami Rama explained how to complete that practice. He came astrally with two male students. From the appearance of the subtle forms of the students, I could tell that they still have physical bodies. The swami has none at this time.

As he showed a technique, one student said this, "You never showed that. We did not know that you do that. Since when is that part of the practice?"

With a curt smile, he replied, "What do you know about my practice? "

The student replied, "But Guruji, we know that what you show here is not your practice. We are with you all the time. We never saw this. It is strange that you know this and this yogi does whatever you instruct."

The swami then said, "You cannot see everything an accomplished yogi does. You do not know anything about my practice."

The swami showed me that if the effort to perceive is totally internalized, the yogi will see in all the parts of his psyche and will by that get practices for full purification.

"Kundalini," he said, "must be completely curbed. Then the yogi can use prana to clear the subtle body, all parts of it, not just the spine and head. First get rid of the nuisance kundalini. Then use prana to directly clear the system. Dismiss the kundalini. Take the tasks of purification into your own hands."

Yogi with Two Bodies

Swami Rama has two bodies, one is the body he used to practice yoga. The other is an astral form which he uses to continue his yoga teacher duties. Because he was a Shankaracharya lineage guru, he maintains an astral body in respect to that. In the meantime, he uses another body in another dimension to do yoga austerities. Some students are unaware of his double life.

When he showed more details of the agnisara practice, he transferred my perception into the dimension where he has another body. He showed how the inside of that body is constructed. That form has no spinal kundalini even though it has routes for channeling subtle energy.

His other subtle body is not a spiritual body. It is an altered siddha yoga body. When a yogi becomes successful in practice, the subtle body changes. It is called a siddha form. That is not a spiritual body. It is a precursor to such a body.

Usually yogis transfer to the siddha form but Swami Rama keeps that form and his previous astral format from before. The different between that siddha body and the standard astral form is this:

The conventional astral form has tendencies which lead the individual back into the birth/death cycle repeatedly. It is hell-bent on gaining benefits from cultural activity in the physical world. The siddha form has no interest in the cultural activities. It has no inclinations for rebirth or participation in human history.

To understand consider helpless infants. They have the tendency to suckle milk from the mother's breasts. Later in the toddler and juvenile stages this tendency disappears. The body becomes changed. It loses interest in suckling.

In teenaged years, my body expressed an interest in alcohol. I was with friends who had similar interest. After a time, there was a disinterest because I focused on spiritual practice.

Because of religious stipulations and social disapproval many people cease drinking alcohol but I stopped because my body lost interest in it. The siddha form causes a loss of interest in certain aspects of existence. That is its value.

Confidence in the Third Eye

The agnisara process does what Swami Rama said it would do. It affects the operation of the third eye in reference to the potential for chit akash, sky of consciousness, perception and other supernatural means of peering into or visiting higher dimensions. By doing agnisara alone, a person can, it appears, reach the supernatural and spiritual zones of existence.

There is a channel from the navel downwards through the bottom of the trunk of the body. At first when one does the breath infusement focusing on just this area alone, the channel appears to be round. It appears to be filled with a dark-grey dusty subtle energy. By the infusement that changes into a light grey energy and then suddenly it seems to catch afire and burns like burning dusty clouds in a sky.

After this the area clears. It has a shimmering gold light. The round shape changes into an oval shaped tube. After more infusion, that oval shape widens. The infused energy then attacks the sex organ chakras which are in the pubic area of the body. The progression of this development might take days, weeks or months even, all depending on the intensity and efficient of the practice.

After a time, the channel begins at the throat under the mouth rather than at the navel. This is when it begins to affect the operation of the third eye. During meditation what happens is this:

Initially when the student does agnisara, there is no effect on the third eye. In fact, there is no effect in the head of the subtle body. Thus, the student may have doubts about the practice, since most students are eager to have kundalini rise into the head with its accompanying experiences. However, as the practice develops, the yogi will find that there are affects in the head.

At first the yogi will be drawn down into the navel area and will find the coreSelf relocated out of the head of the subtle body down into the agnisara channel. The student might wonder what should be done there.

As the practice develops, the yogin will find that when sitting to meditate after a session, the core becomes aware of both the head of the subtle body and the agnisara channel which was bored and which is filled with a gold shimmering light which sometimes has an orange hue.

Then suddenly the student will find that the third eye assumes an orange hue with small flashes of light which are like icicles shimmering a little in sunlight. Then the third eye will open for about 3 seconds or even for as much as 10 seconds. Then it will be shimmering and it may open for less time a second or third time.

Then it will open but the student will derive from this an important confidence, that it is possible by practice to open this third eye and use the third eye just as one could use physical vision.

The value of this is the confidence gained since a student does not have confidence in the ability to use the third eye due to its resistance to the willpower of the student. It is as if the willpower feels relieved to find itself operating the third eye on that level periodically.

This may be compared to a frustrated child who after a number of attempts to make the feet of the infant body walk in a balanced and orderly way, gets frustrated because of repeatedly falling since the feet does not respond to its willpower. Then after a time, the child finds that the feet respond as desired even though it does that only for a few steps and then it again ignores the willpower.

Many persons think that the opening of the third eye is imagination or belief of yogis. If anyone has these experiences, faith in the practice of yoga develops. That helps to accelerate practice.

Agnisara is one of the practices which help in the development of such faith. Just as an infant gradually finds that the feet which were unresponsive to the willpower, eventually over time becomes more and more compliant. The student yogi will find that the higher faculties of the subtle body which were undeveloped and even non-existent come into focus and become useable functions. It is exactly like taking a new body having no control of it and then gradually learning how to operate it as it develops.

Yesterday someone asked how it was that these persons like Swami Rama develop and have more than one body. That student called and asked about the difficulty in simultaneously maintaining two bodies. Actually, to an infant walking is a challenge, and yet to an adult it is done spontaneously.

When the subtle body changes in configuration, a new form of it will be experienced with the corresponding faculties which to us now are impossible.

Raising kundalini into the head and infusing the head with fresh air, will yield the same results, but only if the infusion is thorough. One must have a lifestyle that is compliant with the stipulations of Patanjali regarding yama and niyama disapproved and approved social behaviors. Without that compliance, raising kundalini will result in opening third eye infrequently.

When he discussed the yama restraint actions and the niyama approved behaviors, Patanjali spoke of the great commitment which is that one should not violate these, nor use awkward situations as a reason to ignore these. He wrote that because if one has to violate these while practicing the yoga process one will get a partial result.

Until the yogi shuts down the interest in the benefits of material existence, he cannot get the full success but that does not mean that he should not practice. One should practice anyway but one should not have false expectations thinking that one will get the full result.

In regards to the question about the physical body and cleansing it, yoga has little to do with the physical body. A person can do yoga and derive physical health benefits and even psychological relief from stress, and that same person may get absolutely zero results in the psychic sense of the subtle body.

But the agnisara process is the hard core hatha yoga process. It is not the western hatha yoga teaching which is postures and healthy diet which results in physical beauty and health.

Ha and tha means the sun and moon influences in the body. That is configured by the kundalini lifeForce. It has very little to do with a material body. The value of a material body to an advanced yogi is that it stabilizes the subtle system. Besides that, the physical body is a useless limited appendage.

When the subtle body is in the subtle world, if it is not a yoga siddha form, it is a sensation because it is fickle and jumps from one place to the next. This makes it near impossible to have a steady yoga practice because the subtle body acts like a squirrel always moving about and not staying steady for anything.

The use of the physical body for a yogi is a far cry from its regular usage by others. But come to think of it, what is the use of taking care of a body that will lasts for the most say eighty years?

If I sell you a car and tell you that it will explode in ten days, will you invest thousands of dollars to repair something in it? You would not. In the same way a yogi is not concerned with the physical body but in so far as working on it affects the subtle body, we are eager about that.

My discussion concerns the subtle body even though it is also occurring to the physical body to a great degree. Swami Rama's advanced method does not involve kundalini. It involves the self using subtle energy just as kundalini would have used it. Initially a student yogi must do agnisara with the kundalini. When this is done proficiently, the kundalini moves into the brain. It loses its tight hold on the base chakra, the sex chakra system and the navel chakra domain. Then in the preparation to assume a yoga siddha body the student practices a higher type of agnisara practice.

In the subtle body we are not concerned with muscular locks. There one deals with energy, either heavy subtle energy or light-weight subtle energy. The tubes I mentioned are in the subtle body. That particular one has no corresponding conduit in the physical system. In the physique we have intestines and a colon in those areas. These are coiled tubing. In the subtle body there is a passage from the navel straight down (no coiling) through the body to somewhere between the anus and perineum.

The physical actions of agnisara are for beginner students. That practice is the beginning. It is not the advanced practice which concerns the subtle body.

A point might be raised though as to why focus so much on what is subtle and abstract, why not focus on the physical side?

This is a good argument until the time of death of the physical system, because from then onwards one must deal with the subtle part of the psyche. Yogis should realize the subtle before death.

Physical existence is not the problem for a yogi. Physical history is based on a psychic interest in it. The problem is that psychic interest. To deal with the physical in real terms means to confront the psychic interest.

Part 8

How I Fell in Love in the Previous Life

Boyfriend and girlfriend usually mean that there were past lives of association in the same way as lovers. This is an assumption we should always make. The least we should understand is that if I knew someone in a past life and was sexually attracted to that person and was unable to fulfill a relationship, when I meet that person in this or in a future life, I will be wonderstruck and will again fall in love.

I met someone some years ago about fifty years ago. I did not realize at the time that this person was sexually attracted. Suddenly I had a dream in which I was sexually involved with this person. Why did that happen? I had no feelings of love for that person fifty years ago. The relationship was casual, and somehow that person's affection for me increased exponentially in my fifty-year physical and astral absence. By the force of that increase of affection, I met the person in a dream. This person was all over me. How did that affection change into a conjugal one? Why did that person's subtle body develop the power to pull me into a dream for sexual love?

Both the conscious and subconscious minds are wonder struck by sex attraction and affection. But these two systems of awareness act differently. The conscious mind is concerned with the present situation. In the background the subconscious mind does not care about the present. It has a long-ranged reach into the past energies that are stockpiled. It is the architect which construct the limited circumstances in which I will find myself in the future.

The subconscious is unpredictable. In yoga, one is trained to enter and decipher its operations and compulsions. It can undermine the conscious mind and make a complete fool out of the conscious self which plans fulfillment of desires.

Information and memory energy which is stored in the subconscious may come back to haunt someone, just as something a politician did privately, may be publicized by his rival and be used to disgrace him. The subconscious can attack to make one falter at any time.

Affairs like man and wife, boyfriend and girlfriend are the most difficult situations to resolve. They influence one's behavior in other lives. Conjugal love is the strongest impression in the emotional instincts we carry through these lives. It haunts and taunts us. Love affairs do not end merely because we are at a distance from a loved one. The instincts about it remain and surface at the nearest opportunity, even if one has no conscious impetus.

Most of the hurt one feels because of disagreements and disloyalties in sexual relationships, have to do with disharmonious cultural trappings which the lover acquired after taking the new body. When one fails to work through those cultural differences, flare-ups occur. One gets distress instead of happiness.

Location of Willpower

Agnisara with breath infusion also helps with sorting the various components of willpower. What I term as me, may be a composite of psychic forces? Perhaps it is not really me? Perhaps it is that I am powerless to segregate myself, like when I was an embryo about 2 weeks in my mother's uterus. Then I did not have the power to isolate myself. I had to be one with my mother. I did not know where she began and where, I ended.

For that matter some women become pregnant and do not know of it until months after when their stomachs begin to harden and there is kicking of the infant who grows.

The will power is an important tool used in meditation to focus on particular energies, forces, deities or objectives. Sometimes this willpower just cannot do what we desire it to accomplish.

Are there components to this willpower? Is the willpower like the tongue of a serpent which flickers outside its mouth to detect odors and body heat of other creatures?

Does the willpower reach out of the coreSelf?

What do we mean when we say that Jack's willpower is stronger than Henry's?

A tongue is in the mouth. Where in the psyche is the willpower?

Death of a Yogi

Taking a body is signing a contract to be defeated by death. As soon as the fetal development begins, one is under a threat. In fact, in that position there is absolutely nothing one can do to help or defend oneself. One's initiative is reduced to the impulse to live.

But even then, one is a sitting duck, with death being the marksman who aims with unerring focus. When will it kill the fetus? No one knows for sure. The only thing we know is that death has its aim and will fire at any time, at its convenience.

Can it be dodged? How long can one avoid it? Even a wealthy and famous person is not allowed to stay here forever. For many years now as a safety precaution, I dedicated myself to writing books so that I can leave something behind. I did many things in this life and the one thing that is consistent is spiritual practice of which writing books is a part.

It is not a good idea to depend on the physical body of anyone. That is a kind of madness since we know that everyone who has a material body sits on death row.

It is best to move to the subtle and psychic side of existence, and strive to keep in touch with the yogis in that way, even if one has a material body. Nothing is missed if you develop connection with the subtle body of a yogi, because death of the physical system cannot kill the subtle form.

A student yogi has to reach a point of confidence, where the death of the teacher has no relevance due to psychic connection with that teacher. No one should remain with only physical awareness and physical identity.

You can check your development by asking the yoga teacher questions mentally and then sitting silently and try to absorb any answer-energy the teacher would psychically send your way.

Then ask the teacher the same question by some physical means. When you get that physical answer, compare it with your meditation notes. That is a method for calibrating the psychic connection with the teacher.

Let me share a secret:

A yoga teacher does not have to give attention while answering a question sent by anyone psychically. The body of the yogi can answer those questions by emitting a matching energy even without the yogi deliberately answering the question.

The solutions to practice which are in the body of the yogi because of his practice of those solutions, will automatically send out a response energy.

The yogi's body is like an automatic response system. I did this with some yoga gurus where without verbalizing a question to them even astrally, the answer jumped from the teacher's body to mine. It can happen!!

Consequential Energy

Life on earth is about desires and nature's accommodation of the same. People are driven by desires. It so happens that even though we are part of nature, still it does not fulfill every desire. The ones which it accommodates are fulfilled partially only.

The same person today has the same desires as he did two thousand years ago when he could not fulfill those desires. Now that he may fulfill them, the fulfillment will be partially only. Just as our bodies will die, reality is itself a statement from nature about how much it is willing to respond to our needs. From nature we get desires which nature itself would either fulfill or frustrate.

Making mistakes is something one has a right to as far as nature is concerned. By repeatedly making mistakes we develop instincts and intuitions which guide us away from the behaviors which are not in our long-termed interest.

The other way to look at this is that when I reach a dead-end, I will turn back. I will see that I took a road to nowhere. Nature is in no hurry to expose reality. It does so bit by bit over millions of years. Eventually I get the idea.

Cosmic Contact

Due to following Swami Rama's technique for agnisara, I managed to find a definite way to make contact with cosmic intellect *(buddhi),* but I am not sure that it is cosmic intellect. Due to the angle from which it strikes I am of the opinion that it might be cosmic sense of identity *(ahamkara).*

Usually the lights from cosmic intellect strikes from a lower angle. The cosmic sense of identity strikes from a higher angle.

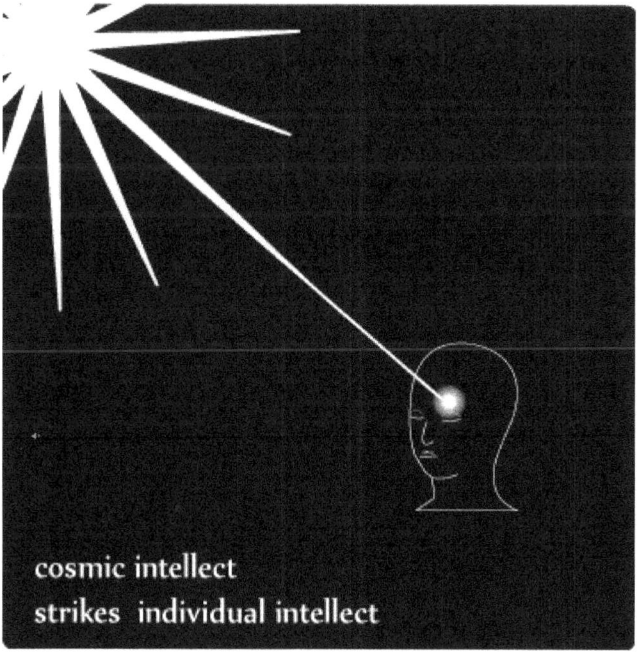
cosmic intellect
strikes individual intellect

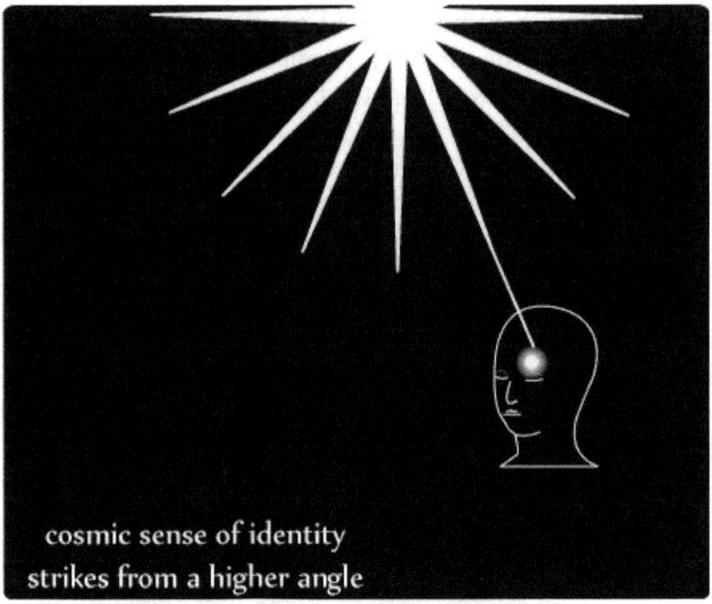
cosmic sense of identity
strikes from a higher angle

In any case, both contacts are desired by a yogi. By these he can cull his existence from the material world. He may escape from these zones forever, getting his social register erased from the historic karmic pool of power which keeps the entities on the merry-go-round of reincarnations in temporary bodies.

It appears that by Swami Rama's method, the sex area chakras and energies can be attacked after the agnisara channel from the navel downward is gutted out and filled with light and high-grade subtle energy. The yogi must push the infused air into the sex area. At a certain point it seems that one feels like there are a few tubes which lift sex energy from the sex organs, the gonads in men and the ovaries in women. When this happens, the yogis use breath infusion to pull that energy. After a time, an advanced yogi removes the sex organs from the subtle body. This is a painless operation but when the surgeon yogi pulls on the genitals to separate them from the subtle body there is a slight sensation when two tubes are pulled out of the subtle body.

The genitals are now useless since the yogi forsakes the opportunity of begetting children in the material world and has no more need for reproductive energy. The part of the sex organs which has to do with excretion of liquids remains but the organ loses interest in sex hormones for reproductive purposes.

When an advanced yogi or a deity person comes to perform the operation on the subtle body, there is flash of light. One sees the last person whom one was irresistibly attracted to. That is the final chance to either go further in the practice and have the subtle genitals removed, or to stay on the lower planes and keep reproducing. The yogi/yogini must decide to do one or the other.

I did this procedure before in more than one past life but I still observed this again so that I could give an up-to-date report to the students.

After this happens, the yogi is free to use the third eye without the hassles and failures of lower meditation. Swami Rama did not come when this happened but he left an energy in my psyche which said this:

> *Soon after the yogi becomes involved in reproduction or in sexual expression, the third eye fails to operate or it operates sporadically. This is why one of the requirements in yoga according to Patanjali is brahmachari celibate status. The energy that is at the third eye is reduced considerably when reproduction and sex become involved. Much of the energy required for operation of the brow chakra, is used up in sex dalliances. As soon as those energies are no longer being used for sex, third eye vision resumes.*

As I said the Swami left that message-energy in my psyche. After doing breath infusion session, I sat to meditate. During the breath infusion kundalini was nowhere to be found, not even in the spine. It vanished. During the meditation, there were no thoughts created by the intellect. The thing was completely silenced by the agnisara practice. I lowered the coreSelf into the area cleared by the infusion.

After about thirty minutes, I focused upward through the third eye but with mild force only, making sure that the willpower ray did not act brashly and was a gentle prod going upwards and out of the third eye area.

Then there were a few flashes of cloud energy, like a grey cloud lit in the sky. After this suddenly a light penetrated which I thought was cosmic sense of identity. But it hit the intellect so I am not sure if it was cosmic sense of identity or cosmic intellect.

That contact was refreshing as it relieved the psyche of stress. It was like when a thirsty man who walked in a desert for many days, suddenly finds himself in a rain shower.

I was like this in the material world for some time now, roaming here and there with everyone else. Now it is time for me to escape.

Special Note:

Cosmic intellect (buddhi) is lower than cosmic sense of identity (ahankara) which is lower than the Supreme Soul (paramatma). The cosmic intellect hits the localized intellect. The cosmic sense of identity hits the localized sense of identity (ahamkara). The Supreme Soul (paramatma) hits the localized individual limited soul, the atma.

Some ascetics think that these aspects can merge but what happens is that they become linked so that the limited one becomes infused with energy from the cosmic one.

All students should hence forth scrap the idea of merging into anything and assume the idea of linking with other realities. Dharana, dhyana and samadhi, or samyama, concerns linking with not merging with. When one links with a higher reality, one's psyche becomes saturated with energy from that other level. This is how it should be understood.

Initially the limited soul is outfitted with a sense of identity, an intellect, a kundalini of sensory energy, and memory. After a time, this composite or psyche, becomes perverted and warped in the numerous transmigrations. The only way to get these psychic accessories back into shape is to re-link them with their cosmic sources. Unfortunately, when one becomes conditioned in the material world, one loses the insight into how to do this.

Managing Consequences

Just as when a person dies in reference to this physical world, the body is left behind to rot here, so when a yogi is liberated, his remaining consequential energies are left on this level of existence. It is then appropriated by others or it might latch on to others regardless of their being aware of it. This is similar to when a wealthy man passes away. His properties are distributed by a probate court.

There is this idea that when a yogi becomes liberated, his consequences disappear. Some spiritual masters thrive on the basis of that statement where they advocate that if one becomes a disciple and follow the system, bad consequences will be neutralized. However, this is not true for all consequences. It is only true for some.

There is a related statement in the *Anu Gita*:

ब्राह्मण उवाच
शुभानामशुभानां च नेह नाशोऽस्ति कर्मणाम्
प्राप्य प्राप्य तु पच्यन्ते क्षेत्रं क्षेत्रं तथा तथा

brāhmaṇa uvāca
śubhānāmaśubhānāṁ ca neha nāśo'sti karmaṇām
prāpya prāpya tu pacyante kṣetraṁ kṣetraṁ tathā tathā (3.1)

brāhmaṇa - the elevated ascetic; uvāca – said; śubhānām – of what is asupicious; aśubhānāṁ - what is inauspicious; ca – and; neha = na (no) + iha (here); nāśo = nāśah = elimination; 'sti = asti – is; karmaṇām – of the cultural activities; prāpya

prāpya = obtaining in sequence; tu – but; pacyante – express energies; kṣetraṁ kṣetraṁ - environment after environment; tathā tathā = so in order (3.1)

There is no elimination of the energy of auspicious or inauspicious social acts. Obtaining bodies in sequence, the activities express energies in various envirnoments in sequence. (Anu Gita 3.1)

A liberated entity cannot remove all the karmic energies which he or she stockpiled and is tagged with from many past lives. That is not possible. Material nature will not allow that to happen. Even God cannot free Himself totally from his involvement with material nature. Krishna as the Supreme Being admitted in the Bhagavad Gita that he must from time to time get involved in the world for establishing righteous lifestyle.

It is not possible to completely severe one's relationship to material nature; even though one may suspend it, where one's relationship with it goes into dormancy for several eternities.

Material nature maintains the relationship to it on the causal plane. Even if one is liberated and one vanishes out of these levels of existence, even then material nature will keep a record of one's activities and her reactions to these. It will be dormant but it will still be there. If one returns into manifestation in nature, that dormant energy will be immediately re-activated.

With material nature, if one desires liberation and if in fact one achieves that, material nature will refuse to close one's account. One can leave but the account remains for the record. If the yogi wants to settle any of it, material nature will agree to do that on its terms which mean one must settle it within nature's time frame.

Here is an example.

I knew a lady during the time when Greece was the most powerful country on earth. This was around 1500 BC. Due to dying on a battlefield during the wars, I died without fulfilling my love for this woman. As my body died, she was on my mind. In the afterlife I wanted to be in her association but at the time in the ancient world, even on the astral side there were wars. My ghost body was captured by the enemy and kept in astral confinement.

Among the prisoners there was a soothsayer priest. He advised us that we could escape and go back to Greece to become children there, but somehow none of us understood what he meant because we felt that our ghost bodies were physical forms.

After that life I had many other bodies here and there in Europe and Eurasia, but once I got a body in the Himalayan region. I learnt about yoga and practiced it.

I forgot the Grecian woman whom I loved. Once when meditating I had a glimpse of her face at my third eye. I again fell in love with her. I asked a yoga teacher if I could meet her but he said that I should forget it. He explained that many images from past lives will be seen at the third eye and they were not worth it.

In any case, despite being told that by the teacher, I still felt a burning desire to be with the Grecian woman. I planned to find her in the astral world. I felt that if I could find her current astral body, I could meet her physically and fulfill the relationship.

I met her astrally but I could not find her physical location because my meditation practice was not advanced enough. I was uneasy about it, thinking that I should leave the ashram and go wandering to find her.

Once in a lecture, the Guruji said this,

> *"If you want her you will have to take ten births. Then nature will allow you to meet her in the eleventh lifetime from this one. Do not leave the ashram now because even if you go here and there you will not find her. She is written in your destiny in chapter eleven, which means that you would have to pass through the ten prior chapters before you can meet her.*
>
> *"Think about it carefully. That would mean signing a commitment with nature regarding a mandatory ten lives to see her. It is best to forget her. Endeavor for liberation. She will remain in the world and so will your fate-energy but you will be gone to the spiritual place. Some other man will be possessed with your fate energy. He can complement the woman. Why imperil yourself seeking her since you do not know what will happen in those ten lives and even in the eleventh one in which you will meet her.*
>
> *"Abandon your fate energy the way people willingly abandon their property when a hostile barbarous army marches through the area. "*

If I explain that meditation does not remove the conseqences of actions, what is the use of meditation?

Its value is that it separates the yogi from most consequences, not all. The consequence energies remain as is but the yogi is segregated from it, for the time being.

The same yogi, if he relapses, will again be afflicted by those deactivated consequences. A particular fate is operative only in a particular zone of existence. If the yogi leaves that zone, he is out of the loop of it. If he returns, it will latch on to him, even if he evolved or changed in the course of time and history.

Meditation puts one out of reach of most consequences but it does not destroy the effect energies. They remain intact in the material world. People like Buddha and Krishna were involved as soon as they surfaced in this world. These two persons are God for all practical purposes and still they became involved.

Regarding Krishna, at his birth ceremony they called an astrologer. The guy after figuring the horoscope and psyching out the Child Krishna said something to this effect,

"I recognize this child. In the past he established righteous lifestyle, He will repeat that behavior. He will wipe out corrupt rulers. Take care to protect him. In infancy people will attempt to kill him."

As far as Buddha is concerned his father had an astrologer speak at his birth ceremony. The astrologer said that Buddha would be either a world conquering monarch or a supreme yogi.

The histories of the living entities are there. If one appears in a certain domain that history will continue as it was before. No one can destroy the consequential energies in material nature, nor the tags which nature has for each individual. If one desires to destroy one's consequence energy, one may do it indirectly by exiting the domain in which that energy is logged.

One can be blessed with the good karmas of yogis who are now liberated. Because the effect-energies of their yogic penances are still in the universe, even if they left it, one can get some of that energy. It could accelerate the practice.

Special Clarification:

A yogi might eradicate particular consequential situations but not all. He or she may do this by two means:

- Acting for the Supreme Being under the influence of and with the power of the Supreme Being
- Acting to settle particular reactions but acting with valid insight and with detachment.

In the *Bhagavad Gita* there is some talk by Krishna about consequences. The acts which Arjuna performed on the battlefield for Krishna, for the Universal Form, were acts which were free of consequences for Arjuna but Arjuna's other activities after the battle were not necessarily covered as acts done for the Universal Form.

Even in the case of the Universal Form which is God in real terms, even that Central Person of it, that Supernatural God, Krishna, has to deal with the consequences which result from his acts and which cause people to hate him, to hate the Supreme Being for disciplining them for socially deviant acts.

Many people feel that perhaps God or Jesus will take away their faulty acts but in the Bhagavad Gita Krishna denounced the idea, saying that he absorbs no results of anyone socially-beneficial or socially-hostile acts.

When on the way to the crucifixion a disciple wanted to carry Christ's cross, he corrected the disciple by indicating that in this existence everyone must carry his burden.

One cannot erase consequences by contemplation in meditation. Material nature runs its own show. No yogi will do anything to change the energy of past acts which are ushered into the present or future.

Predestination

Whatever happens is predestined in the sense that everything occurring is a composite of the past which serves as the foundation of the present. There is some variation and free play in varying percentages according to how much providence utilizes a past circumstance and its ingredients.

Third Eye and the Dark Train

I will focus on the agnisara practice for a while, just to be sure that when I recommend it, I know what I suggests. I test procedures thoroughly before I suggest to others. So far, the agnisara method is impressive.

This morning Swami Rama taught it saying that it is the way to understand how the cosmic kundalini arose in the first place, how the Supreme Being generated the cosmic kundalini.

In the Sanskrit books this force was generated by the Supreme Spirit in the *mula prakriti*. In the instructions to Uddhava, Krishna named it the *sutram* and explained how it came about.

परावराणां परम
आस्ते कैवल्य-सञ्ज्ञितः ।
केवलानुभवानन्द-
सन्दोहो निरुपाधिकः ॥४.१८॥

parāvarāṇāṁ parama
āste kaivalya-saṁjñitaḥ
kevalānubhavānanda-
sandoho nirupādhikaḥ (4.18)

parāvarāṇām = para — superior creatures + avarāṇām — of ordinary creature; parama = paramaḥ — Supreme Lord; āste — He exists; kaivalya-samjñitah = kaivalya — one who is segregated from subtle mundane energy + samjñitaḥ — known as; kevalānubhavānanda-sandoho = kevala — absolute + anubhava — personal evidence + ānanda — bliss + sandoho (sandohaḥ) — mass, totality; nirupādhikah — without mundane qualities.

He, the Supreme Lord of the superior and inferior creatures, exists as a mass of absoluteness, personal existence, and bliss, He is known to be segregated from subtle mundane energy, and is without mundane qualities. (Uddhava Gita 4.18)

केवलात्मानुभावेन
स्व-माया त्रि-गुणात्मिकाम् ।
सङ्क्षोभयन् सृजत्य् आदौ
तया सूत्रम् अरिन्दम ॥४.१९॥
kevalātmānubhāvena
sva-māyāṁ tri-guṇātmikām
saṅkṣobhayan sṛjaty ādau
tayā sūtram arindama (4.19)

kevalātmānubhāvena = kevala — absolute + ātma — self + anubhāvena — by existential power; sva-māyām = sva –own + māyām — bewildering energy; tri-guṇātmikām = tri — three + guṇa — influences + ātmikām — formed of; saṅkṣobhayam — motivates; srjaty = srjati — projects; ādau — at the time of creation; tayā — that; sūtram — sexually-charge mundane energy; arindama — O subduer of the enemies

O subduer of enemies, He, by use of existential power, motivates into activity, His bewildering energy, which consists of three influences of material nature, and at the time of creation, though that, He projects the sexually-charged mundane energy. (Uddhava Gita 4.19)

After the yogi gets rid of kundalini and breaks its choke hold on the muladhara base chakra anchor point, he can directly infuse that area with pranic energy and discover how the kundalini is created in the first place.

Swami Rama said this:

The yogi is not the Supreme Being. He is not Krishna. He does not have a Universal Form to display to Arjuna, but still the yogi can get some idea of how the Supreme Being generated these cosmic circumstances.

Ants are tiny creatures but they can still get some understanding how an engineer builds a skyscraper. By studying their own activities in building mud nests ants can appreciation the work of an architect.

In a way if a person is an atheist, that person disbelieves in his/her person-self because if one understands the person-self, it is very easy to go the next step and understand that there would be a supreme person-self.

When doing the agnisara practice, sometimes it happens that suddenly when the system gets charged there is a flash of energy like lightning or there may suddenly be shifting frosty bliss energy moving up directly from the charged infused force. This is generated directly from the infused energy as contrasted to when that energy strikes kundalini and kundalini produces the flash.

When I sat to meditate after doing the agnisara practice, I checked again after about twenty minutes to see if it affected the third eye. It did. There was at the third eye another dimension but it was as

if I looked through a train window and the train move rapidly so that I could not focus on anything outside the window due to the fast movement. I could not adjust the speed. I was positioned to watch from inside the psychic head through the third eye window.

Then it was night outside the window with just a little moonlight so that I could not distinguish one form from the other.

I will test this to make sure that this is a consistent result from the agnisara practice.

When the third eye opens in this way it is like you look through a bay window either in the daytime or night time but usually whatever you see is there in the distance. There is no movement on your part. Sometimes there is slow movement. Sometimes it is rapid as in this experience.

It is more like you are in a train which is pitch dark inside and you look through the window into a world environment which is either illuminated or lacking visibility.

One conclusion from this is:

The need to develop material existence causes the shutdown of the third eye. The tendency to be here and to take nourishment here causes the shutdown of the third eye. Physical vision equals the lost of psychic perception.

Agnisara is the method for eliminating the digestion and sex hormone systems. That causes the third eye to open. My conclusion is that there is an inverse relationship between keen psychic perception and physical nourishment. The more we pursue and invest in physical nourishment, the less we have psychic perception.

Mind Inside Body

This morning Swami Rama made an important statement about the time it takes to get success in yoga practice. Read this:

Previously a yoga guru would tell a disciple that in a certain time say six months, or one year or twelve years that student would be successful, provided the person stuck to a prescribed method and lived at the hermitage. Usually these places were isolated, so that the student was cordoned from influences.

Thus, why is it that we find that in the modern setting this is not happening? In fact, students who live at ashram become disillusioned when they do not get success in whatever the yoga guru suggested.

The main reason for the failures is the social environment even at the modern ashram. The rigidity of the past is no longer present. Without it, the student is not propped-up with the disciplines and restrictions. That decreases the likelihood of success. We also have a case where the teachers themselves are affected by the social trends and cannot deliver what they intend to give.

There is a process mentioned for the life which is conducive to yoga success. This is in the Anu Gita. *There is a period given for six months. Today that period is much longer. In fact, students might never be successful even in a lifetime.*

There is one key feature when practicing asana postures and when sitting to meditate and that is the keep the attention in the body. There is a statement to that effect in the Anu Gita *in the example of a tourist in a city. You should quote that at the end of this message.*

Students should keep the mind inside the body during the exercises. Mind in this case is the attention. The attention likes to wander outside the body and go to various places during the exercises but a student should use an effective method to keep the mind inside the body during the asana postures and pranayama infusion practices.

One can practice yoga for a million years and if one fails to keep the attention in the psyche, there will never be full success. One will always lack the full proficiency. That will affect the confidence in yoga and the yoga guru.

Train the attention to stay in the body during the exercises. Do not allow it to stray outside the body. Do not allow it to pursue thoughts which come from others during the exercises. Discipline the attention. Be harsh with it if it tries to disobey this stipulation.

दृष्टपूर्वां दिशं चिन्त्य यस्मिन्संनिवसेत्पुरे
पुरस्याभ्यन्तरे तस्य मनश्चार्यं न बाह्यतः
dṛṣṭapūrvāṁ diśaṁ cintya yasminsaṁnivasetpure
purasyābhyantare tasya manaścāryaṁ na bāhyataḥ (4.31)

dṛṣṭa – seen; pūrvāṁ - before; diśaṁ - place; cintya – thinking; yasmin – in which; saṁnivaset – should reside; pure – in the city; purasyābhyantare = purasya (of the city or psyche) + abhyantare (in the interior, inside); tasya – of his; manaś = manah = mind; cāryaṁ - behavior, operation; na – not; bāhyataḥ - outside

When thinking of a place which was seen before, one should reside in the city in which the incidence occurred. The mental operations are within the psyche, not outside of it. (Anu Gita 4.31)

पुरस्याभ्यन्तरे तिष्ठन्यस्मिन्नावसथे वसेत्
तस्मिन्नावसथे धार्यं सबाह्याभ्यन्तरं मनः
purasyābhyantare tiṣṭhanyasminnāvasathe vaset
tasminnāvasathe dhāryaṁ sabāhyābhyantaraṁ manaḥ (4.32)

purasyābhyantare = (purasya of the city) + abhyantare (inside); tiṣṭhany = tiṣṭhani = situated; asmin – in this; nāvasathe = na (not) + avasathe (city); vaset – should reside; tasmin – in this; nāvasathe = na (not) + avasathe (city); dhāryaṁ - absorbed in; sa – with; bāhyābhyantaraṁ = bāhya (exterior) + abhyantaram (interior); manaḥ - mind

Being situated inside the city, he should reside there with his mind absorbed in the exterior and interior features of that place. (Anu Gita 4.32)

प्रचिन्त्यावसथं कृत्स्नं यस्मिन्कायेऽवतिष्ठते
तस्मिन्काये मनश्चार्यं न कथंचन बाह्यतः
pracintyāvasathaṁ kṛtsnaṁ yasminkāye'vatiṣṭhate
tasminkāye manaścāryaṁ na kathaṁcana bāhyataḥ (4.33)

pracintyāvasathaṁ = pracintya = meditating; kṛtsnaṁ - whole reality; yasmin – in which; kāye – in the body; 'vatiṣṭhate = avatiṣṭhate = being situated; tasmin – in that; kāye – in the body; manaś = manah = whole; cāryaṁ - wander; na – not; kathaṁcana – any way; bāhyataḥ - outside

Meditating in that place, the self sees the whole reality being situated in the body. The mind should not in any way wander outside the body. (Anu Gita 4.33)

संनियम्येन्द्रियग्रामं निर्घोषे निर्जने वने
कायमभ्यन्तरं कृत्स्नमेकाग्रः परिचिन्तयेत्
saṁniyamyendriyagrāmaṁ nirghoṣe nirjane vane
kāyamabhyantaraṁ kṛtsnamekāgraḥ paricintayet (4.34)

saṁniyamyendriya = saṁniyamya (completely restraining) + indriya (sensual energies); grāmaṁ - aggregate; nirghoṣe – without noise; nirjane – without people; vane – in the forest; kāyam – body; abhyantaraṁ - inside; kṛtsnam – whole reality; ekāgraḥ - one object of focus; paricintayet – deeply meditate

In an uninhabited and noiseless forest, while completely restraining the aggregate sensual energies, he should deeply meditate within the body on the whole reality as one object of focus. (Anu Gita 4.34)

Force Open Third Eye?

As I said I will report on and constantly check the agnisara practice. Right now, I do not know how long I will have to do it but I will continue until Swami Rama recommends a change in the practice or suggests another level of breath infusion.

This morning session was thorough and complete with the whole bottom of the trunk and even the thighs, legs and feet being infused and flashing with light in every part.

I noticed that kundalini was completely absent in the trunk of the body and still the infusion worked so that the usual sensations which emanate from the infused kundalini occurred, but only based on the infused energy.

This is a way for a yogi to understand and to believe even, that a Supreme Being, a Personal Being, could have infused this universe with energy or could have caused this universe to be surcharged with static electricity and other types of force-charge.

The yogi can accept that if a limited spirit can infuse energy into its psyche, then the Supreme Spirit could have done this to the cosmic psyche. There is no need for ant to doubt that human beings could build skyscrapers. From observing its own ability to build mud structures, the ant can surmise the possibility of a larger more perceptive being doing likewise on a monumental scale.

When I sat to meditate, the intellect was completely silent. In fact, it was like it was absent completely, like it never existed. Absolutely no thoughts, just a black space all around with super-tiny specks of color. When I focused on the invisible intellect or on the space where the intellect is usually in its default location, there was a black-grey space. It had no images, ideas, nor memories, nothing.

When I focused forward towards the third eye brow chakra, the physical eyes were pulled up into the top of the head. These remained there and I made a slight focus into the center of the energy.

The fact that the physical eyes were pulled up means that the third eye and top of the head chakras were active. For about 30 seconds the third eye opened but instead of seeing clearly through it, I saw a cloud passing slowly across. This cloud was like when a cloud is lit at night by moonlight. It was dense so that I could not see through it into the environment it existed in. After this the opening closed.

In these experiences, I could not control the third eye opening. It operated on its own. The only control I have over these experiences is to do the breath infusion thoroughly.

Yogi and Friend in the Next Life

Last night I had another death premonition. A friend from childhood met me in the astral world. He wanted to discuss the way in which we grew up. This person has wished that he could exchange fortunes with me when we were teenagers, even though he has a much better childhood than mine. He saw some benefit in my childhood when around 14 years of age I moved from Guyana where our bodies were born to Trinidad.

He failed to see that he got good fortune since he grew up under the care of his mother and father, while I did not live under the shelter of my parents but was under the shelter of my paternal grandmother. While my father was an irresponsible young man after marriage, his father was responsible and came home every night to the same house in which his children and spouse lived.

Even though the other field is drought stricken and the one in which the cow feeds has ample rainfall, the cow is likely to consider that the grass is greener on the other size.

Of interest in this story, is that some years after we had this friendship in high school, we came to realize that in their adolescent years our fathers were school friends. There is no telling where one will be in the next birth, with what advantage and disadvantage. The winding curvy road of destiny has many surprises. Some are unfavorable. Sometimes the circumstances are ideal.

This friend who met me in the astral is of the mind that in the next life we will again meet as boys. I did not interfere with his ideas. He would be disappointed to know that I have absolutely no interest in being his friend in any life in any material body ever. If I have to do it, I will do it, but it is not what I prefer.

Little does he understand that material nature was very friendly to him in this life and will perhaps be friendly again in the next life, since material nature has favorites. For me, it will probably be the same with a hell of an infancy and childhood with misfortune stalking every chance it could get.

Cosmic Sense-of-Identity Penetration

I checked the Agnisara practice in reference to its ability to open the third eye brow chakra. Yoga practice should be done at least once per day, early in the morning between 3.30am and sunrise. That is the minimum practice required. It is also beneficial if one's lifestyle permits one to do a session in the afternoon.

Yesterday I got a mental command from Swami Rama to do an afternoon session. He said I should check to see the effects of that so that if I would recommend what I experienced.

The afternoon session cleared the agnisara passage from the navel area down. It seemed that a cloudy dark energy accumulated below the navel. Breath infusion cleared it. I did not sit to meditate immediately after because of some other pressing concerns, but ideally the student should sit to meditate after each session of breath infusion.

During the early morning session, some thoughts from others entered the psyche, Swami Rama sent a message signal saying that the thought-energies should be pulled into the agnisara passage and should be flushed out of the psyche by the infused breath. This works. The way to do this is that when there is a thought during the practice; pull that energy into the area where the breath is being infused. The infused energy will dissipate that psychic thought energy which will vanish into thin air.

When I sat to meditate, there were absolutely no thought energies. I focused upwards in the center of the head. There was a gold shimmer light in the center.

After some time, the coreSelf glowed, emitting a white light. The core is itself light but somehow usually it cannot objectively perceive itself nor contrast itself as light.

Soon after this, the cosmic sense of identity penetrated my psyche hitting my sense of identity. It streamed in from the left side hitting through the left top of the head.

Support the spine

While sitting to meditate make sure that the spine has the proper support. The posture should be such that the lower back is fully supported.

One may sit on a spacious couch in which the spine is cushioned while meditating. If it is not supported, the attention will be invested in keeping the spine in a certain posture. That leakage of attention will result in less focus during the meditation.

People who did asana postures, Indian style, since their youth, may have a spine that can sit without drooping but others should use support.

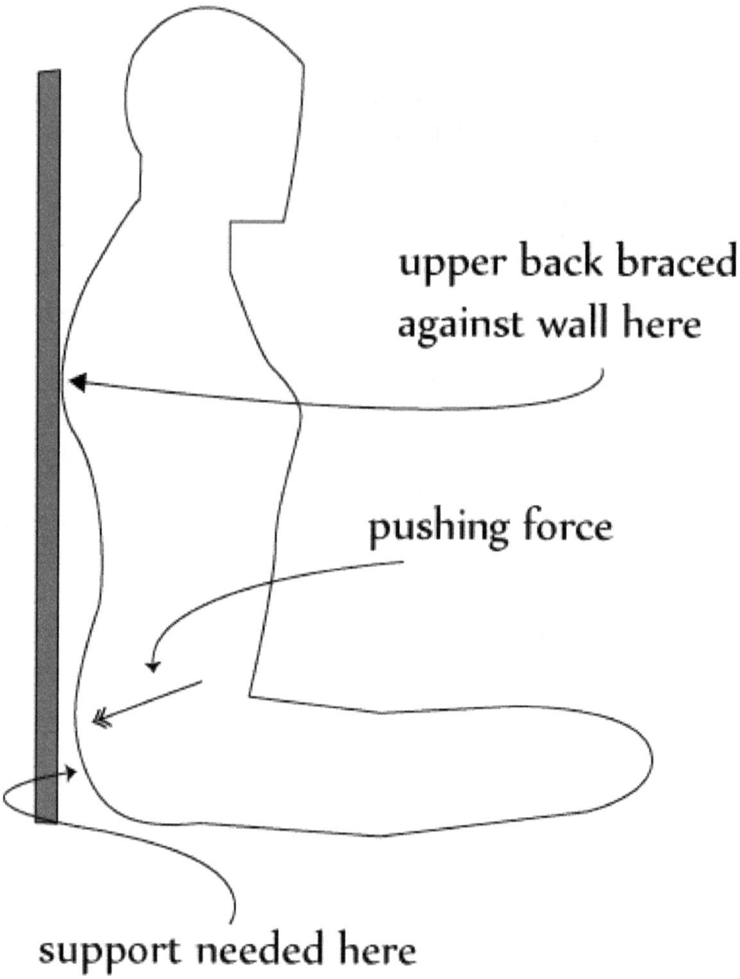
upper back braced
against wall here
pushing force
support needed here

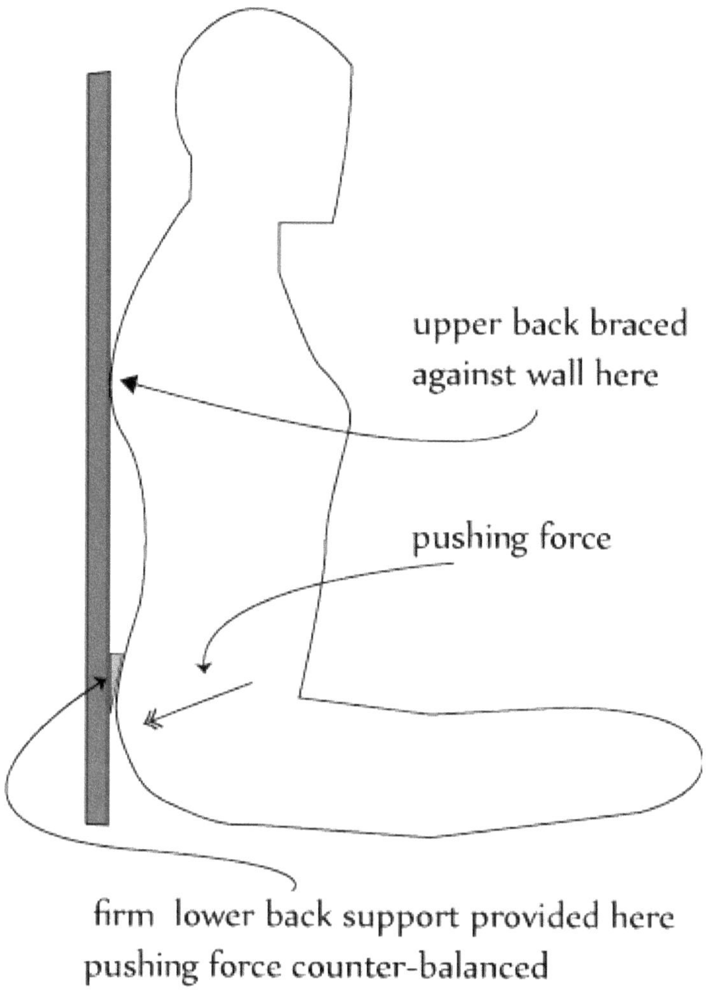
upper back braced
against wall here
pushing force
firm lower back support provided here
pushing force counter-balanced

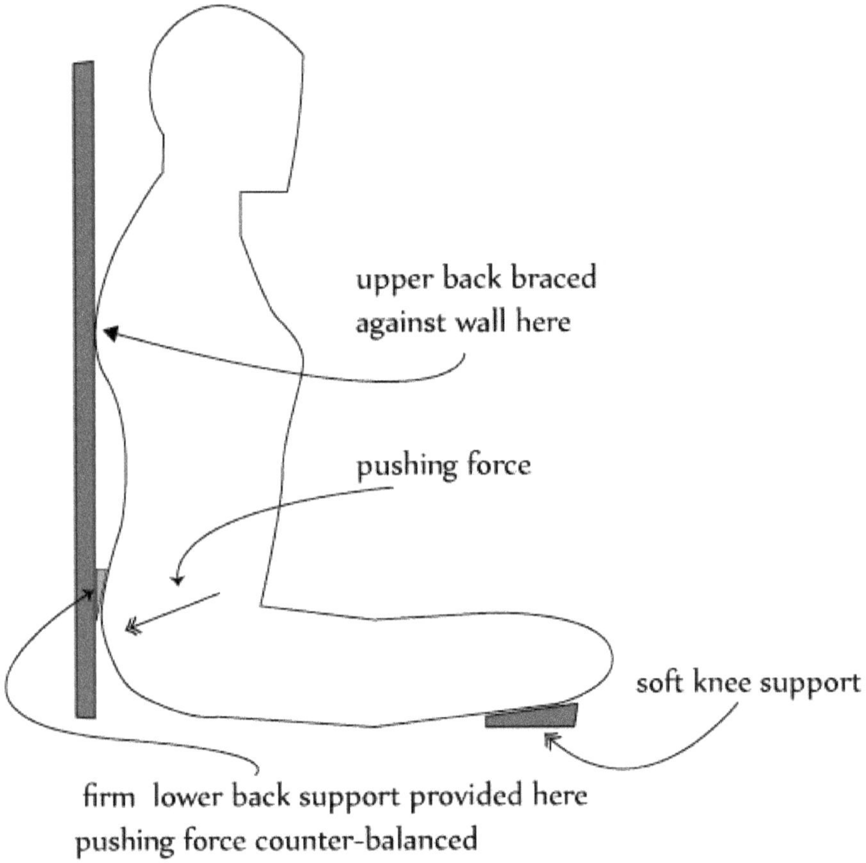

A Bhagavad Gita Verse

नासतो विद्यते भावो
नाभावो विद्यते सतः ।
उभयोरपि दृष्टोऽन्तस्
त्वनयोस्तत्त्वदर्शिभिः ॥२.१६॥
nāsato vidyate bhāvo
nābhāvo vidyate sataḥ
ubhayorapi dṛṣṭo'ntas
tvanayostattvadarśibhiḥ (2.16)

nāsato = na- no + asatas - of the non-substantial things; vidyate- there is; bhāvo- enduring existence; nābhāvo = na — no + abhāvaḥ — lack of existence; vidyate — there is; sataḥ — substantial things; ubhayoḥ — of the two; api — also; dṛṣṭaḥ — perceived; 'ntas = antaḥ — certainty; tvanayos = tu — but + anayoḥ — of these two; tattvadarśibhiḥ = tattva — reality + darśibhiḥ — by mystic powers

Of the non-substantial things, there is no enduring existence. Of the substantial things, there is no lack of existence. These two truths were perceived with certainty by the mystic seers of reality. (Bhagavad Gita 2.16)

Originally, this is from the Upanishads. It is not an original statement of Krishna. It was quoted from the Upanishads. It is said that the Upanishads was the cow. Arjuna was the calf. Krishna as the milkman squeezed the udders of the cow so that the milk entered Arjuna's mouth. Krishna is said to take the milk and cream from the Upanishads, which are representative of the best the Vedas offered humanity.

In the Upanishads, there are two major categories which are sat and asat. Later, Krishna elaborated. Sat means the enduring reality, regardless of whether it can be perceived or not. Asat means that which is perceptible now or was perceived in the past or will be perceived in the future but which is temporary. It does not have perpetual endurance.

There is an argument where some people say that what is temporary is illusion (maya). And that this temporary stuff should be dismissed.

However, we find that it is not practical to do this. The way reality is set up it is a spin off with what is temporary which is supported for the time being by the fabric of eternity which is permanent. Somehow, we should come to terms with what is temporary and also know that under it there is something else which is sat which is really the reality.

Upanishads were written by great minds. Just as Freud and Jung studied the mind, so the ancient yogis of the Upanishadic period studied the psyche. They excelled in the study of psychological reality.

In the Upanishads, Yama is mentioned both as a student and as a deity. He is listed the deity with authority over those who were recently departed from a physical body. He got his position as a deity by being the first human being to consciously astral project. He was the first to study the subtle body, master it and understand how we enter an embryo, depart from a developed physical body and then get another physical form.

Once the advanced spirits started using human bodies, they became restricted to the physical side. Some lost the psychic perspective. It became necessary to study it again. The Upanishads are the first detailed attempt to do that. Some of these yogis published their realization. However, before the Upanishads there were the Rishis around the Pampa forest in India in the time of Rama of Ayodhya. If one reads Valmiki Ramayana, one will know of the austerities and dimensional accomplishments of those yogis. It was the sages of Upanishads who began a rigorous discourse about reality.

Bhagavad Gita is the compressed form of the Upanishads. It takes into account personality which is something that is avoided for the most part in the Upanishads. The special value of *Bhagavad Gita* over the Upanishads is that the Gita takes into account personality.

Christian Yogis in the Astral Regions

Somehow last night I was astrally with some persons who practice the teachings of Paramhansa Yogananda. They met on the astral side in the southern part of the United States, around the states of Alabama, Mississippi and Georgia. There was a large prayer meeting outdoors. At first a lady whom I knew some years ago in Hattiesburg, Mississippi invited me to attend this meeting. I said to her, "You guys are Christian. What have you to do with the Hindu way?"

She replied, "This guy is cool. He supports Christ. He teaches how to do meditative prayers."

She spoke of Paramhansa Yogananda or of a double of him whom he produced in the astral world. As an accomplished yogi, Yogananda can produce doubles.

After a while some people congregated until there were thousands of Western people sitting as if they were yogis. These were people who do no yoga postures or breath infusion practice. They practiced a prayer-meditation method taught by Yogananda.

I said to the lady, "After death, you Christians are supposed to meet Christ in heaven. This guy is not Christ. What happened to your way of salvation?"

She said, "That is the thing. I am not dead as yet. I still use a body but some who died and who are here did not see Christ. They seek alternative methods of spirituality. Since he appreciates Christ and does not criticize and uses a method which is like our prayer system, we use his process."

After this a person who I am related to and who lives in Atlanta Georgia but who is a staunch Catholic, appeared and sat to meditate. She said to me, "If I knew about this years ago, I would have done this previously. I did not realize that you were such a yogi. Anyway, since you are related to us, you can help us to learn this."

Agnisara Tubes in Subtle Body

The Agnisara process is effective. It yeilds psychic penetration during the meditation session after practice. It shifted however in two ways. At first the shift was to the back a little and then it rose up to the chest area on the inside of the chest near the spine. The first shift caused a mini-kundalini to form and when this got white hot with intensity, it flashed and kundalini joined it and came up under the neck into the shoulders. I applied neck lock and suppressed kundalini from entering the head which is what Swami Rama wanted me to do during this particular phase of Agnisara practice.

The idea is to pull kundalini into the head of the body and to cause it not to be in the trunk of the body below the neck. Then the yogi is supposed to generate mini-kundalinis by using the pranic charge confined in various nadis all over the trunk of the body. It begins with finding the subtle excretion track which is from the navel down through the body.

After one finds that, it feels like a tube about one and one-half inches wide but it gets bigger at times and may change into an oval shape. The yogi should target that repeatedly until it completely disappears. That happens after repeated intense infusion with breath, with full focus on the tube so that even if a thought arises in the head of the subtle body, the thought or image is immediately dropped into the tube and is demolished by the infused energy.

After that primary tube is annihilated, another one appears. This goes from the navel front area of the body to the anus, to a little before the anus. This tube is more slanted than the first tube. At the bottom, it leans back more. The yogi should work on this and then blast this one away with the infusion.

What happens is that initially the tube becomes evident to the yogi and the infused energy keeps flowing through it but as the yogi intensifies everything, the dusty cloudy energy in the tube turns white hot like when metal is near the molten stage under intense heat. If the yogi continues the infusion, the intensity causes the tube to disappear.

Then the yogi will find that another tube or a sliver tube, a narrow tube, appears. His attention is shifted to that. It may be in some part of the body or even in the thighs or legs or feet.

The problem facing a yogi who does these procedures is discouragement. This comes in the form of the inability to persist with the practice, and also in the form of a discouragement energy which causes the yogi not to do enough breath infusion to energize the tube.

If the yogi fails to take help from yoga teachers, he will be overwhelmed by the discouragement energy.

A student yogi, all by himself or herself cannot complete these kriyas because the all-surround discouragement energy is more power than the will or desire. Assistance must be taken from the yoga gurus.

A person, who is in a deep hole which has a high vertical wall, cannot climb with no assistance. He or she should not even think about doing it all by himself or herself. One should take help from the yoga gurus.

Agnisara Tubes are Central in the Subtle Body

tube below is from navel
to perineum area (pubic floor)

tube below is from navel to near anus
but not touching anus
this is between anus and perineum area

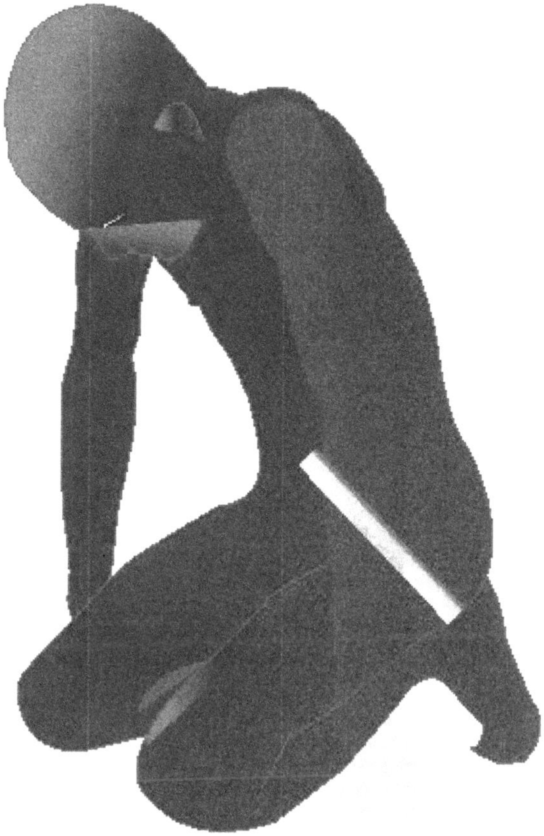

tube is near spine on the inside of the body
centered in the subtle body
it feels like a sliver of molten metal in white heat

Clarification:

The first shift caused a mini-kundalini to form and when this got white hot with intensity, it flashed and kundalini joined with it and came up under the neck into the shoulders. I applied neck lock and suppressed it from entering the head which is what Swami Rama wanted me to so during this particular phase of Agnisara practice.

The idea is to pull kundalini into the head of the body, to cause it not to be in the trunk of the body below the neck. Then the yogi is supposed to generate mini-kundalinis by using the pranic charge confined in various nadis all over the trunk of the body. It begins with finding the subtle excretion track which is from the navel down through the body.

The mini-kundalini mentioned above is not the standard kundalini which governs the construction of the material body and which usually governs the final departure from it at death of the form. This mini-kundalini is one that is created by the infused breath energy when doing the agnisara practice.

This agnisara is not the standard practice which is done with the regular kundalini. This is a practice which is done after the yogi forced kundalini out of the spine into the head. There were previous posts where I described how a yogi caused kundalini to abandon the base chakra, then it hangs in the spine and then from more infusion it retreats up into the head above the neck.

After kundalini does that consistently and lost its bearings in regards to the base chakra location, the yogi can do this advanced agnisara practice. The mini-kundalini is a minor kundalini that is produced on the spot by the infused energy while doing agnisara in a subtle body in which kundalini was drawn into the head above the neck.

The yogi does not create this mini-kundalini but it is created by the action of infused breath. The accumulated compressed infused breath converts into a mini-kundalini at a certain stage of compression, just as in static electricity, there might be a flash of lightning and no one knows where that flash will be. Once the yogi sees the flash in the psyche, he or she should continue the infusion at that location. The breaths should continue until the flash energy disappears completely.

The idea is to first pull the standard nature-created kundalini and cause it to lose its bearings in regards to the base chakra. When this is done and kundalini is kept out of the trunk of the body, the infusion practice changes so that the yogi causes minor kundalinis to form (mini-kundalinis) in various parts of the trunk of the subtle body according to the degree of infusion. These mini-kundalinis are not the standard kundalini.

Radio-Sweep Operation of Third Eye

Meditation this morning after doing breath infusion into the lower part of the body resulted in a different type of third eye brow chakra opening. At first, I noticed that there were no thoughts, memories or images in the mind space which usually displays thought-constructions. There was no attempt of any part of the mind to procure thoughts, images and memories. This is the benefit of a thorough breath infusion session. This is the first result one gets from that.

Instead of sitting to meditate before doing breath infusion, it is wise to do pranayama breath infusion, if you know the practice. Checking and checking for years now, I concluded that Patanjali knew yoga proficiency. He listed pranayama as the fourth stage of yoga.

If one does it before sitting to meditate, one will get benefits in terms of the fifth stage which is pratyahar sensual energy withdrawal and the closure of ideas, images and memories in the mind.

In plain terms a thorough pranayama session causes the yogi to bypass the pratyahar session when he/she sits to meditate. This is if one meditates according to the ashtanga yoga (Patanjali) method.

Doing pranayama is not a waste of time. It causes one to derive a vritti-less impression-less mind-space to work with in meditation. With that one can take the thought/breath/whatever watching or ignoring practices and throw them overboard as being redundant to practice. Of course, one must do the breath infusion in the proper way for this to hold true.

Since there were no impressions in the mind, I did not have to do anything which involved curbing, observing or even neglecting the impressions. I did not have to use mantras, or avoidance techniques or even detachment techniques. You do not have to avoid something which is absent. You do not have to be detached to something which is not present.

In the mind space up front, there were sheets of dark colors which were falling. They would fall. Then they would again appear above. Then they would fall. This continued for a time. This is an operational mode of the third eye. Usually one does not see this as a falling system but rather as a system where there is a disc of color which either approaches one and then disappears or begins to go away from one and then disappears.

These indications tell the yogi that the brow chakra is open, active and ranges into higher dimensions. This is similar to the range knob on a car radio. If one presses or turns the range knob, the radio begins to seek a channel and if it finds one it stops at the frequency and one hear the sounds from that channel. The third eye sweeps to locate other dimensions. This action is perceived by the yogi inside the head, as a cloud of light, usually a dark brown, dark blue, or even purplish light moving away from or approaching or going up or down and then disappearing.

If this happens in meditation where you get this indication of the brow chakra being opened, you should remain focused in the center of it with a slight but not too strong focus. Sometimes, this develops into a clear vision opening where you peer through a large or small window or peer down a funnel or cylindrical channel. One then sees into other dimensions.

If the focus in the center is heavily pushed by willpower or by the idea to force open the chakra that might cause the chakra to disappear completely.

For beginners a breath infusion session should be for twenty to thirty-five minutes. An advanced student can take that much time and double infuse the psyche because of the efficiency of air absorption in the physical body and subtle energy (prana) absorption in the subtle form. However complete sessions for very advanced yogis may take 40 minutes or more. There are tales from ancient yogis in India who did infusion for hours.

Breath infusion must be checked by an advanced yogi, otherwise how do one know that one practiced in the correct way. For myself I am not checked by an advanced yogi in the physical world, except during 1973 thereabouts when I lived in Yogi Bhajan's ashram. I was not checked by him there, even though he did once visit the ashram for two days when I resided there. I was shown the practice by his disciple Prem Kaur (white American body). He did not closely check anything. He told students what to do. There were about four males in the ashram downstairs on a dirt floor basement.

We visited the most advanced student in Denver who was known as Brian but Brain had moved out of the ashram and lived with a teen lover. He had no time to instruct us.

Since I do not have a physical guru, how is my practice checked? I am checked in the astral world. Do not think for a moment that I do this only on the basis of intuition and discovery. Intuition and discovery are parts of this but I am checked by yoga gurus in the astral world. This is afforded me because of many past lives of psychic perception and also austerities for reinforcing that in the present life.

Here are some aspects which should be checked.

- the locks
- the capacity of the lungs to absorb the air
- the bottom of the lungs for absorption of air
- the subtle body's ability to hold in the infused breath until it develops a charge to strike kundalini
- the particular stretches which release toxins and carbon dioxide (apana) out of the bodies (physical and subtle forms)
- the mental locks
- the sex hormone absorption techniques
- control of the objective consciousness when kundalini rises above the neck
- the intellect's change of attitude so as not to want to go down to the genitals for pleasure

These are some particulars.

Breath infusion is a specialize practice which must be checked either physically or astrally. So far, I never paid one dime to be checked by a yoga guru. There are no costs to you except to get to a place to meet with a person who did this for years and progressed thereby.

If one has the hot and heavy feeling from kundalini rising into the head, that means that one did not applying the locks efficiently. One should apply the neck lock? One should apply mental locks in the mind to restrict the attention of the self. One should see kundalini when it makes its first move up the spine? One should perceive it before it enters the head? One should know when it penetrates the intellect.

Mahabandha is a compression system in the lower trunk of the body. It is combined with stomach pull-up pull-in lock, and with anus sphincter and sex region lock. That is okay but it does not do anything for when kundalini passes the neck and goes into the head.

If thoughts persist when kundalini rises into the head, it means that kundalini entered the head in a contaminated lower state. In other words, the student raised kundalini but some other aspects of existence were amiss.

The aspects of one's existence, one's social behavior and such must comply with the yama restraints and niyama behaviors as defined by Patanjali. Kundalini will rise even in the subtle body of a person who is not purified but that is not higher yoga.

Kundalini should be purified first. Life style should be consistent with the *mahavrata* great commitment as explained by Patanjali.

If one has certain social duties hanging, if those are not completed, kundalini will rise in its dirty irresponsible condition and that will give no enlightenment. Please read *Bhagavad Gita* about karma yoga and understand that unless one satisfies that requirement, one's yoga practice will be mediocre.

Arjuna wanted to do yoga instead of fulfilling social duties but the Supreme Being prohibited him from yoga at that time and insisted that he complete social obligations. Krishna told Arjuna that going to do meditate when social duties were pressing is the way of a pretense yogi, who sits to meditate but who in fact only thinks of concerns while practicing.

If one has pressing duties which are not fulfilled, one's meditation will be filled with ideas from the persons to whom one is obligated. Thus, the yoga effort will fail.

In my book *Kriya Yoga Bhagavad Gita,* I discussed the matter of getting a waiver from social duties. Until a yogi gets that, he or she should efficiently service those concerns otherwise the meditation attempt will fail.

This is because the Supreme Being is not involved in our obligations. He cannot protect one from obligations except by urging that one should tend then efficiently. Whatever favors one owes from this or previous lives, one must reimburse as stipulated by providence. Doing yoga is no excuse for not reciprocating. If one fails to pay it will interrupt the meditation practice.

New students should work on the lower two chakras. For about six months at least focus on the two lower chakras, muladhara and svadhishthana (base chakra and sex chakra). When one infuses breath, one should put attention on the base chakra alone. Focus on pushing the air into the very bottom of the lungs. From there push it to the navel. From the navel there push it around the sexual front curve to the base chakra. Put all attention on this while doing the breath infusion. As one does this put all attention in the trunk of the body. Make an attempt to move the attention out of the head into the lower trunk.

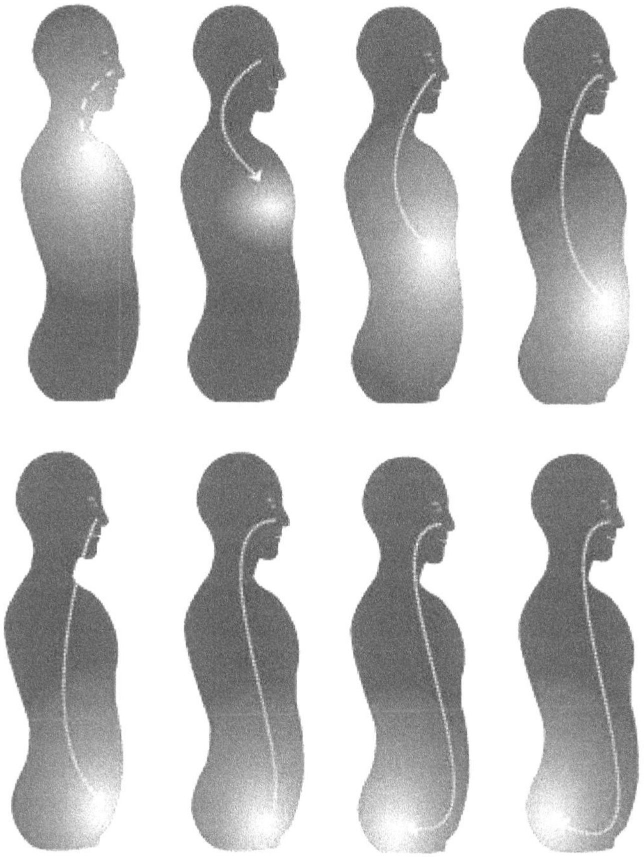

Kundalini may move into the head in the wrong way and with the wrong energy content. To change that one should purify the lower chakras as described above.

One important thing is that if one does standing postures while doing this practice, there is a likelihood that one will lose track of the physical body and it will fall to the ground. One should keep the body in a low posture and if one stands during the session, one should be attentive. The locks should be very tight so that the body does not assume a lax posture which might cause it to fall to the ground if kundalini ascends.

Kundalini should come up as an electrical sensation or as shimmering bright energy (gold or gold-white if perceived visually within the psyche). It may move as bliss energy in tiny crystals.

Be sure to hammer away at the base chakra because that is the sure method for purifying kundalini. A student should focus on kundalini's base. If one successfully gets the infused energy into the base, kundalini will rise as a result. It will rise with a cleansing energy from the breath infusion. It will blast the sushumna nadi channel from the bottom upwards, sweeping the impurities every time it ascends in that way.

Kapalabhati pranayama

Do the rapid breathing but with focus on the exhale only. Make no attempt to focus on the inhale. Put all your power into the exhale so that it is heard loudly as the air is forced out. In the meantime, internally conceive of the air moving down into the body but not coming out. This is like when you air up a car tire. As the air goes in it should not be allowed to escape from the tire, otherwise there will be no air retention.

However, the air that is accumulated is the air on the inhale. The exhaled air is not retained. It goes out. The compression of the air into the system is the compression of the air you take in on the inhale. The lungs should absorb this air and not ignore or be unresponsive to it. This air is compressed in and builds a cumulative force which at a certain point will strike kundalini. If there is a burning sensation while you do the breathing, keep breathing rapidly while pushing into the burning sensation. Stop when you feel you must and apply the locks with a downward mystic thrust. The locks are usually in and up on the pulls. While a lock is the physical muscular action, the mental lock is a downward thrust towards the base chakra. This will cause the infused air to attack the navel chakra in the front part of the body (not the navel chakra on the spine). When this front navel chakra is attacked repeatedly, there will come a time when it will explode in the subtle body. From then onward the energy will always pass through the navel easily.

Bhastrika Pranayama

For bhastrika everything is the same as for kapalbhati except that bhastrika is with focus and forcefulness in both the inhale and exhale. Do not attempt bhastrika if you have not mastered kapalbhati and if kapalbhati has not become a reflex for you. This is because otherwise your attention will be split in too many directions. As soon as you did kapalbhati say for about 6 months to 2 years, you can do bhastrika. In fact, if one does kapalabhati, it will change by itself into bhastrika.

Social Obligations of a Yogi

Social obligations from this life only are not the concern in yoga. A yogi should tap into previous lives. Many consequences from the past lives leak into the present existence. The past is woven into the present and comes before us as the present. In other words, despite what people say and believe, the past haunts us. It demands services. I recently did a translation and commentary on the *Anu Gita* where this was explained to Arjuna.

There is psychic interference into one's life because of obligations one has to ancestors, those of this present life and those from other lives. Besides these, there are other pressing psychic influences. These must be serviced, otherwise the meditation practice will be nothing but a joke.

Observation of Kundalini Arousal

Kundalini must be guided but first one should observe how it becomes aroused and where it wants to route itself when it is energized. If it goes where desired one should allow it, otherwise one should use locks and mental pressures to divert it in the required passage.

Kundalini cannot be trusted. It is like the self is the king and the kundalini is the prime minister from a lower class of people. If the king thinks that the prime minister will spontaneously work in his interest, that king will be misled.

Kundalini will from time to time do something that is in the spiritual interest of the self but when one least expects it will revolt so that it remains in charge of the kingdom with the king or self as a crippled puppet.

Siddha teachers like Gorakshnath gave bandhas or locks for the reason of keeping kundalini under control, so that it does nothing crazy which will in the long run puts the self into an awkward position or makes the self take an awkward body like that of crocodile.

Many people have no idea that the soul can take an animal body. They think that soul can only take a human format, but that is not a fact. If one is not careful and if one does not supervise kundalini and keep it tied to divine interest, one will descend the evolutionary tree of life and take animal forms.

If for instance I am attached to material existence, then say for example if this planet becomes uninhabitable for life either by human destructive acts or by astronomical events, it means that I will be out of luck and will not take even a fish form so that I can again be a physical being. But if somehow some other planet fosters life and it is somewhere nearby in this galaxy, I may be attracted to that place psychically. If no human forms are manifested there, I will take whatever beastly format I can get. My desperation for physical existence will itself cause me to follow kundalini into a crude lifeform where

I can get physical existence. In the human life, one should harness kundalini so that it has no freedom to pursue physical existence.

Compress and restrict kundalini. Force it to come into the head in the central spinal passage. That is the first objective. Be sure that when it enters the head it is not allowed to attack the intellect, the thought-manufacturing psychic mechanism in the subtle head. If you are careless with this, the coreSelf will go into a subjective state and the physical body will fall to the ground.

This is not an alarming development but be attentive for it. Kundalini is sex-crazed which means that its highlight is sexual climax. If you divert it from sex, it will still need excitement. It will try to get that by fusing with the intellect in the head of the subtle body. A yogi should acutely observe, and regulate kundalini's rise through the spine so that it does not sever the connection between the coreSelf and the intellect, because that will result in temporary loss of motor control of the physical body.

Chit Akash Access

Chit akash has several levels. It consists of several bliss environments where divine persons and energies abound. Those inhabitants use supernatural or spiritual bodies which can be seen if one uses a similar body.

In this world, we experience three dimensions. We may consider what it would be like if we shifted to four dimensions but in chit akasha, dimensions are multiple beyond what we can calculate.

The place where you really want to go in the chit akash is where there are environments with life, with everything which is life. This is called *akshara dham* or *vaikuntha*.

I have an existential register on this physical side. Now and again I am on the astral side in various dimensions there but the real place for me is the chit akash in a dimension where there are only divine beings in a divine environment with divine vegetation and elements with no physical or psycho-physical substance.

Peering into the chit akash is the main business of a siddha yogi but the problem is that there are pressing social concerns on this side. These duties consume the life of a yogi. They keep his development stunted.

Naad Sound Absorption

Naad sound occurs differently for different persons. It is heard originating from mental locations as well. Naad sound should not be taken lightly. It is the real *Om* sound which is not made by anyone. It is the resonation from where the material existence borders the spiritual existence. A yogi should keep naad nearby as the constant companion and reference.

If one can, one should go deep into naad. One may cross through a naad vortex to another side of existence. If possible, this should be done frequently

When in meditation if one is lost or if one is controlled by a thought, one should take help from naad by fleeing into it. When there are distractions from wherever or whoever, run to naad.

We take up social positions in this world where physical well-being is the top priority. For that physical eyes are important. Once we get the hang of it that this world is simply a *fly by night* thing, we may shift interest to the subtle body. After we master that, we realize that the subtle world is psychic physical existence which means that it too will eventually fiz out.

At first, we have this physical body. It may take us for about eighty years. In my case sixty plus of those eighty years are finished. At that time when the track of this life runs course what is next? It will be the subtle body but how far can that take me?

There are two routes once the physical body is finished, either I develop as another physical body or I stay in the astral existence and wait for that to expire in about fifteen billion years. Assuming that I am a yogi of worth and that I am lucky, I can assume that my subtle body may survive for another fifteen billion years. Okay but then what will happen?

Then I must find another way of existing or I will be extinct. This is why the great yogis slighted the subtle body as being a disgusting adjunct. It is because that body has fear of a cosmic light-out. Even if it can sidestep the blowout of the sun, it definitely cannot out-live the galaxy. This Milky Way will not last forever. Just as we think that there must be something other than the physical form which is for eighty years there has to be some other shelter that one can use besides the subtle body.

Two nights ago, I was with a friend in the astral South America. He showed a place where people stay in the astral. They live very simply. There is no violence. Everyone is peaceful there. They have cars which are like the cars used in the 1940's. He invited me to go there as soon as my body would die. Both of us were about sixty years of age at the time. He and I were the only ones at that astral place who were not deceased.

I did not tell him anything but I have no intentions of living in such a place. I do not intent to put myself in such a place. Being here in the physical situation with its eighty-year limit, is enough stress for me. My friend was all smiles about the astral place as if he found paradise.

In meditation, in astral projection and dream states, we have to make sure that we understand the flaws of the subtle body. It is better than the physical system for sure but it has its downside. Hence in meditation do not use the physical eyes and if one can, one should not use the two subtle eyes. At first one should use those subtle eyes and be excited about them but later as one advances, one should reduce their usage. Instead, one should develop pranaVision, third eye singular vision, intellect organ vision, sense of identity vision and coreSelf direct vision. These are distinctly separate visions even though when one fuses with the other, it becomes difficult to distinguish.

A yogi should practice disabling the physical eyes by depriving that optic system of energy. He should learn how to close the two eyes of the subtle body by shutting down the psychic energy which runs through those orifices. These practices are part of the fifth stage of yoga, which is pratyahar, withdrawal of sensual energies from places which cause the yogi to back-track into another material body.

If one fails to purify the lower chakras, to infuse that area with a high level of subtle energy, the progress made in other ways will be meaningless because the lower areas will pull one back to a lower level, after one transited to a higher one for a short period of time.

Flash erratic enlightenment is what it is, as being a flash experience. It will not sustain the yogi on a higher plane but if he can remove or eliminate or even upgrade the lowest parts of your psyche, he can have some permanent elevation.

Index

A

Abraham, 99
absoluteness, 160
abstract location, 120
Adi Shankar, 77
adjuncts,
  details, 135, 141
  necessary, 68
  relationship, 185
affection, 172
African savannah, 24
agnisara, 212
air conditioning, 59
akashic records, 22
Alabama, 157
alcohol, 200
alcoholic, 99
almonds, 98-99
Alzheimer, 32
Amitabha, 156
amusement part, 181
anahat naad, 33
anatomy, difference, 37
ancestors, 23
Angeles City, 193
ants, 63, 100, 231
Anu Gita, 44, 146
aphids, 100
Arjuna, 146, 192
army, 186
arteries
arthritis, 149
asat, 237
ashram, 154
asphalt, 115
astral body,
  atomic, 12
  influenced, 127
  language, 14
  sitting separation, 27
  speed, 25
  uncontrolled, 18
astral building, 195
astral Canada, 91
astral flying, 173
astral fruit, 43
astral Guyana, 127
astral hell, 80
astral land, 112
astral language, 26
astral money, 195
astral paradise, 87
astral police, 43
astral projection,
  author, 153
  detail, 11
astral realm, freaky, 20
astral student, 37
astral travel,
  pressure, 20
  speed, 26
astral world, hidden, 24
astral zones, 139
astronaut, 15
atomic body, 12
author,
ancestry, 101
astral travel, 14-15
cosmic experience, 126
deity seen, 105
diet, 96, 97, 198
father in astral, 112
killed chicken, 96

past lives, 194
practice check, 245
author, continued,
rebirth, 76, 137
repairman, 50
ship experience, 183
Autobiography of a Yogi, 194
Ayodhya, 237

B

Babaji, 44, 192
baking powder, 101
Balarama, 78
bananas, 98
Bardon, 77
base chakra, 45, 57, 113
batter, 102
bean curd, 98
beans, 98
bears, 24, 100
beef, 198
belief, 17
berry trees, 43
Beverford, 44, 193
Beverford, astral land, 60
Beverford, astral visit, 51
Bhagavad Gita, 146, 237
Bhaishavya, 156
Bhajan – see Yogi Bhajan
bhakti yoga, 204
Bhaktivedanta, 125
bhramari mudra, 208
Bikram Choudhoury, 44
binocular, 143
birth, various, 96
black pepper, 101
blackeye peas, 98
black-out, 140
bladder, 27
blank existence, 139
blind follower, 125
blindfold, 37, 108
blood pressure, 153
blood smell, 102
Blue Beach, 125
blue boy, 144
blue pearl, 144
blue star, 182
body,
bomb, 114
elderly, 153
lack of control, 19
property, 115
snatching, 77
switching, 79-80
bomb, 114
bones, 102
books, 193
brahmachari, 145
brahmaloka, 138
brahman level, 93
Brazil nuts, 99
breast breath infusion, 204
breast tube, 84
breath infusion
astral practice, 83, 133
attack kundalini, 124
detail, 106
diagram, 109-111
effective, 243
elderly body, 124
Brian, 245
British diet, 101
brow chakra, 175, 244
bubble body, 36, 163
Buddha,
austerities, 113
births, 96
deities, 156
son, 115
teacher of, 165
buddhi, 136
buddhi yoga, 45
bull, 116
Burma, 26
butcher, 96
butter, 101

C

cakes, 101
calf, 237
camouflage, 24

Canada, 91
cape, 116
carnivorous diet, 96
carrot, 98-99
catfish, 101
cauldron, 186
causal body, 21
causal energy, 37
causal plane, 102, 192
causal zone, 92
caveman, 100, 184
chanting, detail, 16
Charles Darwin, 188
Chaurangi, 189
chicken,
  author killed, 96
  egg, 96
  history, 100
  thigh, 99
Chinese bean curd, 98
chit akash, 52
chives, 101
chlorophyll, 98
Choudhoury, 44
Christ, 190
citron, 102
citrus fruits, 98
Clark Air Base, 193
collard green, 98
colon, 74
color, as sound, 48
commission, 87
commitment, 246
compassion, 123
components of consciousness, 47
concentration force, 11
conjugal love, 216
consciousness, components, 47
consequence, 172
constipation, 73, 98
consumption, 209
content of thought, 143
coreSelf,
  adjuncts, 66
  billed, 90
  bull, 116
  diagram, 18
  experiencer, 47
  intellect needed, 141
  naad, 18
  passive, 38
  power supply, 185
  relocation, 17
  surrounded, 72, 86
cosmic body, 12
cosmic circuit, 125
cosmic collapse, 102
cosmic intellect, 62, 179
cosmic kundalini, 179
cosmic light, 180
cosmic light-out, 251
cosmic sense of identity, 179
cosmic spirit, 179
cosmology, 93
cows, 98
crabs, 101
crickets, 17
crocodile, 249
crystal ball, 143
cultural prejudice, 14-15
cyst, 19

D

dairy products, 96
dakinis, 145
dance, 148
darshan, 191
Darwin, 188
daydream, 25, 143
death row, 218
death,
  absolute, 217
  already known, 90
  base chakra, 45
  experience, 81
  omen, 137
  psychic existence, 38
deduction, 9

de-exist, 102
deities, 191
deity, possessed, 160
deity, yantra, 83
dementia, 32, 181
dervish, 148
Descartes, 66
desire, 207
desires, fulfillment, 51
Devaki, 78
Devi, 190
diabetes, 153
diagram, person, 83
diet, 101, 198
disciples, teacher quarrel, 189
disharmony, 49
divine body, 105
divine world, 250
dog, 58, 91
double, 238
dream journal, 168, 177
dream, sexual, 24
dream, imagination, 25
drug dealer, 41
drug use, 60, 69
dungeon, 144
dynasty, 192

E

eagle, 91
ear canal, 8
earth, gravity, 75
earth, vaporize, 133
eat for practice, 199
effect-energies, 207
eggs, 96, 99, 101
ego, 141
elderly person, 153
embryo, development, 188
end of life, 190
energy, universal, 30
enlightenment, 252
environment, 196, 250
evolution, 100
existence? 53
exorcism, 41
explosives, 42
exposure, 201
eye of fish, 100
eyes, 208

F

fabric of eternity, 237
fall in love, 216
false ego, 141
fantasy of individual, 63
feathers, 102
figurines, 60
firefly, 52
fish, 97, 100, 101, 198
fistule, 19
flash experience, 252
flesh, 96, 102
follower, 125
food, flesh, 96
food, rank, 101
foot prints, 205
foot spark, 197
foundry, 186
four-handed Form, 105, 192
foxes, 100
Franz Bardon, 77
Freeman Farr,125
Freud, 237
fruits, 98

G

galaxy demolished, 183
ganja, 21
Gautam, 156
gayatri, 15
geyser, 54
ghosts, 196
glass, 51
glove, 186
God's diet, 101
godsend, 165
goggles, 53
gold, 195
gonads, 220
good shepherd, 99
Gorakshnath, 77, 189

grass greener, 232
gravity, 75
Great Masters of the Himalayas, 194
Greece, 223
greens, 99
grocery, 96
grouse, 100
guru, 41
gush-way, 173
Guyana, astral, 127, 183

H

habit of practice, 166
hamsa, 15
Hare Krishna, 125
hashish, 21
hassles, 89
heart trouble, 98
heaven, diet, 101
helium, 75
help, required, 164
hen's reproductive fluids, 99
hereafter, duration, 206
heroin, 20
hide and seek, 24
highway, 115
hum, 157
human body diet, 96
humbug sexual energies, 160

I

I am dead, 75
iceberg, 181
idea, location, 134
Ila, 79
illusion, 237
imagination, detail, 24
impression, 48
India, author, 14
individual, 40
individuality, 63, 65
Indraloka, 191
influenced experiencer, 47
inhibition, 207
inner Mongolia, 60
inner vision, 121
insight, 106, 115
intellect,
    color 134
    details, 136
    disabled, 144
    disempowered, 37
    invisible, 134
    kundalini, 67
    location, 8, 176
    orb, 6
    perception of, 52
    seer, 68
    self bewildered by, 120
    spins, 26
    targeted, 47
    vision instrument, 34, 133
interference, 115
intestinal system, 74
introspection, 107-108
iSelf, object, 6
isolation, 202
Italy, 52

J

janaloka, 138
Japanese martial arts, 194
Jesus, 138
jewels, 186
jnana chakshu, 136
jnana dipa, 136
journal, 177
Jung, 237

K

kale, 98
kamarupa, 72
Kamsa, 204
Kashyap, 87
king, 186
Kirpal Singh, 16, 125
knowledge, defined, 40
Krishna, 78, 138, 190
Krishna, divine cowherd boy, 106
kriya system, 45
Kubera, 79
kumblaka, 189

kundalini,
arousal, 148, 161, 169, 183
assigned, 140
attacks, 124
base, 70, 187
bearings 242
biological, 185
body thrown, 160
command, 47
configuration, 132
controlled, 184
death condition, 95
diamond, 94
discouragement 238
downward, 29
elimination, 102, 227
end, 114
fingers, 121
front, 120
instinct, 124
intellect, 67
jumps, 121
kundalini
mini, 238
neck, 54
pearl drops, 26
pratyahar, 130
rebirth influence, 73
reform, 73
reliance on, 184
seen 246
sensations, 248
sex urge, 22
sexual arousal, 28
sexual climax, 171
sleep, 170
stub, 129
tendency, 128
thighs, 54
trunk, 28
untrustworthy, 249
uprooting, 45
urination, 27
willpower, 70
kundalini yoga, practice check, 245
Kuru, 192

L

Lahiri Mahasaya, 45
lamprey, 113
language, astral, 14
laser beam, 184
leech, 113
legs, infusion, 80
lemon peel, 102
leopard, 91
lifeForce, - also see kundalini
lifeForce,
desperation, 48
migration, 74
light, 8
lightning, 183
lights-in, 141
lights-out, 141
liquor, 99
live wire, 10
Lobsang Rampa, 77
location of thoughts, 142
location, 49, 120
locks, 141, 248
Lord's Prayer, 99
love, 216
LSD, 20, 59
lucid dream, detail, 10
lusty energy, 72

M

mahabandha, 246
Mahabharata, 44
maharloka, 138
mahavrata, 246
mammal, 188
mandala, 83
mantra,
naad, 125
prop, 17
ultimate, 34
marijuana, third eye, 59
Markandeya, 44, 194
marooned sailors, 63
martial arts, 194

Martinique, 183
matador, 116
math, 172
Matsyendranath, 77, 189
maya, 237
meals, 98
meat, 98
meditation,
  blindfold, 37
  transcendent, 24
memory,
  mix, 171
  vivid, 104
mental chatter, 9, 166
message-energy, 221
methods of release, 192
microscope, 12
milk, 73, 98, 237
milk, diet of mother, 198
milkman, 237
mind,
  body, 229
  chamber, 139
  contents, 135
  environment, 195
  physical reality, 38
  self, 47, 103
mine, 42
mini kundalini, 242
mistakes, 219
molars, 98
money, 195
Mongolia, 60
monks, astral quarrel, 89
moons, 191
morality, 207
morphine, 20
mortality, detail, 169
mother, diet, 198
Muhammad, 190
Muktananda, posture, 149
Mukti Baba, 26
mystic power, 79
mystic skill, 11

N

naad,
  boring, 125
  core attached, 48
  core attracts, 18
  details, 33, 250
  drift, 35
  final resonance, 16
  focus details, 35
  Kirpal Singh, 16
  loud buzz, 205
  meditation, 15
  pronounced, 52
  radiance, 59
  shrill frequency, 17
nadi shodana, 57, 81
Narayana, 192
narcotics, 21
nature, closed system, 102
navel, design, 9
neck, kundalini flush, 138
Nityananda Baba, 147
Nityananda, bubble body, 164
nomad, 73
non-corruptibility, 194
nostalgic needs, 113
notes, 81, 168
nothing, 133
notion, 9
nuclear bombs, 161
nuts, 98

O

obligations, 249
observer, core, 38
old man, 147
Om hrim, 15
Om mani padme hum, 15
Om mani padme hum, 157
Om namo Bhagavata vasudevaya, 15
Om namo shivaya, 15, 157
Om, 15
omen, 137
oneness, 138, 160
onion, 101

opium, 20, 73
optic nerves, 208
orb, location, 176
organic food, 97
out-of-the-body experience
ovaries, 220
overseer, 43

P

Pacific, 125
Padmanabha, 105
pain killers, 73
Pampa forest, 237
Paramhansa Yogananda, 238
paradise, 87
param atma, 179
paranormal, 115
parents, appreciated, 177
park, 181
Paramhamsa Yogananda, 192
passionate force, 72
pastry, 101
Patanjali, 208
peak of youth, 124
peanut butter, 98
pearl drops, 26
peasant, 186
penis, Stuna, 79
pepper, 101
perception, types, 252
person, 40
person, diagram, 83
personal energy, 29
person-self, 227
petri dish, 201
Philippines, 125, 193
physical body value, 214
physical existence, 191
physician, 41
pikes, 117
pill, 41
pinto beans, 98
pistachio, 98
place for working, 195
placenta, 187
point of perspective, 47
point of visualization, 125
polar bears, 24, 100
police warden, 43
pond, 36
popsicle, 130-131
portends, 205
possession, 159
posture, male/female, 37
potato, 97, 99
practice habit, 166
prana will show, 199
pranava, 33
pranaVision, 252
pranayama, 86, 244
pranotthana, 198
pratyahar, stages, 131
prayer meeting, 238
predestination, 226
prejudice, 14-15
Prem Kaur, 245
pride, 177
primitive mat, 172
printer, 81
prison, 144
privacy, 13
probe, 12
probiscus, 12
projective, 14
prostitute, 42
protein, 98
providence, 115
psilocybin, 125
psyche, 39, 101, 166
psychiatrist, 41
psychic sensitivity, 28

Q, R

queen, 186
Rama, 138, 237
Ramayama, 237
Rampa, 77
rank food, 101
rankness, 102
rations, 43
reading, 193

rebirth,
ancestor, 30
author, 137
expense, 78
ignorance, 32
process, 181, 206
resistance, 190
siddha help, 82
tendency, 74
rectum, 74
reference, 91
reincarnation,
author, 76
detail, 19, 207
relationship advance, 203
remnant of self, 53
repairman, 50
residence, psychological, 39
revelation, 191
rheumatoid, 149
rice, 98
ripping away, 157-158
Rishi Singh Gherwal, 44, 56, 194
Rohini, 78

S

sadhu, 132
Sahara, 176
Sai Baba, 26
sailors, 63
salt, 98, 101
samsara, 207
samyama, 5, 45
sanga, 132
Sanskrit, 78
Santa Barbara, 60
sat, 237
satyaloka, 138
savannah, 24
savior, 190
school friend, 232
segregation, 67, 184
self,
adjuncts, 66
details, 139
environment contrast, 195
mind, 47, 103
origin, 64
questions, 24
reform, 164
remnant, 53
semen upward, 111
sense of identity, 128
senses, kundalini controls, 185
sex chakra, 41
sex hormone route, 109-110
sex organ chakra, 41
sex urge, 112
sex you! 30
sexual climax, 162, 171
sexual dream, 24
shadow universe, 52
shaft of energy, 51
shaman, 41
Shankar, 77
Shatakratu, 192
shepherd, 99
ship wreck, 63
ship, 183
Shiva, 190
siddha, 45, 187, 191, 193, 206
siddha body, 212
siddha status, 137-138
siddhi, 11
signatures, 178
silver cord, 75
sitting duck, 217
sky of consciousness, 52, 72
slaves, 101
sleep, 170
small of back, 161
smoking, 51
snow leopard, 91
social association, 200
social obligations, 246
social person, 40
solutions, 218

sound current, 16, 125
South Korean woman, 60
soybeans, 98
spaceship, 15
Spain, 119
species, think, 9
spices, 101
spinach, 98
spiritual world, 250
spiritual zone, 139
spring, 61
squid, 101
squirrel, 215
star, 181
stone axe, 184
stool, 74
string beans, 98
stub kundalini, 129
student notes, 81
student, students, 145
Stuna Karna, 79
subconscious mind, entry, 21, 81, 216
subjectivity, 64
sublimal desire, 207
subtle body,
- assets, 80
- breath infusion, 83
- duration, 251
- escapist, 20
- heavenly type, 69
- independent, 20
- interposed, 168
- locks, 215
- possession, 160
- relationship advance, 203
- shrinks, 188
- unrestrictive, 23
- ventilation, 59
- willpower, 207

subtle world, sex, 112
sufi, 148
sugar, 101
sun deity, 154
sun planet, 52
supersoul, 179
support, 51
Supreme Beings, 78
Supreme Person, 165
surfer, 50
surgery, 19
sutram, 179
Swami Rama, bodies, 214
swargaloka, 69
sword, 117, 186

T

tag-team, 128
tantric mantra, 15
Taoism, 81
Taoist figurines, 60
tapaloka, 138
teacher, 94, 218
thinking,
- existence, 66
- involuntary, 9
- species, 9

third eye,
- details, 64, 175
- experience, 123
- perceptions, 181
- sex involvement, 221

thought,
- breath infusion, 155
- core, 36
- creation, 67
- intellect location, 8
- location, 134, 142, 176
- missiles, 49
- neutralization, 13
- none, 9
- organ, 143
- projective, 14
- response, 155
- speed, 8, 133

thunderclap, 126
tide, 191
tigers, 24
time bombs, 114
time limit, 30
time, astral, 191

time, variant,13
tinnitus, 33
tobacco, 51
toe, 142
tofu, 98-99
tool kit, 43
tour guide, 81
toys, 73
treasury, 78
tundra, 91
turnip greens, 98

U

uncertainty, 63
universal consciousness, 63
Universal Form, 192
universe, shadow, 52
Upanishad, 237
urdhvareta, 111
urination, 27
USA, 26

V

vagina of Ila, 79
Valmiki, 237
Vasudeva, 192
vegetarian diet, 96, 198
Venture, 194
vinegar, 101
Vishnu, 105
Vishnu Gosh, 44
vision, types, 252
vrittis-less, 244

W

water spring, 61
wheat, 98
whiskey, 41
white-out, 140
whole wheat, 98-99
wild goose chase, 184
willpower, 207, 217
wire, 10
woman, infant, 73
woman, Korean, 60

X, Y, Z

yama, 237
yams, 98
yantra, 83
yitchnoids, 136
yoga,
  astral practice, 133
  stages, 208
Yoga Sutras, 45
yoga teacher, disembodied, 94
Yogananda, 44, 192, 238
Yogesh, causal plane, 192
Yogi Bhajan,
  ashram, 154
  contact with, 194
  Kirpal conpared, 125
  siddha, 193
  student, 105
yogi,
  bodies, 211, 214
  frustrated, 147
  hideout, 112
  insight, 115
  progress, 151
yogurt, 201
youth, aim, 124

About the Author

Michael Beloved (Yogi *Madhvāchārya)* took his current body in 1951 in Guyana. In 1965, while living in Trinidad, he instinctively began doing yoga postures and tried to make sense of the supernatural side of life.

Later in 1970, in the Philippines, he approached a Martial Arts Master named Arthur Beverford. He explained to the teacher that he was seeking a yoga instructor. Mr. Beverford identified himself as an advanced disciple of *Śrī* Rishi Singh Gherwal, an Ashtanga Yoga master.

Beverford taught the traditional Ashtanga Yoga with stress on postures, attentive breathing and brow chakra centering meditation. In 1972, Michael entered the Denver, Colorado Ashram of *kundalini* yoga Master *Śrī* Harbhajan Singh. There he took instruction in bhastrika pranayama and its application to yoga postures. He was supervised mostly by Yogi Bhajan's disciple named Prem Kaur.

In 1979 Michael formally entered the disciplic succession of the Brahmā-Madhava-Gaudiya Sampradaya through *Swāmī* Kirtanananda, who was a prominent sannyasi disciple of the Great Vaishnava Authority *Śrī Swāmī* Bhaktivedanta Prabhupada, the exponent of devotion to Sri Krishna.

However, yoga has a mystic side to it, thus Michael took training and teaching empowerment from several spiritual masters of different aspects of spiritual development. This is consistent with *Śrī* Krishna's advice to Arjuna in the *Bhagavad Gītā*:

Most of the instructions Michael received were given in the astral world. On that side of existence, his most prominent teachers were *Śrī Swāmī* Shivananda of Rishikesh, Yogiraj *Swāmī* Vishnudevananda, *Śrī Bābāji Mahasaya* - the master of the masters of *Kriyā* Yoga, *Śrīla* Yogeshwarananda of Gangotri - the master of the masters of *Rāj* Yoga (spiritual clarity), and Siddha *Swāmī* Nityananda the Brahmā Yoga authority.

The course for kundalini yoga using pranayama breath infusion was detailed by Michael in the book *Kundalini Hatha Yoga Pradipika*. This current book was composed from meditation and breath-infusion notes which were originally shared in staple bound booklets as Yoga Journals.

Michael's preliminary books relating to this topic are *Meditation Pictorial*, *Meditation Expertise*, and *Meditation ~ Sense Faculty* (co-author). Every technique (kriya) mentioned was tested by him during pranayama breath-infusion and *samyama* deep meditation practice.

This is a result of over forty years of meditation practice with astute subtle observations intending to share the methods and experiences. The information is published freely with no intention of forming an institution or hogtying anyone as a disciple.

Publications

English Series

Bhagavad Gita English

Anu Gita English

Markandeya Samasya English

Yoga Sutras English

Hatha Yoga Pradipika English

Uddhava Gita English

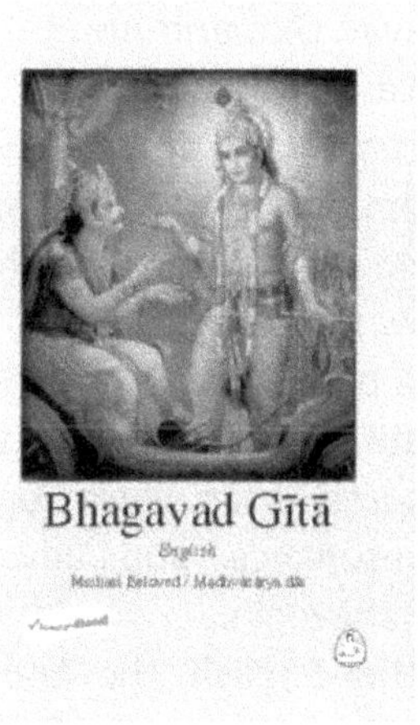

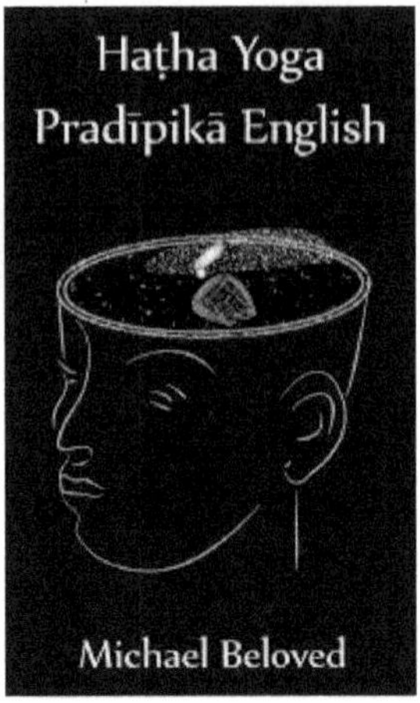

These are in 21st Century English, very precise and exacting. Many Sanskrit words which were considered untranslatable into a Western language are rendered in precise, expressive and modern English.

Three of these books are instructions from Krishna. **In Bhagavad Gita English** and **Anu Gita English**, the instructions were for Arjuna. In the **Uddhava Gita English,** it was for Uddhava. Bhagavad Gita and Anu Gita are extracted from the Mahabharata. Uddhava Gita was extracted from the 11th Canto of the Srimad Bhagavatam (Bhagavata Purana). One of these books, the **Markandeya Samasya English** is about Krishna, as described by Yogi Markandeya, who survived the cosmic collapse and reached a divine child in whose transcendental body, the collapsed world was existing.

Two of this series are the syllabus about yoga practice. The Yoga Sutras of Patañjali is elaboration about ashtanga yoga. Hatha Yoga Pradipika English, is the detailed information about asana postures, pranayama breath-infusion, energy compression, naad sound resonance and advanced meditation. The Sanskrit author is Swatmarama Mahayogin.

My suggestion is that you read **Bhagavad Gita English**, the **Anu Gita English, the Markandeya Samasya English,** the **Yoga Sutras English,** the **Hatha Yoga Pradipika** and lastly the **Uddhava Gita English**, which is complicated and detailed.

For each of these books we have at least one commentary, which is published separately. Thus one's particular interest can be researched further in the commentaries.

The smallest of these commentaries and perhaps the simplest is the one for the Anu Gita. We published its commentary as the Anu Gita Explained. The Bhagavad Gita explanations were published in three distinct targeted commentaries. The first is Bhagavad Gita Explained, which sheds lights on how people in the time of Krishna and Arjuna regarded the information and applied it. Bhagavad Gita is an exposition of the application of yoga practice to cultural activities, which is known in the Sanskrit language as karma yoga.

Interestingly, Bhagavad Gita was spoken on a battlefield just before one of the greatest battles in the ancient world. A warrior, Arjuna, lost his wits and had no idea that he could apply his training in yoga to political dealings. Krishna, his charioteer, lectured on the spur of the moment to give Arjuna the skill of using yoga proficiency in cultural dealings including how to deal with corrupt officials on a battlefield.

The second Gita commentary is the Kriya Yoga Bhagavad Gita. This clears the air about Krishna's information on the science of kriya yoga, showing that its techniques are clearly described for anyone who takes the time to read Bhagavad Gita. Kriya yoga concerns the battlefield which is the psyche of the living being. The internal war and the mental and emotional forces which are hostile to self-realization are dealt with in the kriya yoga practice.

The third commentary is the Brahma Yoga Bhagavad Gita. This shows what Krishna had to say outright and what he hinted about which concerns the brahma yoga practice, a mystic process for those who mastered kriya yoga.

There is one commentary for the **Markandeya Samasya English**. The title of that publication is Krishna Cosmic Body.

There are two commentaries to the Yoga Sutras. One is the Yoga Sutras of Patañjali and the other is the Meditation Expertise. These give detailed explanations of ashtanga Yoga.

The commentary of Hatha Yoga Pradipika is titled Kundalini Hatha Yoga Pradipika.

For the Uddhava Gita, we published the Uddhava Gita Explained. This is a large book and requires concentration and study for integration of the information. Of the books which deal with transcendental topics, my opinion is that the discourse between Krishna and Uddhava has the complete information about the realities in existence. This book is the one which removes massive existential ignorance.

Meditation Series

Meditation Pictorial

Meditation Expertise

CoreSelf Discovery

Meditation Sense Faculty

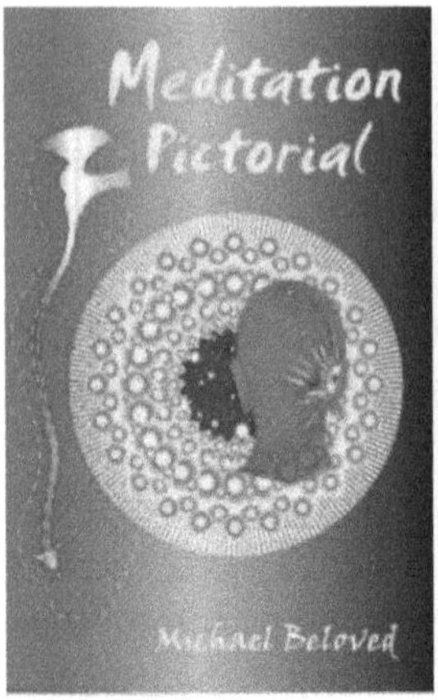

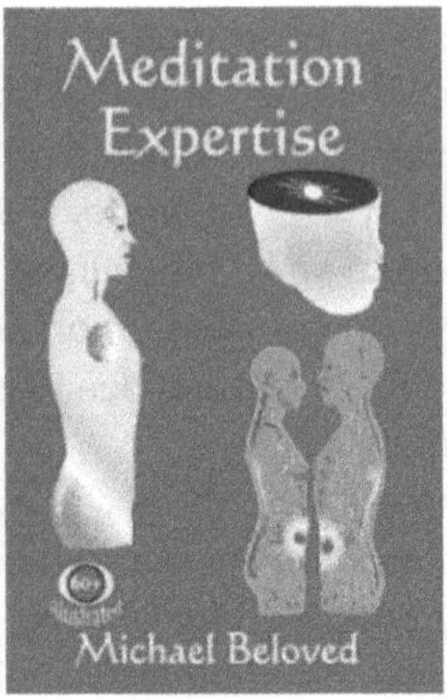

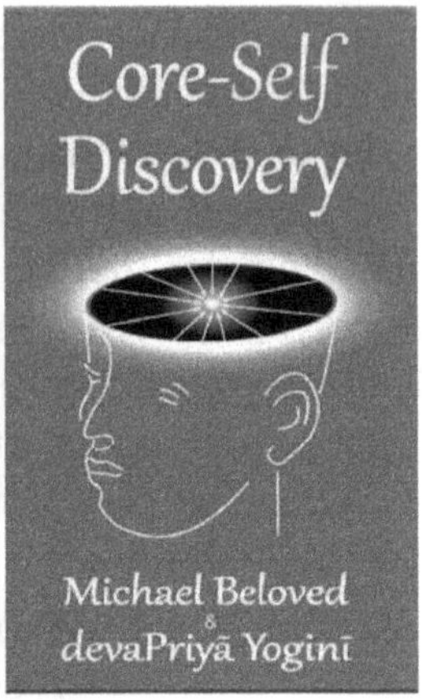

The specialty of these books is the mind diagrams which profusely illustrate what is written. This shows exactly what one has to do mentally to develop and then sustain a meditation practice.

In the **Meditation Pictorial**, one is shown how to develop psychic insight, a feature without which meditation is imagination and visualization, without any mystic experience per se.

In the **Meditation Expertise**, one is shown how to corral one's practice to bring it in line with the classic syllabus of yoga which Patañjali lays out as the ashtanga yoga eight-staged practice.

In **CoreSelf Discovery**, (co-authored with *devaPriya Yogini*) one is taken though the course of pratyahar sensual energy withdrawal which is the 5th stage of yoga in the Patañjali ashtanga eight-process complete system of yoga practice. These events lead to the discovery of a coreSelf which is surrounded by psychic organs in the head of the subtle body. This product has a DVD component.

Meditation ~ Sense Faculty (co-authored with *devaPriya Yogini*) is a detailed tutorial with profuse diagrams showing what actions to take in the subtle body to investigate the senses faculties. The meditator must first establish the location and function of the observing self. That self must be screened from the thoughts and ideas which usually hypnotize it.

These books are profusely illustrated with mind diagrams showing the components of psychic consciousness and the inner design of the subtle body.

Explained Series

Bhagavad Gita Explained

Uddhava Gita Explained

Anu Gita Explained

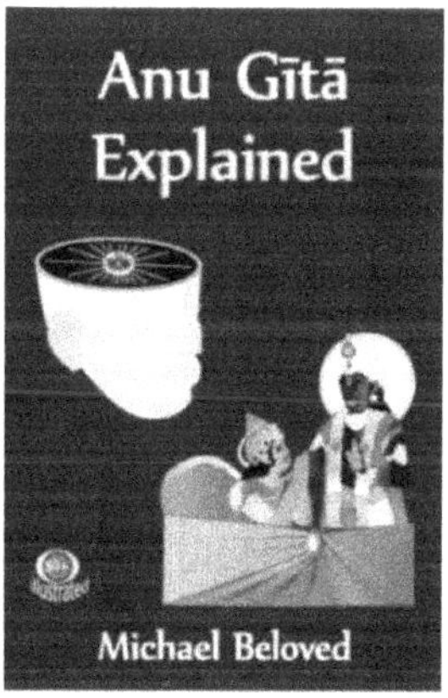

The specialty of these books is that they are free of missionary intentions, cult tactics and philosophical distortion. Instead of using these books to add credence to a philosophy, meditation process, belief or plea for followers, I spread the information out so that a reader can look through this literature and freely take or leave anything as desired.

When Krishna stressed himself as God, I stated that. When Krishna laid no claims for supremacy, I showed that. The reader is left to form an independent opinion about the validity of the information and the credibility of Krishna.

There is a difference in the discourse with Arjuna in the Bhagavad Gita and the one with Uddhava in the Uddhava Gita. In fact these two books may appear to contradict each other. In the Bhagavad Gita, Krishna pressured Arjuna to complete social duties. In the Uddhava Gita, Krishna insisted that Uddhava should abandon the same.

The Anu Gita is not as popular as the Bhagavad Gita but it is the conclusion of that text. Anu means what is to follow, what proceeds. In this discourse, an anxious Arjuna request that Krishna should repeat the Bhagavad Gita and again show His supernatural and divine forms.

However Krishna refuses to do so and chastises Arjuna for being a disappointment in forgetting what was revealed. Krishna then cited a celestial yogi, a near-perfected being, who explained the process of transmigration in vivid detail.

Commentaries

Yoga Sutras of Patañjali

Meditation Expertise

Krishna Cosmic Body

Anu Gita Explained

Bhagavad Gita Explained

Kriya Yoga Bhagavad Gita

Brahma Yoga Bhagavad Gita

Uddhava Gita Explained

Kundalini Hatha Yoga Pradipika

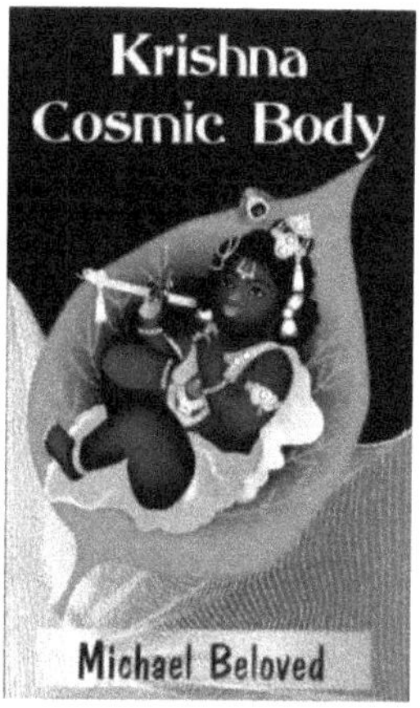

Yoga Sutras of Patañjali is the globally acclaimed text book of yoga. This has detailed expositions of yoga techniques. Many kriya techniques are vividly described in the commentary.

Meditation Expertise is an analysis and application of the Yoga Sutras. This book is loaded with illustrations and has detailed explanations of secretive advanced meditation techniques which are called kriyas in the Sanskrit language.

Krishna Cosmic Body is a narrative commentary on the Markandeya Samasya portion of the Aranyaka Parva of the Mahabharata. This is the detailed description of the dissolution of the world, as experienced by the great yogin Markandeya who transcended the cosmic deity, Brahma, and reached Brahma's source who is the divine infant, Krishna.

Anu Gita Explained is a detailed explanation of how we endure many material bodies in the course of transmigrating through various life-forms. This is a discourse between Krishna and Arjuna. Arjuna requested of Krishna a display of the Universal Form and a repeat narration of the Bhagavad Gita but Krishna declined and explained what a siddha perfected being told the Yadu family about the sequence of existences one endures and the systematic flow of those lives at the convenience of material nature.

Bhagavad Gita Explained shows what was said in the Gita without religious overtones and sectarian biases.

Kriya Yoga Bhagavad Gita shows the instructions for those who are doing kriya yoga.

Brahma Yoga Bhagavad Gita shows the instructions for those who are doing brahma yoga.

Uddhava Gita Explained shows the instructions to Uddhava which are more advanced than the ones given to Arjuna.

Bhagavad Gita is an instruction for applying the expertise of yoga in the cultural field. This is why the process taught to Arjuna is called karma yoga which means karma + yoga or cultural activities done with yogic insight.

Uddhava Gita is an instruction for apply the expertise of yoga to attaining spiritual status. This is why it explains jnana yoga and bhakti yoga in detail. Jnana yoga is using mystic skill for knowing the spiritual part of existence. Bhakti yoga is for developing affectionate relationships with divine beings.

Karma yoga is for negotiating the social concerns in the material world. It is inferior to bhakti yoga which concerns negotiating the social concerns in the spiritual world.

This world has a social environment. The spiritual world has one too.

Currently, Uddhava Gita is the most advanced and informative spiritual book on the planet. There is nothing anywhere which is superior to it or which goes into so much detail as it. It verified that historically Krishna is the most advanced human being to ever have left literary instructions on this planet.

Even Patañjali Yoga Sutras which I translated and gave an application for in my book, **Meditation Expertise**, does not go as far as the Uddhava Gita.

Some of the information of these two books is identical but while the Yoga Sutras are concerned with the personal spiritual emancipation (kaivalyam) of the individual spirits, the Uddhava Gita explains that and also explains the situations in the spiritual universes.

Bhagavad Gita is from the Mahabharata which is the history of the Pandavas. Arjuna, the student of the Gita, is one of the Pandavas brothers. He was in a social hassle and did not know how to apply yoga expertise to solve it. On the battlefield, Krishna gave him a crash-course on yogic social interactions.

Uddhava Gita is from the *Srimad Bhagavatam (Bhagavata Purana),* which is a history of the incarnations of Krishna. Uddhava was a relative of Krishna. He was concerned about the situation of the deaths of many of his relatives but Krishna diverted Uddhava's attention to the practice of yoga for the purpose of successfully migrating to the spiritual environment.

Kundalini Hatha Yoga Pradipika is the commentary for the Hatha Yoga Pradipika of Swatmarama Mahayogin. This is the detailed process about asana posture, pranayama breath-infusion, complex compressions of energy, naad sound resonance intonement and advanced meditation practice.

This is the singular book with all the techniques of how to reform and redesign the subtle body so that it does not have the tendency for physical life forms and for it to attain the status of a siddha.

These books are based on the author's experiences in meditation, yoga practice and participation in spiritual groups:

Specialty

Spiritual Master

sex you!

Sleep Paralysis

Astral Projection

Masturbation Psychic Details

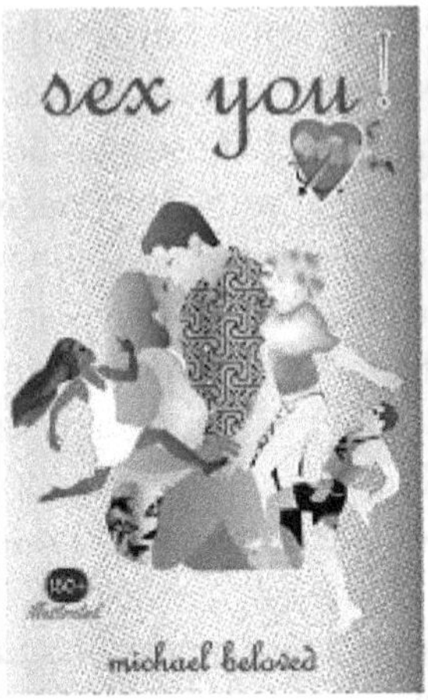

In **Spiritual Master**, Michael draws from experience with gurus or with their senior students. His contact with astral gurus is rated. He walks you through the avenue of gurus showing what you should do and what you should not do, so as to gain proficiency in whatever area of spirituality the guru has proficiency.

sex you! is a masterpiece about the adventures of an individual spirit's passage through the parents' psyches. The conversion of a departed soul into a sexual urge is described. The transit from the afterlife to residency in the emotions of the parents is detailed. This is about sex and you. Learn about how much of you comprises the romantic energy of one's would-be parents!

Sleep Paralysis clears misconceptions so that one can see what sleep paralysis is and what frightening astral experience occurs while the paralysis is being experienced. This disempowerment has great value in giving you confidence that you can and do exist even if one is unable to operate the physical body. The implication is that one can exist apart from and will survive the loss of the material form.

Astral Projection details experiences Michael had even in childhood, where he assumed incorrectly that everyone was astrally conversant. He discusses the lifeForce psychic mechanism which operates the sleep-wake cycle of the physical form, and which budgets energy into the separated astral form which determines if the individual will have dream recall or no objective awareness during the projections. Astral travel happens on every occasion when the physical body sleeps. What is missing in awareness is the observer status while the astral body is separated.

Masturbation Psychic Details is a surprise presentation which relates what happens on the psychic plane during a masturbation event. This does not tackle moral issues or even addictions but shows the involvement of memory and the sure but hidden subconscious mind which operates many features of the psyche irrespective of the desire or approval of the self-conscious personality.

inVision Series

Yoga inVision 1

Yoga inVision 2

Yoga inVision 3

Yoga inVision 4

Yoga inVision 5

Yoga inVision 6

Yoga inVision 7

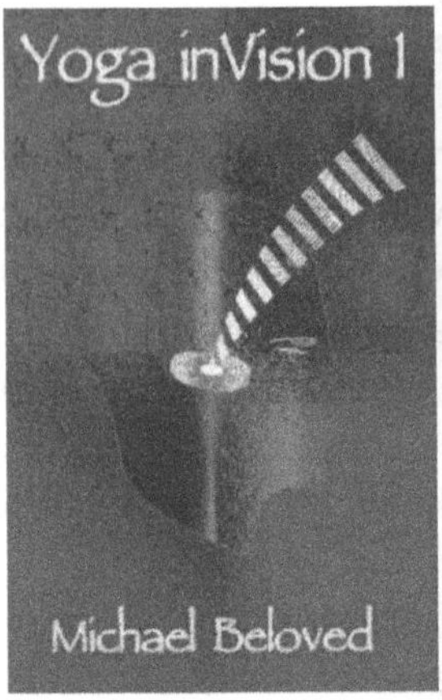

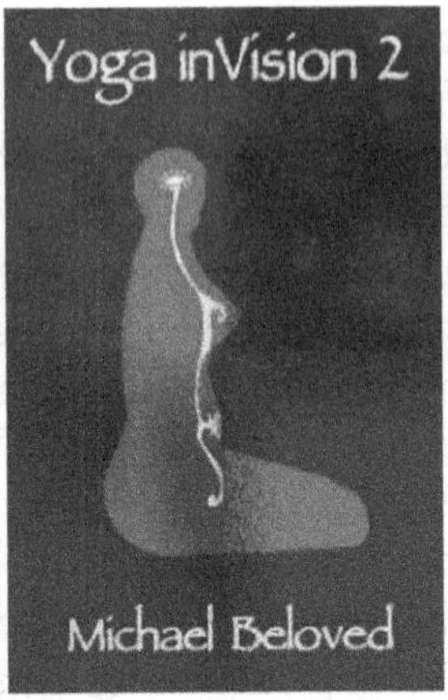

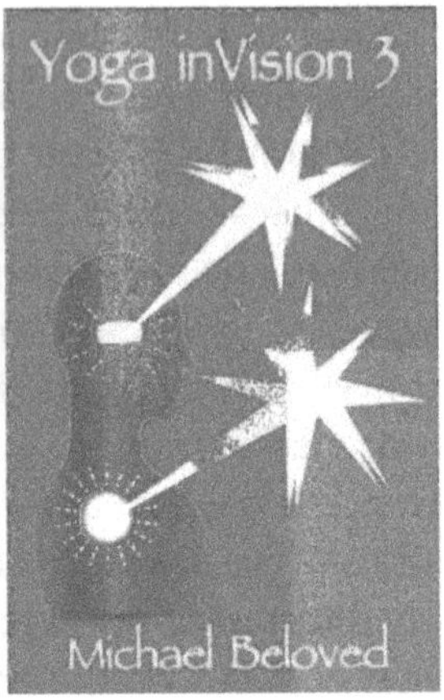

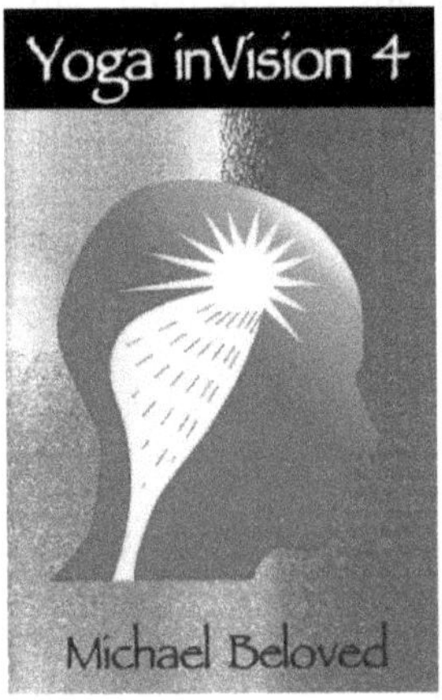

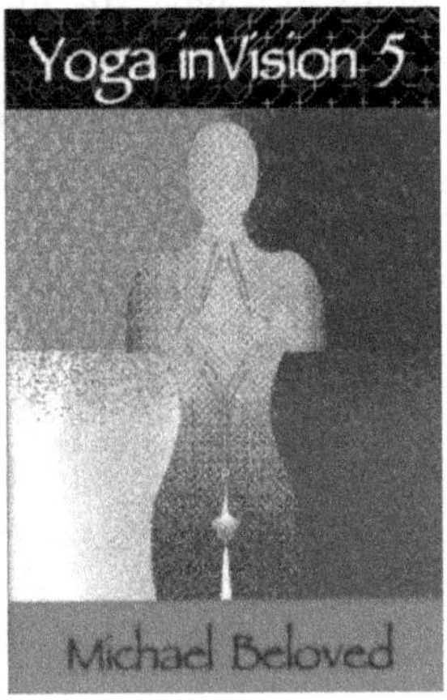

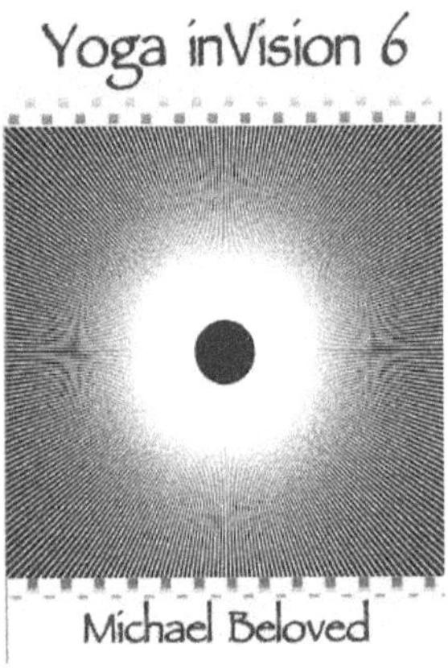

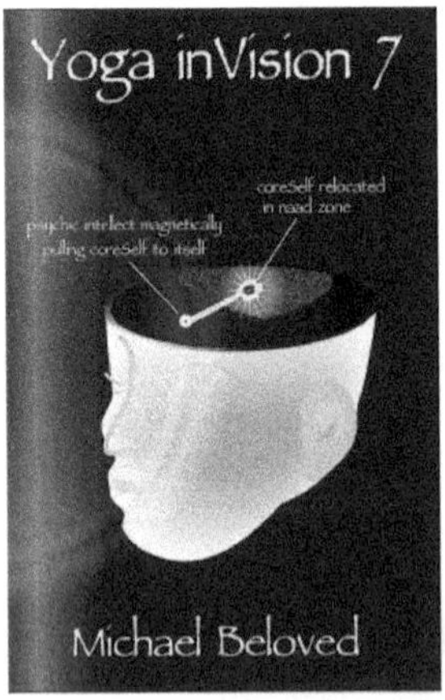

Yoga inVision 1, the first in this series, describes the breath-infusion and meditation practices during the years of 1998 and 1999. There are unique, once in a lifetime as well as recurring insights which are elaborated. inFocus during breath-infusion and the meditation which follows is an adventure for any yogi. This gives what happened to this particular ascetic.

Yoga inVision 2 reports on the author's experiences from 1999 to 2001. Each day the experience is unique, illustrating the vibrancy of practice. Many rare once-in-a-lifetime perceptions are described.

Yoga inVision 3 reports on the author's experiences from 2001 to 2003.

Yoga inVision 4 reports on the author's experiences from 2006 to 2009.

Yoga inVision 5 reports on the author's experiences from 2006 to 2008.

Yoga inVision 6 reports on the author's experiences in 2010.

Yoga inVision 7 reports on the author's experiences in 2011

Online Resources

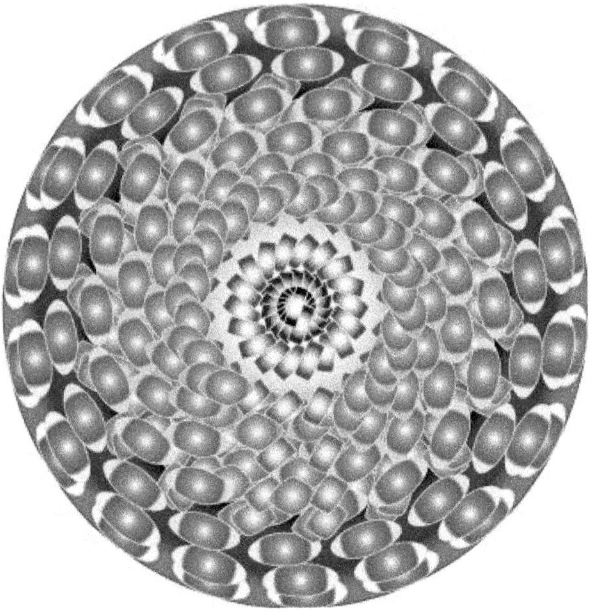

Email: michaelbelovedbooks@gmail.com
axisnexus@gmail.com

Website: michaelbeloved.com

Forum: inselfyoga.com

Posters: zazzle.com/inself

www.ingramcontent.com/pod-product-compliance
Lightning Source LLC
Chambersburg PA
CBHW072339090426
42741CB00012B/2852
9781942887225